Home Truths

Property Ownership and Housing Wealth in Australia

Blair Badcock and Andrew Beer

MELBOURNE UNIVERSITY PRESS

MELBOURNE UNIVERSITY PRESS
PO Box 278, Carlton South, Victoria 3053, Australia
info@mup.unimelb.edu.au
www.mup.com.au

First published 2000

Typeset by Syarikat Seng Teik Sdn. Bhd., Malaysia in Sabon 10/13
Printed in Australia by RossCo Print

National Library of Australia Cataloguing-in-Publication entry

Badcock, B. A. (Blair A.).
Home truths: property ownership and housing wealth in Australia.
Bibliography.
Includes index.
ISBN 0 522 84893 1.
1. Home ownership—Economic aspects—Australia. 2. Housing—Economic aspects—Australia. I. Beer, Andrew Philip. II. Title.
333.3380994

Contents

Illustrations

Tables

Foreword

Hugh Stretton

Houses and their equipment are the capital for more than a third of work and output in rich democracies. But because most household work does not attract formal wages, orthodox economists don't count it as work. Because its output is not sold for money, they don't count it as national product. And from both those inexcusable omissions many of them conclude that although housing is necessary for people's welfare, building it diverts resources from productive investment. That slows economic growth and leaves people poorer than they might otherwise be.

There is worse to come. Most of the goods and services produced by household work don't sell for money. So they don't finance the purchase of the capital which is used to produce them. That mostly has to be financed from income earned in paid employment. So the markets for houses and housing finance can't promise the classical efficiency—the efficiency which allocates available capital funds to their most productive uses—which orthodox economists rightly look for in the rest of the private sector.

Within the limits that they can afford, people should have full market freedom to choose the housing and household equipment that suit them best. But the land and money markets together determine *what* they can afford. Prospects of tax avoidance and capital gain invite rich people to buy grander houses—or more houses, in town, country and seaside—than they can make full use of. Meanwhile many low-income households can't afford basics which they would use willingly and well, both for their own benefit and to contribute sociable, energetic, productive children to society's human capital.

So there is double scope for public policy. Well-designed measures to improve the supply of public and private housing and the market access and options of younger and poorer households can distribute housing resources more equitably and compassionately than unaided markets can. And those same measures are likely to distribute them more productively, for the households concerned and for the economy as a whole. Some of the gain will appear in orthodox measures of the distribution of wealth and income. But some—the bigger total of household output and its better distribution—will not.

Economists' neglect of these issues has left work for other disciplines. Our knowledge of Australian inequalities and their sources through the last half-century owes less to academic economists than to sociologists, political scientists, town planners and—in Badcock, Beer and others—geographers.

Blair Badcock has long been an Australian leader in this research and Andrew Beer is an able recruit to it. *Home Truths* is the latest, best, most original and most thorough study of the complex interactions between the distributions of housing wealth, total wealth, and the income that matters most: that is, income after tax and housing costs, and its distribution through the phases of household life and between succeeding generations.

It is important that policy-makers read and understand this book. The tax-cutters and welfare-shrinkers won't like it. It makes very clear the improvident and unequalising effects of current policies. So it may be specially important that they and the public hear its message from journalists, broadcasters, independent welfare organisations and others who still enjoy free speech, loud voices, a social conscience and—with this book's powerful help—economic competence.

Hugh Stretton

Acknowledgements

WE HAVE TRIED to make this an accessible book. As well as serving as a first point of contact for tertiary students, it will also, we hope, appeal to the general reader with questions about real estate but little formal understanding of how the property market works and contributes to the concentration of housing wealth. If so, it should help to spark renewed interest in questions about the significance of housing for all Australians. In our view, there has never been a greater need for politicians and policy-makers to be aware of the consequences of their policies.

The book arose out of a three-way collaboration that goes back almost fifteen years, to when Andrew Beer left the University of Adelaide with his honours degree to begin a PhD at the Australian National University. As an external supervisor, Blair Badcock found there was a nice convergence between his ongoing interest in residential property markets and the wealth they generate for home owners, and Andrew's Canberra study. Then, in the late 1980s, Blair received funding from the Australian Research Council for a major project called 'Getting Ahead: Housing Careers and the Amassing of Personal Wealth'. Lisel O'Dwyer worked as research officer on that project and then started her own PhD, this time under Andrew's supervision, at Flinders University of South Australia. Her research is some of the first to be done in Australia on the all-important question of inherited housing wealth. We both thank Lisel for her contribution to this volume.

We owe a huge debt of gratitude to professional colleagues. Firstly, Hugh Stretton, who so kindly agreed to write the Foreword, has provided inspiration to all those working to improve housing provision in Australia. Chris Hamnett, University College London, familiarised us with British housing studies when Blair was a Visiting Fellow at the Netherlands Institute of Advanced Studies in 1992–93. Judith Yates commented on an early draft of Chapter 7, and shared much wisdom with Andrew while they worked together on an Australian Research Council Collaborative Research Grant. Chapter 8, which places housing wealth in a much broader policy context, grew out of a seminar that was held in the Department of Human Services in December 1998. We acknowledge not only the comments and suggestions that came from the participants that day, but also the interest and support extended to us by those same people over the years. They know who they are!

We have been helped and encouraged by departmental colleagues at the University of Adelaide, Flinders University of South Australia, and Plymouth University where Andrew Beer spent some of his study leave in 1997. In particular, both of us have profited from the insight of Clive Forster—a fellow urban geographer in the School of Geography, Population, and Environmental Management at Flinders—over the years. A Teaching Release Fellowship funded by the Adelaide Research Centre in the Humanities and Social Sciences, Faculty of Arts, University of Adelaide, enabled us to meet the publisher's deadline. Commissioning Editor Teresa Pitt and the rest of the team at Melbourne University Press were another vital element in bringing the project together at the end.

We are grateful to: Arnold Publishers for permission to reproduce Figure 3, which originally appeared in B. Badcock, 'Urban and Regional Restructuring and Spatial Transfers of Housing Wealth', *Progress in Human Geography*, 18, 1994, pp. 279–97; Pion Limited, London, publishers of *Environment and Planning A*, 24, 1992, for permission to reproduce Figure 4 from B. Badcock and M. Browett, 'Adelaide's Heart Transplant, 1970–88: 3. The Deployment of Capital in the Renovation and Redevelopment Submarkets', pp. 1167–90; Hans Baekgaard for the graphs of house price trends in Figures 6a and 6b; the Planning Research Centre at the University of Sydney for the use of Figures 7a and 7b; and Carfax Publishing for permission to reproduce Figure 1 from J. Yates, 'Is Australia's Home Ownership Rate Really Stable? An Examination of Change Between 1975 and 1994', *Urban Studies*, 37 (20), 2000, pp. 319–42.

The book has taken shape during some personally difficult times for both of us and we acknowledge the love and support that we received from our partners, Carole and Christine, while it was being written. But we have decided to reserve the dedication for those Adelaide home owners who responded so graciously to the questionnaires that we mailed to them, and to those others who agreed to share something of their own housing histories with us orally and pictorially. Without their co-operation there would be less learnt, and less known to inform the shaping of housing policy in the future.

Blair Badcock and Andrew Beer
January 2000

Introduction

As home ownership levels go, Australians take the prize as the world's greatest hoarders of housing wealth during the twentieth century. The home they are paying off, or already own outright, is undoubtedly the average Australian's nest-egg. The accepted course of action for successive generations of wage and salary earners has been to sink their life savings into bricks and mortar in preference to other forms of investment. This has been characteristic, for longer than elsewhere, of the pattern of household savings and private wealth accumulation in Australia.[1] By contrast, middle-class households in the United States have traditionally held more of their private wealth in a liquid form, as stock, shares and bonds.

Until the 1990s, housing wealth as a share of all private wealth in Australia hovered between 60 and 65 per cent. Australia heads a league table of countries with housing systems dominated by owner-occupation (Table 1). Most Australians regard the standard of housing they have come to enjoy as part of the postwar success story. However, on the eve of the new millennium the picture is being transformed. Not only is the home ownership rate falling in Australia, but housing's share of household wealth is also coming under challenge from other assets like superannuation and equities.

Our book helps to explain in simple terms the major part that home ownership has traditionally played in both the creation and the distribution of housing wealth in Australia. Our study is shaped by two over-arching questions. Firstly, has the favoured status granted to home ownership by successive Australian governments enriched owners, or entrapped them? This is not to imply that we will come down on one side or the other of this question. But it focuses attention on the winners and losers in the housing stakes—and all forms of redistribution worked out by governments have their winners and losers.

Our second main question follows naturally from the first. In view of recent signs that the postwar housing system might be coming unstuck, we ask what of the future of home ownership and housing wealth for Australians? Will the 1990s prove to be a watershed decade which marks the beginning of a fundamental reshaping of the Australian housing system?

Table 1: Housing tenure, including owner-occupation, in selected OECD countries, mid-1990s (%)

Country	*Owner-occupation*	*Private rental*	*Social/public rental*[a]
Australia	70	24	6
Britain	68	11	21
Canada	63	30	7
Denmark	60	21	19
France	57	19	24
Germany	39	42	19
Netherlands	45	13	42
Sweden	41	21	38
United States	65	30.5	4.5

[a] Including Local Authority/Council, State Housing Authority, Housing Authority, Housing Associations, Housing Co-operatives, publicly subsidised.

Sources: Various national databases, including ABS, *Housing Australia: A Statistical Overview*, 1996; UK DOE Housing and Construction Statistics; US Bureau of Census; L'Observatoire European du Logement Social, *Social Housing in the EU 1995*.

Figuring out the property market

In spite of their attachment to home ownership, 'Most people really don't understand property'.[2] Nor do they understand how housing markets in our cities work to redistribute housing wealth. By and large, owners who bought in the 1960s and 1970s would agree that it was the best thing they ever did, even though they may not have much idea about how their biggest lifetime investment has performed in financial terms. That their home appears to have held its value against surrounding house prices, or that they obtain more than the official government valuation at resale or auction, is often reason enough for gratification. This helps to sustain the popular illusion that home owners benefit equally from the rates of capital growth that are periodically reported by the media for the state capital housing markets.[3]

It is this widely held sense of the beneficence of the housing market that gives rise to the popular notion of the 'housing escalator'. Real estate agents sometimes use this metaphor in promoting the benefits that owning promises to bestow. The prospect in store can be made especially enticing for first-time buyers by appealing to their desire to succeed in life. With the pay rises that go with promotion, they might reasonably expect the initial burden of mortgage repayments to be short-lived. Once they have their foot on the bottom step, they will be carried upwards in the property market along with house price inflation—almost as night follows day. And when it comes to selling, why, of course, these change-over buyers can use the capital gain as a new down payment to jump a few steps higher on the escalator. Called 'trading up', this is only one of a number of options available to owners.

The housing escalator is seen at its best when a buyer deliberately sets out to play the market and the conditions are right for it. Unless they strike it lucky by chance, this is the only way home owners are going to get the capital growth that 'working the cycles' sometimes delivers to professional or institutional property investors. That it does not happen more often is due to the lack of practical flexibility in the lives of ordinary home owners. They are in no position to respond opportunistically to surging and dipping asset values in the housing market. Therefore, the key to real success when it comes to buying and selling is to 'be in the right place at the right time' (Chapter 1).

Practical needs, 'psychic utility' and resale value

Housing is unlike any other commodity that we purchase. Buying a house allows the occupants to consume the normally inexhaustible services that a house in its local surroundings provides. Housing gets its *use value* from satisfying these practical needs during the course of a lifetime. Naturally someone living alone has different needs to a family growing up. Regardless of where that places you personally, most readers have probably never given much thought to what a remarkable form of consumption their home actually is.

Think of all the things that are taken for granted about the flow of housing services that come with the purchase of a standard land-and-home package; that is, besides the dedication of particular rooms to sleeping, the preparation of food and eating, storage, or just mucking about the house. Some home buyers pay a premium for convenient access to their workplace, or to be close to private schools and handy to shops. The importance of private schools as a locational magnet in Melbourne's exclusive eastern suburbs adds a premium to house prices.[4] For others, it is the added amenity of superlative views, beach and lake frontage, or established parklands nearby. And, given the Antipodean inclination to doing-it-yourself, the typical suburban bungalow with its backyard and workshop in the garage doubles as a site of domestic production.[5]

As well as the practical utility of the average house, there are other intangibles and unpriced benefits that come with property ownership. Although it is hard to identify the satisfaction of putting down roots, forming bonds with neighbours, and a growing sense of attachment to place, we all recognise this as one of the dividends of owning our own home. When economists talk about 'psychic utility', they have in mind the emotional uplift that adds to our overall sense of well-being. All this is bound up with our sense of oneness with where we live, with financial peace of mind, with being safe and sound in the protective cocoon of our own home.[6]

The often unspoken attachment to 'home', to 'our place', or maybe 'my place', is a composite of all sorts of special meanings that well up from time to time from our private store of memories.

This becomes especially powerful in the twilight years. Memories of the elderly are bound up in this place where they raised their children.[7] Moving house at this stage becomes even more of a wrench. For second-generation Australians, it can mean a reluctance to part with the home in which their parents created a new life for themselves. Indeed, much late twentieth-century Australian writing anchors an exploration of identity in this sense of place and the meaning of home.[8]

Here we hasten to add that home owners are not the only ones to benefit from this heightened sense of well-being. Where there is the assurance of long-term stability and security, as with European social housing, tenants develop a similar degree of attachment to their housing and neighbourhood.[9] But crucially, it is legal possession that gives occupants the right to design and create a living space of their own choosing. Tenants enjoy this liberty only up to a point.

To build or remodel a home themselves, to get it the way they want it, is a source of extra pride for home-making types. We all know people who fabricate their lives around their housing. This is the case regardless of class. A drive around any Australian city, through traditional working-class suburbs as well as the ostentatious real estate of the *nouveau riche*, will reveal equally house-proud occupants. Thus our housing also serves to signify achievement and self-worth. On the one hand, a retired couple's spic-and-span cottage speaks of quiet achievers; on the other, a palatial spread behind high walls proclaims 'Look, we've made it'.

All the while, owner-occupiers are paying off an appreciating asset. Usually, regardless of the amount of wear and tear it gets, and so long as market conditions remain favourable, the typical suburban bungalow will continue to increase in value. No doubt most owners give some thought to possible resale value when they buy, but it is not until the house is placed on the market that owners are confronted once more with the market's judgement of what their housing investment is worth. This is known in the trade as its *exchange value*.

Whether or not owners actually make money when they sell their house, owner-occupation enjoys a reputation amongst ordinary Australians as perhaps the most trustworthy form of personal investment possible. In the case of the generation making a new start after World War II, home ownership was the key to achieving comfortable circumstances at the end of their working lives. For many survivors of the Great Depression, owner-occupation amounted to little more than the desire to have a roof over their heads which no one would ever take from them. For people leaving war-ravaged Europe it was a chance to rebuild, secure in the knowledge that possessions like a home would never again be destroyed in that way. The time-worn saying 'as safe as houses' assured this generation that there would be something worthwhile left to hand on to the children at the end of their lives.[10]

Conditions favouring capital gains

A bonus accompanied this confidence in the immutability of hard-won savings locked up in the family home. For almost three decades after World War II owner-occupation proved to be a very effective hedge against inflation. Despite the roller-coaster rise and fall of the property market in Australia, owner-occupiers came to appreciate that, so long as they did not find themselves forced to sell at an inopportune time, their investment was insulated against the boom-and-bust property cycle. Better still, often there was an unexpected bonus of windfall gains if they did sell in a seller's market, or if the value of their home happened to outstrip the prices that other housing was bringing.

Much the same story can be told for home buyers in the United States:

> During the post-war period . . . young couples with almost no money to their name bought houses with a minimal down payment, and over the years, with the steady build up of equity and a little inflation, before they knew it they were rich. The value of owner-occupied homes [in US dollars] at the end of 1986 was $3.758 trillion and the net equity was $2.113 trillion—an average owner had an equity of over $50 000.[11]

This raises an intriguing set of questions about how housing wealth is actually created, and then transferred between home owners. In Chapter 1 we argue that, even though governments set the broad economic parameters for wealth creation, it is in the operation of the property market that the answers are to be found. More particularly, timing and position are the keys to capital gains. The message of Chapter 1 is that wealth accumulated in the housing market depends crucially upon when and where home owners buy and sell: that is to say, *when* you buy in relation to the ups and downs of the property cycle and the cost of a home loan, and *where* that house is located geographically.

Soon after World War II the level of home ownership in Australia climbed to above 70 per cent. To be precise, it rose from 52.6 per cent in 1947 to a peak of 71 per cent in 1966, where it has hovered ever since.[12] This impressive feat can be attributed both to government efforts to make up for the dire shortage of housing that was carried over from the war years, and to a veritable Dad's army of owner-builders.[13] Estimates suggest that the proportion of home owners might even have reached 90 per cent for groups of households born between 1950 and 1970.[14] Despite the initial hardship faced by many aspiring home owners, this surely was 'the stuff that dreams are made of'.[15]

Generally speaking, the generation of home buyers in the 1950s, and those who followed in the 1960s and the 1970s, profited in real terms from the capital formation taking place in the ever-expanding suburbs. Some of the surveys that we draw upon in Chapter 2 suggest this was mainly due to the good fortune of home owners, rather than to the deliberate crafting of an investment strategy on their part. On the whole, though, home buyers from this earlier era were recipients to some degree of the 'wealth dividend' bestowed by the housing system that evolved in Australia in the postwar years.

By contrast, during the 1990s the experience of both first home buyers and changeover buyers has been much more mixed. The steady economic conditions that had favoured home ownership and capital gains changed for the worse. Deregulation of the home finance system, and then the willingness of the banks to lend in pursuit of market share in the heady days of the late 1980s, permitted some borrowers to overextend themselves. Although outright owners were sheltered from the soaring interest rates at the end of the decade, others were crippled.

Location also plays an inescapable part in the way the housing market monetarily rewards or punishes home buyers. As well as all the neighbourhood investment that impacts positively upon house prices as it is capitalised into the value of housing, a variety of effects called negative externalities can pull down upon property values. Australians seem to be especially tenacious, even paranoid, in defence of their property values. In some Melbourne suburbs what is viewed as excessive townhouse or home unit development has resulted in city-wide mobilisation under the auspices of Save Our Suburbs (SOS!). The installation of microwave towers for mobile phones is fought tooth-and-nail by local residents around Australia. The opposition is based mainly on the risk to health, but another reason is the decline in value of nearby housing as future home buyers are scared off. We say much more in Chapter 1 about these underlying market effects upon capital gains and capital losses in the housing market.

Having hinted at some of the hazards facing home buyers, we hasten to add that this book is not meant as a home hunter's guide to what to look for or avoid in housing, nor as an investor's checklist to playing the market. All the same, there are a few preliminary questions that buyers should ask themselves if they are in a position to exercise options over where they live: are you planning to buy in a depressed state or a prosperous state, a suburb on the way up or a suburb on the way down, a good street or a poor street?

One of the research tasks for those interested in the creation and distribution of housing wealth is to identify who actually wins and who loses in the process. From there it is a natural step to ask whether or not capital accumulation in home-owning societies like Australia is making them more or less equal. These are the questions shaping the chapter given over to 'Winners and Losers' (Chapter 2).

'Snakes and ladders'

The depiction of owner-occupation as housing escalator has the support of some influential housing specialists.[16] There are others, though, who argue that, with such a sizeable owner-occupied sector in countries like Britain, the United States, and Australia, the experience of home owners is bound to be much more varied than this implies. In their book *Homeownership: Differentiation and Fragmentation,* the British housing experts Ray Forrest, Alan Murie and Peter Williams suggest there is a need to widen perspectives 'beyond a simple imagery that equates home ownership universally with ladders, opportunity, mobility, the accumulation of wealth'.[17] It is no longer good enough to presume that home ownership is an escalator for everyone, or to assign home owners to a class position and leave it at that.

We believe that the game of Snakes and Ladders (Figure 1) provides a more appropriate metaphor for the processes behind

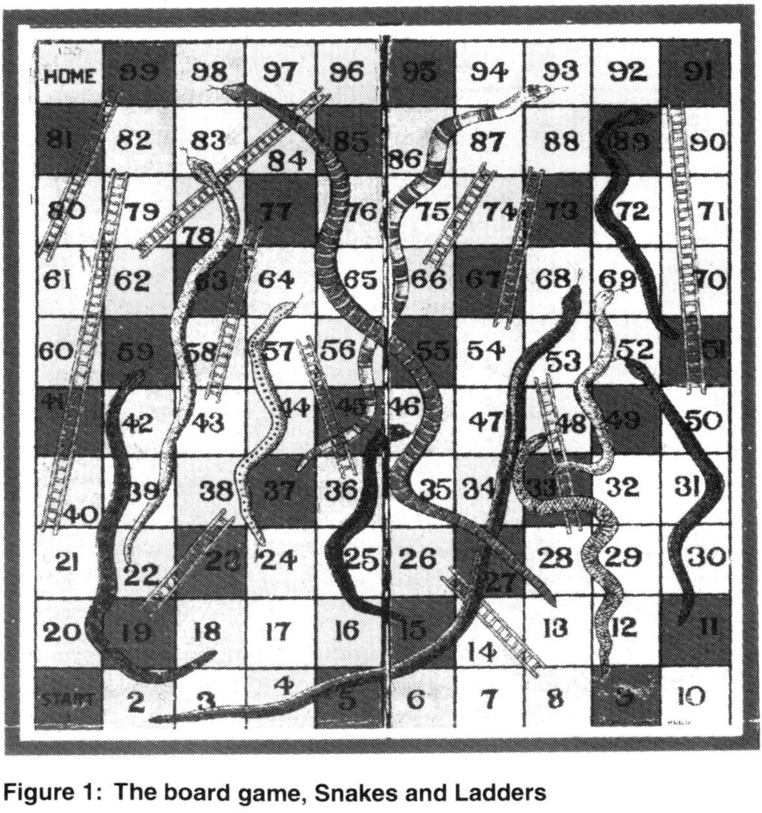

Figure 1: The board game, Snakes and Ladders

the accumulation of housing wealth. This is based upon conclusions drawn from research undertaken by one of us in the early 1990s.[18] Studies are presented in Chapter 2 of the sequence of moves by home owners through the housing market and their record of wealth accumulation. What these case studies of winners and losers show is that wealth accumulation owes much to events during the life course, or to the age, gender, and ethnic breakdown of the household.

To put it more starkly, not everyone enjoys the fruits of capital accumulation: the economic fortunes of home owners may range all the way from the extremes of *enrichment* to *entrapment*. Home buyers encounter structured constraints and opportunities within the housing market not unlike those designed into a snakes and ladders board (Figure 1). Unless they happen to inherit, tenants, of course, do not even get to play the game. We should not push this metaphor too far, though; we do not suggest that housing wealth is solely determined by the roll of the die as in Snakes and Ladders! Yet a home loan can entail an element of risk beyond the temptation to bite off more than you can chew in order to get the dream home that you have set your heart on. Just as certainly, events can conspire to put a damper on the otherwise reasonable expectation of capital gains in the process of investing in home ownership.

The story of housing wealth does not stop here. Do the households that share the best jobs in the labour market also extract the most wealth from the housing market? Are these the same people who invest in the private rental market? Or is the suggestion of a systemic class bias to accumulation upset by events during the life course, or by gender effects, or by the cultural practices of post-war migrants settling in Australia? What is the effect of other factors, such as government programmes like the War Services Home Scheme, the prevalence of owner-building in the 1950s, the sale of public housing, discrimination against women as mortgagees, second incomes, divorce and family dissolution, and reciprocity within migrant families (the sharing of money, skills and materials)? How has the interaction of all these factors ultimately affected the distribution of housing wealth within the Australian community?

On top of this, the prospect of bequeathing wealth to the next generation raises vital questions about the role of housing inheritance in countries like Australia (Chapter 3). For example, are these transfers of housing wealth between the generations helping to soften or exacerbate social inequality? Is there a gender bias to the pattern of housing inheritance? What informal arrangements exist within the family circle to help children make a start? What are the possibilities for releasing home equity in old age, especially as the burden of costs for health and welfare provision shifts from the state to the individual in the 1990s? And lastly, under what economic and regulatory conditions do these outcomes arise?

Structures of housing provision

There is nothing preordained about owner-occupation as the preferred tenure of Australians. Significantly, the high levels of domestic property and proportion of private wealth held in the form of dwelling capital that we take for granted in Australia are found in only a few so-called property-owning democracies (Britain, the United States, Canada, and New Zealand).[19] It is the dominance of owner-occupation in these Anglophone nations that lends them their distinctiveness as capitalist societies. One of the key themes threading its way through the book is that the housing system that has evolved in these societies is the product of a specific form of housing provision, or 'structures of housing provision'.

This way of comparing the housing systems of different societies was originally developed by a British political economist with an interest in housing markets. Michael Ball sought to draw attention to what he believed was an imbalance in the way housing matters were being construed at the time. With the political spotlight perpetually upon issues of distribution, there was a natural tendency to dwell upon housing consumption at the expense of the means by which the housing was produced. It occurred to Ball that, 'Instead . . . of simply being one way in which housing may be consumed, owner-occupation has become associated with a particular way in which housing is provided; and with all the forms of land ownership, building, finance and market exchange that exist there'.[20]

This definition was broadened following exchanges between Ball and his critics:

> A structure of housing provision encompasses the interrelations between all the agencies involved in the production, exchange, finance and consumption of housing in a particular way . . . International variations in forms of housing provision help to explain the different experiences of housing tenures and why they have developed in different ways.[21]

Besides, part of the point of referring to other property-owning democracies is to show that the benefits and wealth conferred by property ownership ultimately stem from the ideological predisposition of civil society, and the way this is interpreted by the state in the process of developing the policies and institutions for housing provision. Perhaps the most uncompromising explanation for the dominance of home ownership in Australia asserts that it has been excessively promoted by postwar governments ahead of, and at the expense of, other tenures.[22] This is the 'state sponsorship of the tenure' thesis.

Since World War II in Australia, home ownership has been accorded the status of a privileged circuit of capital within the economy. This is a direct outcome of the housing policies pursued by the federal and state governments and the institutional arrangements created for providing housing. 'Viewed in the broadest sense, Australian housing policy ensures that home ownership is the dominant tenure by providing very little support for private renters, only a marginal public housing sector, and substantial tax incentives for home owners.'[23] Nonetheless, the force of the 'state sponsorship of the tenure' thesis needs to be relaxed somewhat to properly acknowledge the underlying demographic and economic pressures at work in the 1950s and 1960s.

The key to understanding how housing provision is structured in Australia is the realisation that the advantages of owner-occupation really do cut both ways. Surveys of satisfaction levels amongst home owners, and of the aspirations of tenants repeatedly reveal that owner-occupation is overwhelmingly the tenure of first choice for Australians.[24] Due to this popularity, within the space of a generation home ownership has become one of the most important, and at the same time structurally embedded, means available to the average Australian household for creating personal wealth.

However, it has also suited governments to pump funds into the housing sector from time to time to help kick-start domestic or regional economies. Some states have even been accused in the past of force-feeding the housing industry to provide additional stimulus to a sagging regional economy. In 1983, the federal Labor Party was elected to pull the economy out of recession. Such was the package of incentives offered to first home buyers by the Hawke government in its first term of office that the subsequent turnaround in economic activity is often described as a housing-led recovery.

These so-called multiplier effects are really just the tip of the proverbial iceberg. The dominance conceded to owner-occupation by governments in the property-owning democracies has an underlying significance for the performance of these economies that is not sufficiently appreciated. In Chapter 4 we show how the housing finance system has evolved in Australia and make the case for owner-occupation as a privileged circuit of capital. Of particular interest is the impact of financial deregulation upon access to home ownership and asset prices in the 1980s; and then, what this has done in turn to the concentration of housing wealth.

Beyond this are the larger questions about the role of the housing sector within the economy (Chapter 5). How does the concentration of private wealth in housing complicate economic management in Australia? What contribution to gross national product does the housing sector make? How has the financial system responded to the almost insatiable demand for housing finance over the years? Are housing outlays non-productive, and do they draw capital away from more productive sectors of the economy? What revenue is forgone by governments in the form of tax incentives or concessions to home owners? Is overconsumption encouraged by these measures to expand home ownership?

Chapter 5 draws to a close with a discussion of housing in relation to the welfare system in Australia. We argue that the high levels of housing wealth that the postwar generation of Australians have generally enjoyed came as part of a social compact whereby governments would spend less on welfare provision and related services. But this has been a one-sided deal, which favours home owners at the expense of tenants in their old age. Retired home owners can draw upon the wealth dividend and purchase residential care and health services of their choosing. Elderly tenants are not so lucky with regard to the quality of care that they can access.

As home ownership rates begin to dip in Australia, the federal government will be faced with a dilemma. The commitment to an expanded private rental sector combined with rent relief for poorer tenants has the effect of redirecting housing outlays within the economy. Lower levels of home ownership will almost certainly require both a greater welfare bill and a higher tax burden overall. Taken together, these measures could significantly reshape the Australian economy over the next couple of decades.

Three generations of home owners

Demographers like to demarcate the generations by following the biological cycle, spacing them about fifteen years apart—though these days few mothers have their first child at this age. In rough terms this spacing makes for three identifiable postwar generations—Baby Boomers, their parents and their children. According to the social researcher Hugh Mackay, the economic and social restructuring that has been taking place in Western societies over the last twenty-five years has helped bring into focus some of the differences that exist between these generations.[25]

In Chapter 6 we ask how home ownership and housing wealth figure in the differing stories that can be told about these three generations. We are especially interested in the role that housing wealth is playing, or is likely to play, in the lives of typical households drawn from each successive generation. Because of this, in Chapter 6 we give the generations labels that relate to their respective housing decisions and outcomes.

The first generation of home owners to emerge in Australia after World War II is called the Safe and Sound generation. After the trauma of the war years, state-supported housing assistance was fashioned as an element of cradle-to-grave social security in welfare state societies like Australia. Although there were long delays due to the rationing of home finance and building shortages, *once they were in their own home* a couple who married in the 1950s or 1960s were safe and sound. As a generation, they have carried that expectation with them into old age, and woe betide any government that now tries to undermine their sense of security.

The Baby Boomers dictated housing provision as 25–40-year-olds between about 1970 and 1985. Through sheer weight of numbers they have been a potent force for change in the postwar era. During the prosperous years of the long boom, federal and state governments were in a much better position to fund the schooling, health care and housing that their parents' generation had missed out on. Despite the shadow of Cold War tensions, the social and cultural currents that shaped the times inspired a certain optimism in the future. This aura of confidence made for a generation that characteristically has done everything to excess.

From time to time, when they came to buy or change their homes, rampant inflation in house prices really did tempt some middle-class Baby Boomers to try to run up the housing escalator. Either way, unless a divorce forced the splitting of assets, this pampered generation has mostly profited from home ownership. In the 1990s, if they choose, they can borrow against that accumulated equity in the family home. Baby Boomers also stand to inherit the balance of their parents' estate at a stage when they are likely to have paid off their own homes. If they behave consistently, they will probably spend the windfall on non-essential consumption, or on more housing, or diversify their share portfolio. However, periodically throughout the 1980s and 1990s workforce restructuring did not always treat Baby Boomers kindly. Unlike their parents, they still need to earn, and along with their children have to come to terms with globalisation, corporate downsizing and redundancies.

As with most other things in life, the children born to Baby Boomers will no doubt elect to keep their options open when it comes to home ownership. In fact, while these young adults born in the 1970s are known as Generation X, Hugh Mackay prefers to call them the Options Generation.[26] Their generation has been buffeted most by the winds of change blowing through the Australian economy in the 1990s. Permanent full-time employment is rapidly becoming a thing of the past. Even those members of Generation X with highly sought-after qualifications and skills face the prospect of short-term contracts and greater geographical mobility if they are to be where the work is. Job insecurity mitigates against the long-term financial commitment of a mortgage.

Not surprisingly, then, the dramatic decline in the purchase rate that has been observed among adults under thirty-five years—the figure fell from 70 per cent in 1975 to 55 per cent by 1994—can be traced to several shifts in the life experience of Generation X. Given the current deferral of home purchase by this generation, Judith Yates, one of Australia's most respected housing economists, concludes that 'there is no reason to assume that the existing pattern of ownership, with home ownership rates of over 80 per cent amongst the over-65s, will hold for future generations'.[27]

The future of housing wealth in Australia

One of the key points of difference between these home-owning generations relates to a general feeling that an important generational shift is taking place. Over the last fifty years or so a structure of housing provision evolved in Australia which gave precedence to owner-occupation over alternative forms of housing tenure. For mainstream Australia that structure of housing provision served households tolerably well. But the housing system is now under stress.

The demographic and economic conditions that fed owner-occupation and delivered a wealth dividend to previous generations of home owners are in a state of flux. The traditional factors that drive the underlying demand for housing in general, and the purchase of new dwellings in particular, have lost some momentum. Wide-ranging changes are afoot in the labour market. The size and composition of the migrant intake has been altered. The population is ageing, while the diversification of household structures taking place in Australia is without precedent. All these developments are segmenting the housing market and changing access to, as well as the affordability and adequacy of, owner-occupied housing. Home ownership, and the opportunity to build up some kind of asset—however modest—is a receding dream for increasing numbers of Australians without long-term job security.

On a second front, people buying their first home in the 1990s have been forced to rethink their expectations in relation to capital gains. By the late 1980s borrowers could select from an extensive array of competitive and flexible mortgage and home equity products. Home loan interest rates had fallen to a thirty-year low by the middle of 1997. But because of the lingering uncertainty about long-term job security, demand pressures, and therefore house price inflation, have remained comparatively subdued. The federal Treasurer has said that in his view 'the old boom-and-bust cycle of the Australian economy may be over, barring some unexpected "external shock"'.[28] Consequently, the opportunities for capital growth are less promising than they were during periods of house price inflation in the 1970s and 1980s.

Investment conditions have reverted to something like the 1950s and 1960s, when house prices were reasonably stable, and occupiers gradually built up equity in their homes in the process of paying them off through principal-and-interest loans. As long as general inflation is kept in check, the capital-city housing markets are less likely to overheat as they did in the past. But some sub-markets will still outperform general trends in house prices, and lift property owners in some favoured districts above the ruck.[29]

The muted growth in capital-city house prices during the 1990s coincided with a growing diversion of household investment into shares and superannuation. In the five years 1993–98, the All Ordinaries index of share prices surged by around 80 per cent. By contrast, an index of established house prices in Australia posted only an 18 per cent improvement (or just 7 per cent in real terms).[30] According to the Australian Stock Exchange, potential first-time home buyers—affluent young singles, couples with less than $25 000 in assets—are among the 34 per cent of Australians who owned scrip in 1997.[31] As young Australians make a break with the past they are opting for more mobile forms of investment that will not tie them down in the same way that home ownership does. Whether or not a correction in the stock market will precipitate a flight of capital back into the relative security of fixed assets, including home purchase, as it did in 1987 is yet to be seen.

If these economic and demographic trends continue into the new millennium, the 1990s will stand as a watershed decade for the Australian housing system. And if indeed the Golden Age of home ownership in Australia is drawing to a close, what does that portend for housing wealth in the future? In Chapter 7 we fast-forward a generation to wonder how these changes to the housing system might have affected ownership patterns and housing wealth by 2030. Everyone knows that projecting trends far into the future is hazardous, even if the underlying premises are reasonably sound. But it can help to alert politicians and bureaucrats to some of the long-term consequences if present trends and policies are left to run their course.

Towards fairer shares of housing wealth

The kind of housing that a society gets is ultimately a matter of public choice. The idea that owner-occupation is one of the essential pillars upon which an egalitarian society is built remains strongly implanted in the popular consciousness of the postwar generation of Australians. Our high level of home ownership at once mirrors, and helps to determine, the structure of Australian society.

Home ownership has been pushed close to its limits in Australia. The rate has hovered around 70 per cent since the early 1960s. This is despite repeated efforts by the federal and state governments to extend access to low-income households who would otherwise have missed out. Not only do they often need help with the initial down-payment in order to bridge the deposit gap—the difference between purchase price and what the bank will lend on a home—but these households depend upon the earnings of workers who cannot be sure of continuing employment. During the last two decades, there has been a sharp rise in the numbers of households falling out of home ownership due to financial hardship or divorce.[32]

In spite of this, a majority of Australians currently enjoy enviable housing standards and the fruits of wealth accumulation. By the time they retire, three out of four Australians own their homes outright.[33] Yet many commentators now hesitate to characterise Australian society as genuinely egalitarian. For one thing, it is simply wrong-headed to suggest that housing in Australia—as distinct from owner-occupied housing—is sufficiently equitable in its distribution to qualify.

For example, despite the existence of special housing programmes in each of the states, comparatively few indigenous Australians enjoy the housing standards that the rest of us take for granted.[34] Of the 81 579 dwellings occupied by Aboriginal and Torres Strait Islanders in the mid-1990s, only 26 per cent were owner-occupied.[35] The two-thirds of indigenous Australians who cannot afford to buy their own home face a lifetime of renting from private landlords (31.6 per cent), or one of the state housing authorities (31.1 per cent). At the time of writing, very little else is known about the experience of indigenous home owners beyond the tentative estimates of dwelling adequacy obtained as part of the 1994 national survey of Aboriginals and Torres Strait Islanders.[36]

Those Australians who cannot afford to buy their own home, and for whom renting *is not a matter of choice*, remain trapped on one side of a housing divide. Although private renting has always been regarded as a transitional tenure—a sort of trampoline—nearly 40 per cent of private tenants now rent for more than ten years.[37] Not only is this group at risk in housing terms, but long-term tenants have the least wealth to show from their housing. They miss out on the tax breaks and the potential for generating personal wealth inherent in home owning. Chapter 8 begins, therefore, by asking what is making our housing system more unequal. Part of the answer lies in the abandonment of any semblance of a strategic approach to housing provision in Australia. Where governments used to co-ordinate the needs of poor Australians and the supply of affordable housing, they are now leaving them to the operation of housing markets.

We conclude by asking what ought to be done. A likely decline in the home ownership rate, together with the downsizing of the public rental sector, will put increasing pressure on the private rental market. The Howard government appears content to play a wait-and-see game with the looming supply problem in the private rental sector. At present the returns are simply not there to attract long-term investment; and in the meantime, the poorest households get squeezed by rising rents. Addressing these stresses in the housing system will require several strategies: mechanisms that offer more protection to home buyers at risk in the labour market; the restoration of funding to the state housing agencies; a much more sophisticated approach to targeted subsidies that work on the supply side of the private rental sector. Lastly, we touch on some of the political options for taxing housing wealth and inheritance.

CHAPTER 1

Timing and Position: The Keys to Capital Gains

How is housing wealth actually created and then redistributed among home owners and small-time and institutional housing investors? Although we aim to shed some light on this question, there is no hiding the complexity of the processes involved. In large cities residential property markets are constantly adjusting. This can be caused by events in the wider economy or by urban development activity.

Although land economists and other academics with interests in property have gone some way towards sorting this out in their minds, it is much harder to quantify in dollars and cents. Land economists make use of sophisticated models to help in the task of identifying and measuring the different determinants of property prices—or their proxies, land values or rents. In the end they have to settle for estimates that can only claim the status of approximations.

Where do capital gains come from?

There are two main sources of capital accumulation in the housing market. The monetary policy of governments is the first source. Obviously home owners have no control over this. The second source is the tax breaks that governments extend to owners and buyers to encourage the spread of home ownership. Here there is some scope for property owners to arrange their financial affairs to maximise the opportunities for income tax relief and enhance returns on investment. Because the role of monetary and taxation policy in expanding housing wealth within the economy is dealt with more fully in Chapters 4 and 5, these sources of redistribution only receive a brief mention here. What sets them apart from the wealth effects that will occupy most of our attention in this chapter is that they are generally *non-spatial* in their impact.

A third source of housing wealth is often overlooked, yet it is vitally important to the transfers of value that take place within the housing market between home owners and other housing investors. It is one thing for your asset to accrue value along with the general movement in aggregate house prices. It is quite another to be on the receiving end of planning gain, the betterment that flows from the capitalisation of public investment into the value of your own private property. Or, alternatively, to be faced with a development proposal that threatens to seriously reduce the value of your home.

We will examine these significant effects upon property values shortly. They contribute to the differences that arise from place to place in capital gains and losses. Unlike monetary policy, or the various tax measures applied by governments to housing investment, these effects are definitely *spatial* in nature. But before considering how housing wealth is created and redistributed by these effects, we should be clear about the nature of the potential value that resides in real estate.

The value stored in real estate

Capital accumulation in the property market relies on the creation of value. With the exception of the construction phase, or the sweat equity that goes into home improvement activity, value creation in the property market owes very little to the labour process. This sets it apart from, for example, the value adding that takes place in manufacturing production. There, value is added by inputs of labour when raw materials are processed and transformed.

In broad terms, the value stored in real estate derives from the intrinsic qualities of the land itself—position, suitability for development, natural features, etc.—and from the investment in the assets that are built upon the land. When urban development takes place, the proceeds from the investment activity surrounding a property are capitalised into the value of real estate. We say much more about these processes shortly.

Until British home owners experienced the late 1980s property boom, there had been a tendency to dismiss underlying movements in house prices as paper gains or losses.[1] The prevailing view was that only a few categories of owners could really capitalise on bullish market conditions. These included speculators, those few profit-takers who deliberately trade-down, and ageing owners selling for good. Other changeover buyers quickly find, irrespective of how much their house has gained in value since they bought it, that they usually have to outlay the same amount to obtain comparable replacement housing.

The fact remains that in the long-term all home owners get to convert the value increments stored in an inflating asset. Even in a slump, so long as owners can sit tight until the market rebounds, there is an expectation that they will eventually break even. In that case, whether or not their savings would have been better off in other investments while they rented is really beside the point for most home owners.

The experience in Britain in the aftermath of the property market collapse at the end of the 1980s, and to a lesser extent in the United States and Australia, exposed some of the flaws in this kind of thinking. As a result of the plunge in house prices in Britain (Figure 2), many first home buyers were still repaying mortgages that greatly exceeded the going value of their homes in the mid-1990s. This phenomenon, which has been called negative equity, is discussed more fully in Chapter 5. Even if these home owners did manage to sit it out as house prices gradually recovered to pre-boom levels, the mortgage repayments in the meantime represented much more than just paper losses. They were paying too much for an asset that had been discounted by the market. The boom-bust regime that has tended to characterise property markets in Britain, the United States and Australia over the last twenty-five years or so is responsible for profound shifts in the capitalisation of the housing stock through time.

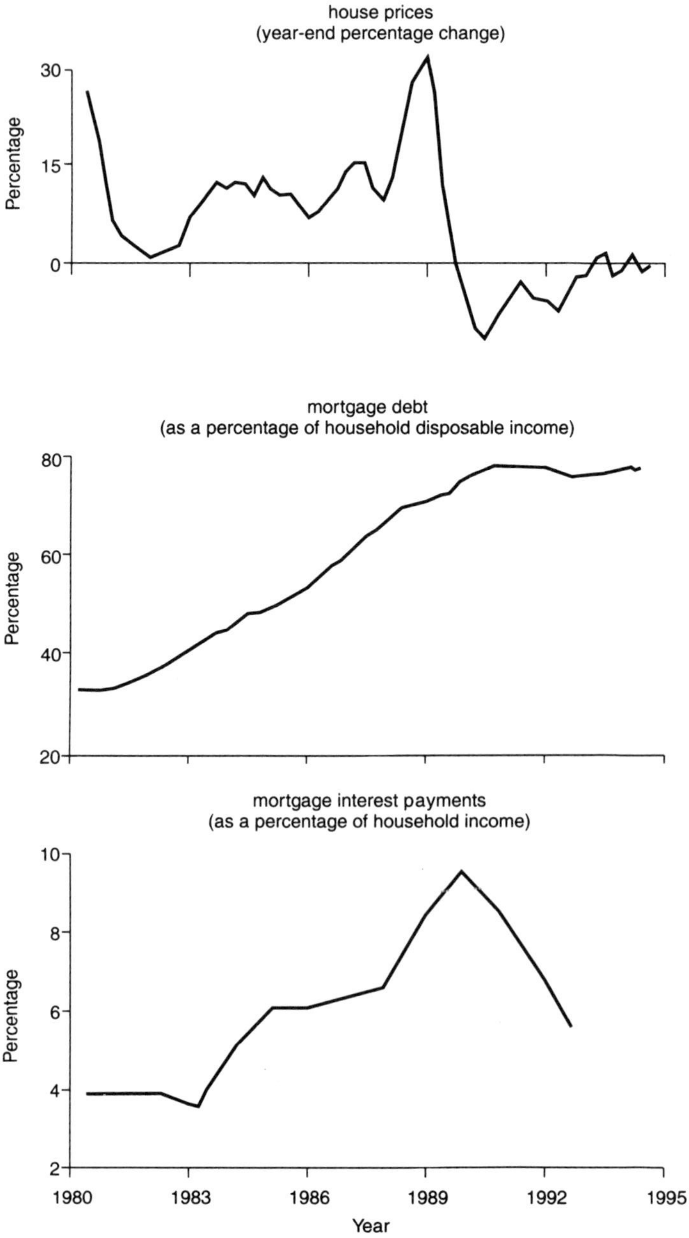

Source: Reserve Bank of Australia, *Bulletin*, September 1995.

Figure 2: House prices and housing finance in Britain, 1980–95

General house price inflation and capital gains

The general movement of house prices determines when, and to what extent, the aggregate value of national housing wealth is expanded or diminished (Figure 3). According to British research, 'a large increase in lending is a *sine qua non* for a house price boom'.[2] The three house price booms in Britain—the early 1970s, late 1970s, and late 1980s—were all associated with a growth in the money supply. Australia's property boom in the early 1970s was also fuelled by excess liquidity when an expansionary budget coincided with the collapse of mining stocks in 1972. This left idle money searching for safer investments. Although the immediate cause was quite different in the late 1980s—the liberalisation of Australia's financial system—once again the outcome was a foregone conclusion. Newly licensed overseas banks jostled with the Australian banks to capture market share. In the process, prudential requirements were relaxed and more loans were placed by the banking system than the economy could possibly absorb.

In October 1987 the stock market crashed and the value of equities on the Australian exchange was written down by almost $100 billion. Despite the loss-taking, capital was moved into

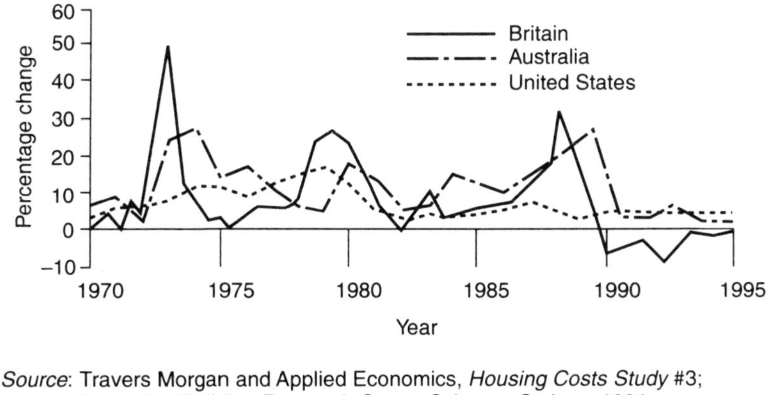

Source: Travers Morgan and Applied Economics, *Housing Costs Study* #3; Australian Building Research Grants Scheme, Sydney, 1991; A. E. Holmans, *House Prices: Changes Through Time.*

Figure 3: Movements in nominal house prices in Britain, Australia and the United States, 1970–95

property, including the residential sector: 'The big switch to property occurred after the October 1987 share collapse . . . in the belief that [property] was a safer form of investment'.[3] More than a decade later, circumstances are so similar that once more some analysts are advising that equities have gone far enough and that a correction is bound to take place soon. But today the big difference is in the conditions that set the stage for underlying demand. The rates of inflation and wage growth are low, and the migration intake is 20 per cent lower than a decade ago.

Although financial deregulation in the 1980s significantly altered the structure of financial markets in countries like Britain and Australia, it is the amount of credit available for housing investment in relation to the underlying demand that ultimately determines the general movement of house prices relative to other commodities within the economy. Who are the main beneficiaries, then, in an overheated housing market? Existing owners benefit from the upward movement in house prices resulting from the extra pressure of demand by new home buyers. Also, in a volatile market, prospective buyers tend to bring forward their purchases of land and houses in order to avoid further escalation of housing costs. They end up paying for the larger mortgages from future wage rises, or by scrimping on other expenses. Eventually the rise in house prices fuelled by plentiful credit is checked when house prices get too far ahead of earnings. Then the ratio between house prices and earnings tends to fall back and stabilise around a long-run equilibrium which, for example, in Britain is about 3.5 to 1.

The real increase in Australian capital house prices over the fifteen years 1979–93 was caused by a combination of the growth in real wage incomes (primarily due to employment growth) and an expansion of net overseas immigration.[4] If income is rising relative to other costs, new home buyers can meet the higher entry costs. This pushes up house prices, and existing owners get the benefit when they sell in the form of capital gains. In this way, capital growth in the residential property market is fuelled by rising real incomes, and the readiness of some wage earners to devote a greater part of their increased earnings to housing expenditure. Thus value is transferred from a new generation of buyers to earlier generations. How big or small that transfer ultimately proves to be is determined by the amplitude of the property cycle. This is the gap between price levels when they reach their peak, as opposed to when they have dipped to the bottom of the cycle.

Tax breaks for home owners

Another often under-rated source of wealth accumulation within owner-occupation takes the form of tax breaks. These differ from country to country (Table 2). The taxation expenditures tied to home ownership in Australia are dealt with more fully in Chapters 4 and 5. By now, taxation expenditures have come to represent an almost unassailable part of the electoral compact between parties on both sides of politics in the United States, Britain, Australia, and New Zealand, although the Blair government voted to remove the tax relief on home mortgages in the 1999–2000 budget. Governments forgo tax revenues in pursuit of the votes of comfortably-off home owners and retired citizens; these forgone revenues help to underwrite what Galbraith calls the 'culture of contentment' in Western societies.[5]

Governments determine the scope for income-tax relief and create the schemes that help households to buy. In Australia and Canada, for example, there is no tax relief for home buyers. At the other extreme, US home buyers can deduct the interest on mortgages worth up to $US1 million from their taxable income. Admittedly there is provision for clawing some of this back by levying capital gains on houses at the point of resale. In practice, though, ordinary home owners in the United States pay little if they plough the proceeds back into a house of at least the same value when they move. Known as roll-over relief, this eliminates a possible brake upon labour mobility in the US economy.

Unlike the geographical transfers of wealth that occupy the remainder of this chapter, tax breaks for owner-occupiers tend to be spatially neutral in their distributional impact. Exceptions may arise when governments deliberately set out to assist a particular category of home buyer, or where subsidies or price discounts are tied to particular locations to attract new home buyers. For example, in the early decades of Canberra's existence, public

Table 2: Tax breaks for home owners

Country	Tax relief on home purchase (maximum allowed)	Capital gains tax	Annual property tax	Maximum loan available as % of house price
Australia	No relief	no	no	85–90
Belgium	Interest payments deductable against income from property and securities	no	yes	90
Britain	Interest on loan up to £30 000[a] (≅ $75 000)[d]	no	yes[b]	95–100
Canada	No relief	no	yes	up to 75
France	Annual interest payments up to FR 40 000 for 5 years (≅ $10 000)[d]	no	yes	60–80
Germany	5% of value of house, up to maximum value of DM 300 000 for 8 years (≅ $250 000)[d]	no	yes	80
Italy	Annual interest payments up to 7m lire (≅ $5 800)[d]	no	yes	50–60
Japan	Tax credit of 1% of loan up to ¥ 20m + 0.5% of next ¥ 10m (≅ $245 000)[d]	yes	yes	85
United States	Interest on loan up to $1m (≅ $1.5m)[d]	yes[c]	yes	80

[a] Removed in the 1999/2000 budget.
[b] Council tax based on value of property.
[c] With rollover relief.
[d] As at May 1999; equivalents in Australian dollars.

Source: Based on *Economist*, 'I owe, I owe, so off to work I go', p. 95.

servants were the beneficiaries of a series of explicit and implicit subsidies to compensate them for the transfer to the Australian Capital Territory. Then, as new home buyers, they were able to capture part of the lavish federal investment in the built form of that city.[6]

The Australian approach to infrastructure pricing for subdivision on the outskirts of our cities has also delivered implicit transfers to the prior owners of the raw land and the initial buyers of serviced allotments.[7] On the one hand, prior owners like market gardeners on the edge of the city can extract a premium for their land once it has been rezoned for subdivision. On the other hand, where less than full cost recovery is charged for the new infrastructure—headworks, roads, water and power connections—new building blocks have tended to be larger and cheaper per unit than they would otherwise have been. 'The fibro cottage on the 850 square metre block stands as a monument—albeit a somewhat unfair one—to the Australian way: cheap land, substitutes for expensive building materials and a lot of "sweat equity".'[8]

Lastly, from time to time when the building industry is really in a slump, governments have made direct grants to, or waived fees for, first-time and low-income home buyers in an effort to stimulate demand. Such measures are partly a response to economic slow-down, and partly a response to the pleas of the housing industry. Even though housing was more affordable in 1996–97 than at any time in the last twenty-five years, prospective home buyers in South Australia appeared reluctant to commit themselves. In January 1997, in an attempt to stimulate the housing industry, the South Australian government offered a one-off $5000 deposit to low-income home buyers and extended a tapering stamp duty concession on first homes and home units up to a value of $150 000. In Australian cities this amounts to an indirect transfer to the outer zone sub-market because so much of the new building still takes place at the edge. But although it is important not to lose sight of the value of these tax breaks as a source of wealth accumulation to home owners, this chapter is much more concerned with the capital gains or losses that result from the operation of property markets.

Sources of geographic variations in capital gains and losses

Different rates of change in house prices from area to area provide a third source of capital accumulation for home owners. From the home buyer's perspective, it is timing and position that hold the keys to capital accumulation. The timing refers to when the house is bought and then sold in relation to highs and lows in the property cycle; the position refers to its geographical location in both national and local housing markets. Looked at from this standpoint, if home buyers go about it consciously their decisions can have a very big bearing on the capital gains or losses that their home attracts while they occupy it.

Some of the most glaring variations in house prices, and rates of change in house prices, are to be found between the regions that form a nation's territory. If allowance is made for the lags, these geographic—or place-to-place—variations in capital gains and losses often provide an index of how healthy a region's economy is. It is clear from national property market indices that the rate of inflation in house prices varies significantly from city to city, and within any one city, several reasonably distinctive geographical sub-markets perform at different rates of appreciation. The high and low performers within a city's housing market normally comprise suburbs that share similar developmental and social class backgrounds, or have been targeted for special attention by investors or home seekers.

For example, suburbs at the low end of the market are affordable for a stratum of home buyers who qualify for home purchase assistance. But these are the suburbs that are especially vulnerable to economic downturn. Some local property owners, for example, get caught up in a vicious circle of retrenchment, financial hardship, mortgage arrears and defaulting, and then a spate of mortgagee sales that depress local house prices. In contrast, from time to time a specialised sub-market outperforms all other residential property. This happened in the 1970s and again in the early 1980s with condominium development on Queensland's Gold Coast. It was repeated during the 1990s with the rise and rise of an apartment sub-market at the heart of Australia's largest cities.

What processes determine who gains and loses, and by how much, from the periodic and spatially uneven movement of house prices? This question was seriously addressed for the first time in the early 1970s. On the one hand, it was part of the conceptual reasoning underlying a theory of residential location developed by urban economists. And on the other, it was included as part of a broader account of the redistribution of real income in cities. In pursuing this interest in the redistribution of income within cities, an urban geographer, David Harvey, pointed to some of the processes that contribute to the capitalisation of public and private investment into house prices.[9] In each case, these early thoughts formed the building blocks for more elaborate sets of proposals about the root causes of place-to-place variations in capital gains and losses.

Three general arguments have been developed from the various attempts to explain the marked geographical variations in house price inflation and capital gains and losses, and the part these play in the creation and transfer of housing wealth. They rest on three factors: the exclusivity of high-status suburbs in the urban housing market; the capitalisation of public and private investment into house prices; and the linkage between labour and property markets. Although the first two arguments focus upon the variations in capital gains and losses internally *within* cities, the third is more concerned about the underlying causes of *regional* disparities in property values. This third argument links wealth effects in the housing market to the growth and decline of regions.

Social exclusivity, demand pressures and capital growth

The first of these early attempts to account for spatial variations in house prices stressed the residential desirability and social prestige of individual suburbs.[10] Each city has its exclusive suburbs in which well-heeled captains of industry and establishment families want to live. In the case of the most sought-after real estate, which rarely comes onto the market, aspiring owners are usually willing to pay a premium. The sheer scarcity of these jewels in the property market crown guarantees their status as price leaders in any Australian city. Some of the cliff-top homes fronting Sydney Harbour in the eastern suburbs now command prices between $10 and $20 million. Melbourne's equivalent are the tightly held seaside properties at Portsea and Queenscliff on the tip of the Mornington Peninsula. Although they are out of the range of all but the wealthiest families in Australia, newly-moneyed wannabes are keen to live close by and are certainly conscious of the cachet that attaches to particular postcode areas.

The intensity of feeling that can be aroused over any threat to a coveted address surfaces in conjunction with the redrawing of postcode or suburb boundaries.[11] In 1997, when the Victorian government's Place Names Committee set about clarifying some disputed suburb boundaries in Melbourne, their recommendations were met with cries of outrage from some residents. Melbourne City Council received almost 400 submissions arguing for the retention of East Melbourne's historic name. On the other side of the city, about 1800 angry Yarraville residents formally expressed their dismay at the proposal to rename a wedge of their suburb Kingsville. A local real estate agent reckoned that Yarraville commands up to 20 per cent more than neighbouring West Footscray. On the basis of past experience, agents estimated that realignment could add or subtract as much as $20 000 to or from house prices in Melbourne's more established suburbs.

A suburb like Toorak, Melbourne's most expensive patch of residential real estate, is a desirable address for an ever-increasing number of business or managerial couples with incomes in the top bracket. Although they might be able to afford the price tag, they still have to compete at auction for a handful of properties that only infrequently come onto the market. Evans, a British urban economist, develops the concept of 'social agglomeration' to describe the express desire of home buyers to live among social class peers, and in surroundings they feel are in keeping with their perceived self-image.[12]

More generally, this imbalance between excess demand and a finite supply of housing within certain suburbs can drive house prices upwards in a given geographical sub-market. This is precisely what has happened in short bursts throughout the inner suburbs of Sydney, Melbourne, and Adelaide. These are the Australian cities that have been comprehensively gentrified over the last twenty-five years or so—certainly more so than Brisbane, Perth, or Hobart.[13] During the height of the property boom of 1973–74, couples looking to renovate, home improvement specialists, and speculators, fought over inner Adelaide's brick and bluestone terraces and villas. This remnant stock is concentrated in the nineteenth-century suburbs abutting the Parklands encircling the City of Adelaide (Figure 4).

Soaring turnover rates in the property market are symptomatic of a 'feeding frenzy'. As the charts illustrate for a selection of Adelaide's inner suburbs, they generate steep price hikes in a comparatively short space of time (Figure 4). Suburbs like North Adelaide, Norwood–Kent Town, and Unley–Hyde Park offered plenty of possibilities. At the beginning of the 1970s such a place could be bought for $12 000 to $15 000. Twelve to fifteen months later, the same house was fetching $22 000 to $25 000. One of the authors bought from an estate agent who had been playing the market for all she was worth during those crazy months of 1973–74. Over an 18-month period she and her husband reportedly made twelve moves—buying, making cosmetic changes to the property, extracting their sweat equity and moving on. Now that really is running up the escalator!

Property markets eventually regain their equilibrium. But since these effects have been cumulative, and sustained across several cycles, the long-run yields obtained by home owners in the inner-zone sub-markets of the three gentrifying Australian cities have been very impressive on the whole. The category of home owners that was not treated so well by the inner city sub-market was the changeover buyers who got caught when Sydney's property boom ended in 1989. As house prices climbed progressively higher during 1987 and 1988, many changeover buyers borrowed highly geared finance or cashed in shares to trade-up to a lavish inner-city apartment or townhouse that they had their eye on. They did not allow for the sharp lift in mortgage interest rates from 13.5 per cent in 1987/88 to over 17 per cent in 1989/90 as the federal government tried to dampen economic activity (Figure 5). Those who could no longer meet their mortgage repayments were forced

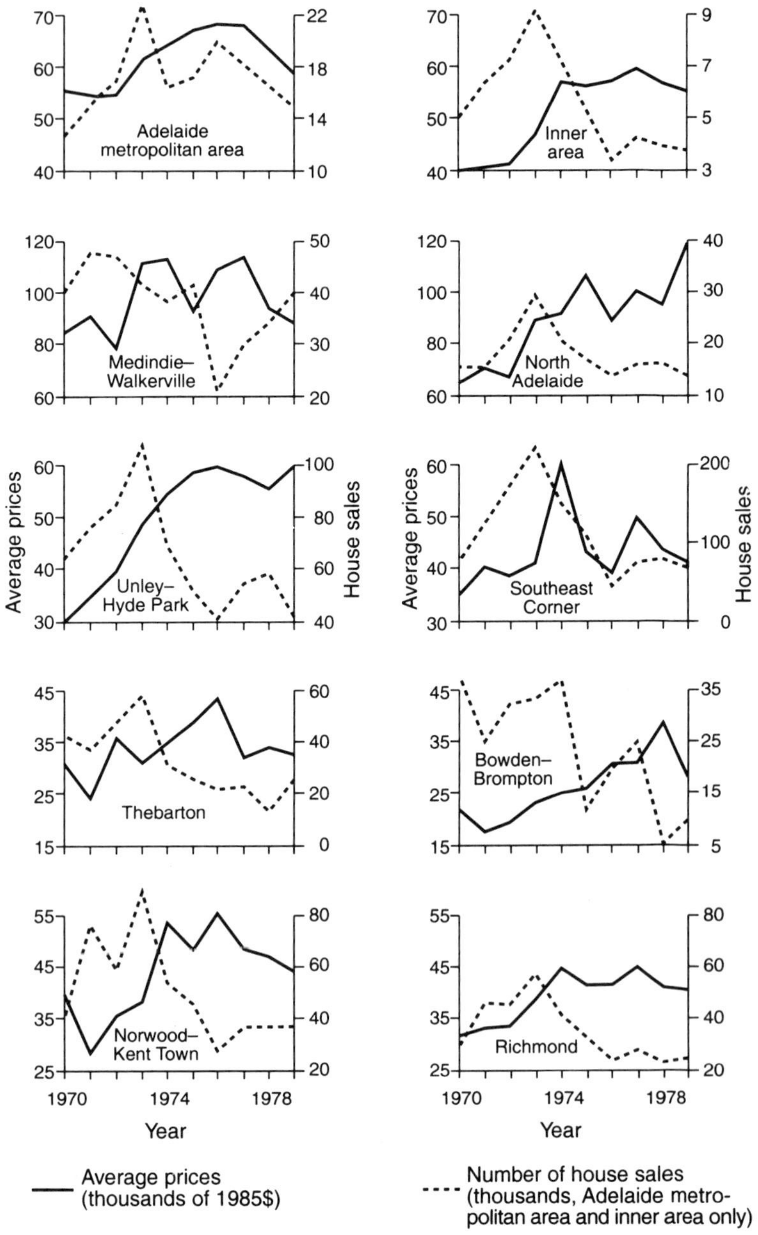

Source: South Australian Department of Lands, *Accumulated Sales Reports*.

Figure 4: House sales and price change in inner Adelaide, 1970–80

to sell in 1990/91, just when the property market was beginning to dip. House prices fell by as much 23 per cent in parts of inner Sydney during the year.

There was mounting pressure on inner-zone house prices again in Sydney and Melbourne in the second half of the 1990s. Even so, house prices in Sydney's top-end suburbs outstripped the gains reported in comparable segments of the market in all other Australian capitals. Median house prices in suburbs like Mosman, Woollahra, Waverley, and North Sydney—all within the inner zone—climbed by 60 per cent in real terms. In Melbourne, although median house prices took longer to recover after the collapse in 1990, top-end suburbs more than made up for that lost ground during 1996/97. In the year ending June 1997, real median increases between 20 and 25 per cent were reported in a broad arc of suburbs adjacent to the city core—though not Melbourne's inner west. This almost matched the 30 per cent gain reported for inner Sydney housing.

The gains were partly fed by the high executive salaries in growth sectors like financial services, communications, and information technology. Pace-setting corporations now have to compete for their senior management in the global marketplace. Property analysts expect this top-end demand for inner-city town housing and apartments in Sydney and Melbourne to be maintained over the next couple of years as shareholders pull funds out of the stock market to reinvest in investment property. In commenting upon the strength of the inner-zone sub-market in Sydney and Melbourne in 1996/97, the chief executive of the Real Estate Institute of Australia noted that 'The real estate market has been highly segmented—as it always is in the early stages of a boom. Location and the type of property has been the key. And there has been a strong geographical element to it as well—strong activity has been confined to the inner parts of Sydney and Melbourne.'[14]

As a result of the demand that has been concentrated in the inner-city housing market over the last ten to fifteen years, capital growth has outstripped most other parts of metropolitan Sydney. For example, the Planning Research Centre at the University of Sydney estimates that real price growth for housing in the inner zone of Sydney exceeded that for outer zone locations by a factor of 2.5 between 1982 and 1990.[15] Then, between 1990 and 1996,

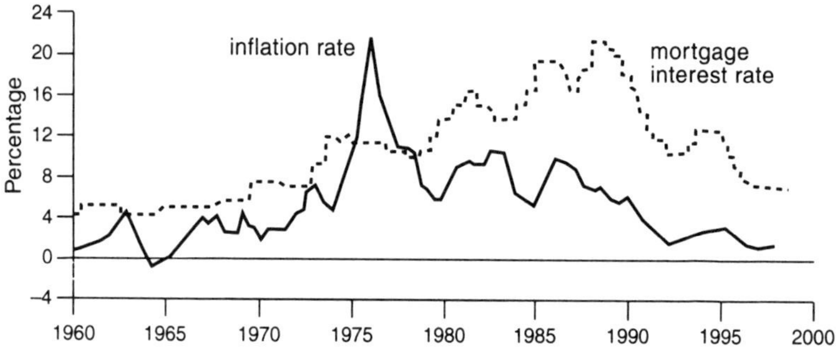

Source: Reserve Bank of Australia.

Figure 5: Mortgage interest rates and inflation rates, Australia, 1960–98

the ratio of house price growth for the inner and outer zones widened even further, to seven to one. In the process, implicit transfers of housing wealth are taking place between home owners in Sydney's outer suburbs and owner-occupiers and investors in the inner zone.

The capitalisation of investment into house prices

The foregoing account of the source of capital gains as a component of housing wealth fails to pay sufficient attention to the processes of value creation and transfer in the property market. 'Value creation' can be equated with urban capital formation. Between them, public sector agencies and private businesses make the major investment decisions that help to capitalise different parts of the city.

This can take the form of new physical infrastructure, such as the plant and equipment provided by public utilities, a regional shopping centre, or community facilities. In the residential sector, it generally takes the form of new dwellings and the additions and alterations that owners carry out from time to time. Part of this investment activity gets capitalised into the value of adjacent housing.

In this situation, urban economists talk about property owners benefiting from the positive externalities that urban development generates nearby. In the broad context of suburban development in Australia, there is no doubt that the pioneers in any new housing subdivision are probably the ones who stand to benefit most from this process. In developing large housing estates, project developers bank on asking higher allotment prices for each successive land release as the suburb becomes more established and appealing to prospective home buyers. Naturally the developer also expects to take an unearned increment off the top as a result of this process of betterment. In the industry it is known as the 'development gain'.

It pays to be aware, however, that beneficial neighbourhood effects are by no means guaranteed in developing suburbs. A large component of public housing in your neighbourhood is bound to dampen capitalisation. This is one of the reasons for keeping the presence of public housing in new growth corridors, like Golden Grove in Adelaide, to 12–15 per cent. In some sleepy rural shires at the outer edge of our big cities there is sometimes a long delay before the social investment that boosts property values eventuates. Home buyers pay a premium to back onto the bush in Sydney's Kuringai Chase or the slopes of Adelaide's Mt Lofty, but there is no scarcity of access to bush in the Canberra satellite town of Tuggeronong.

On the downside, there are a range of developments that can take place close to your home that produce negative externalities. Within large cities, freeway and airport proposals are among the most contentious. The shadow effects along the corridor or under the flight path disrupt community and daily life so much that property values are bound to fall. Recent examples include the City Link tollway in Melbourne, which connects the Tullamarine and South-eastern Freeways and provides a long-awaited bypass around the central business district for the huge volumes of traffic flowing east–west through Melbourne. The addition of a second parallel runway at Botany right in the heart of the Sydney region is another recent case. This decision, which could be delayed no longer due to the growth of air traffic at Sydney International Airport, generated immense political turmoil at both the federal and the state levels because of the numbers of marginal seats lying beneath the flight path.

Well-endowed and residentially stable neighbourhoods are not necessarily more vociferous than transient, poorer communities in defence of property rights and values, but they are usually more resourceful and politically effective. For example, the movers and shakers of Albert Park devised a sophisticated campaign strategy to oppose the building of Melbourne's Formula One motor racing circuit in their backyard. They marshalled support from some of Australia's most powerful corporate and media personalities.

What sets urban externalities apart from externality effects in general, then, is that they assume the form of spatial fields.[16] This is also called the neighbourhood effect. The freeway and flight-path cases are especially dramatic, but urban externalities cover a multitude of localised effects that can raise or discount property values. In fact, the valuation of your property might be susceptible to both positive and negative effects that offset each other to some extent. But make no mistake, the market does price these effects. An interesting study of the property market in Boston by two American urban economists shows that house prices there reacted positively to the accessibility afforded by a nearby thruway and proximity to regional shopping centres, and negatively to proximity to industrial estates.[17]

In a more general sense, it is the continual restructuring of urban space—simultaneously fixing new capital investment in one part of the city while running down old building assets in another (disinvestment)—which gives rise to a transfer of value in the residential property market. When value is transferred in this way via the property market, home owners can enjoy localised price rises in excess of those normally set by the forces of supply and demand.

David Harvey outlined the processes thought to be responsible for the transfer of value within the housing market in his work on the redistribution of income within cities.[18] He was especially interested in changes over time in the relative accessibility of different localities within large cities. Harvey noted that this occurs with population growth within a transport corridor, as congestion slows travel time, or alternatively when route upgrades reduce travel time. The rising levels of car ownership that opened up Australian suburbs during the 1960s and 1970s flattened accessibility contours and also helped to advance the write-down in value of inner-area housing stock.

In Sydney, for example, the period 1931–68 was one of major road and bridge building.[19] Then, after the end of petrol rationing in 1950, the real price of petrol fell—by about 20 per cent between 1956 and 1968. The main beneficiaries were commuters to the central business district and property owners in the outer areas. This phase of Sydney's growth, therefore, was characterised by greater capital growth in the outer suburbs and diminishing real gains, if not losses, in the inner suburbs.

Surprisingly, when compared with the experience of typical United States cities, between the mid-1970s and 1989 the gradients of house and land prices began to steepen again in the Sydney region. Major road construction was postponed during the period by anti-freeway governments, which nevertheless let the public transit services deteriorate at the same time. Unlike the United States, the orientation of the transport system in Australian cities remains strongly radial. This is due in no small part to the failure to invest in circumferential roads that would help to draw more activity and jobs from around the core. As a consequence, commuting costs probably rose by about 55 per cent in Sydney between 1977 and 1989.[20]

There is no doubt that the steepening of the price gradients in Sydney (and Melbourne) is also connected with the spurt of growth in finance and business services and jobs that took place in the 1980s. In Australia these congregated in the prestigious central office sector. In United States metro areas, despite the impressive rebuilding of Manhattan's financial heart, most of the expansion of office and business space took place in Edge City nodes strung like beads around the ringroad system. Meanwhile the New South Wales government was spending billions on the redevelopment of Darling Harbour adjacent to the central business district. As well as creating a vast waterfront mecca for overseas tourists and relaxing locals, this project generated multipliers that continue to ripple through inner Sydney's property sector. In summary, estimates suggest that at least half the increase in Sydney's price gradient was due to increased congestion and increased travel times, and another 10 per cent to the effects of the housing reinvestment that has accompanied the gentrification of the inner suburbs.[21]

Regional price differences and links between labour and housing markets

A third approach links the movement of house prices with the fortunes of the local economy, except that now the focus switches to regional variations in capital gains and housing wealth. Of course, in so far as the economic base of a city also shapes its regional economy, this is also an important determinant of the wide range in house prices that frequently exists from city to city.

In studying the impact of industrial restructuring on different regions within the British economy since World War II, a sociologist came to realise that changes taking place in regional labour markets seemed to spill over into the domestic property market.[22] David Thorns was not alone in noticing the growing divide between the 'areas of persistent decline' in northern England and southern Scotland—Clydeside, Merseyside, Greater Manchester and Tyneside—and the broad belt of 'structurally favoured' areas in the south. He must be given credit, however, for suggesting that a process of cumulative and progressive regional disadvantage in both the labour and housing markets may redistribute housing wealth nationally and open an increasing gap between the more affluent and depressed regions.

The gap between house prices in the south-east of England and Greater London, and the north, widened alarmingly in the 1970s and showed no signs of abating. On this basis, Thorns suggested:

> The results of such marked changes upon owner-occupiers in these declining areas is to reinforce their losses sustained by the labour market change. Not only have they lost their job, but also their main private investment, their own house, is also of declining value and virtually unsellable except at a price which would represent a substantial loss to the household . . .

> In contrast to these areas, those that have received the benefits of restructuring in the form of jobs and higher wage levels are also those areas which have benefited the most from the price escalation of the 1970s in house values.[23]

The assumption of a widening gap between house prices in the north and south of Britain was subsequently refuted. Although price inflation was led by London and the south-east, and rippled outward, 'it is so lagged in the regions of lower house prices as to be almost countercyclical'.[24] Indeed, in the early 1990s there was a strong reassertion of this cyclical variation in regional house prices, including a narrowing of the price gap between the north and the south. While southern and eastern house prices fell by an average of 23 to 30 per cent from their peak in late 1988, those in the northern regions dropped by no more than 3 per cent on average. The firming of house prices in the north coincided with greater economic resilience in the regions of Scotland, the north-west, Yorkshire and Humberside during the 1992–93 recession.[25]

The effects of structural adjustment within the regional economy on local housing markets are neatly illustrated in a case study comparing the experience of home owners in Glasgow and Luton.[26] Between 1989 and 1993, workers in Luton were twice as likely to have their take-home pay cut as those in Glasgow, and two-thirds more likely to lose their jobs. When the recession came, Luton suffered much more than Glasgow. With an economic base of light manufacturing and services, Luton had managed to capture much more job-creating investment in the booming 1980s but then had to shed labour in the downturn. The impact upon home owners was very uneven. Among 30–49-year-olds in Luton, 23 per cent missed mortgage repayments over the four-year period, compared with 4 per cent of a similar group of Glaswegians. At the same time, Luton house prices went into a slide, whereas house prices in Glasgow firmed.

The same connection between regional cycles and sizeable differences in the movement of city house prices has been observed in the United States. In a very readable book on wealth and the American electorate in the aftermath of the Reagan Administration, Kevin Phillips concludes that 'the decade's revaluations in the US housing market had quietly redistributed hundreds of billions of dollars (at least on paper)—and done so with even more bias than income shifts'.[27] Compared with the previous two decades, when house prices in most cities moved at about the rate of inflation and regional differences were reasonably modest, the 1980s and 1990s were turbulent times for single-family home owners in the United States.[28] House prices soared in the north-east, California, Hawaii, Seattle, and Washington, DC, while home owners in Alaska and parts of the south-west were forced to write down the value of their property. By the beginning of the new decade, the real estate booms in the north-east and California were all but over.

Figures 6a and 6b display the different rates of house price appreciation for Australia's state and territory capitals between the middle of 1993 and 1998. Because the chartmaker Hans Baekgaard sets each index against the same baseline (June 1993) it is easy to compare the respective performance of the capital-city housing markets.[29] Over the five-year period, median house prices climbed by about forty points in Sydney, Melbourne, and Perth; by nearly twenty points in Brisbane and Darwin; and by no more than five points in Adelaide and Hobart. Canberra's median house price index actually fell by ten points in the same period.

Although the links between regional cycles and the movement of capital-city house prices have not been explicitly drawn for Australian cities, a general case can be made for some of these price disparities in the 1990s on the basis of the differing impact of economic restructuring. Nationally, Sydney has emerged as the country's only serious contender for status as a global city. It is now the preferred location in Australasia for the regional head-quarters of corporations with a global reach in financial services, investment banking, foreign-exchange dealing, communications, and information technology. This is pushing incomes at the top of the occupational ladder to levels that cannot be matched in the same numbers elsewhere in Australia. Melbourne, with a more diversified economic base, and Brisbane have attracted lesser shares of the growth in these sectors of the new service economy. But cities like Adelaide and Hobart are suffering increasingly from their peripheral location and resource-dependent state economies.

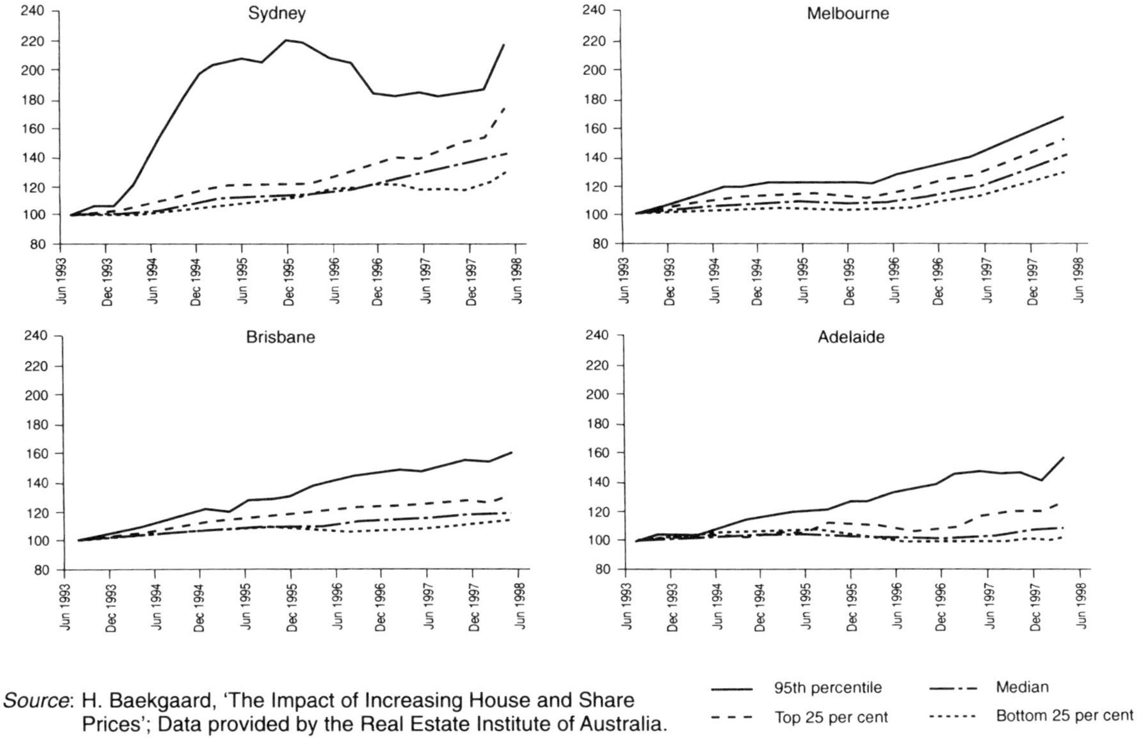

Source: H. Baekgaard, 'The Impact of Increasing House and Share Prices'; Data provided by the Real Estate Institute of Australia.

Figure 6a: Established house sales price percentiles in Sydney, Melbourne, Brisbane and Adelaide, 1993–98 (Index June 1993 = 100)

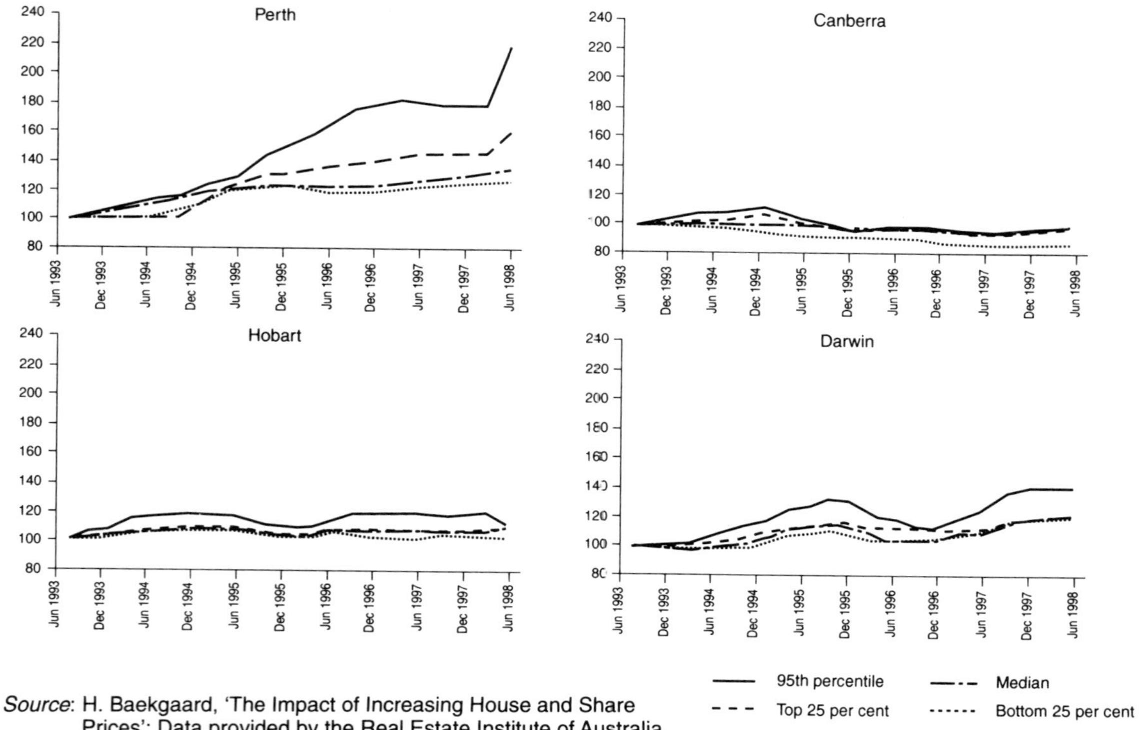

Source: H. Baekgaard, 'The Impact of Increasing House and Share Prices'; Data provided by the Real Estate Institute of Australia.

Figure 6b: Established house sales price percentiles in Perth, Canberra, Hobart and Darwin, 1993–98 (Index June 1993 = 100)

Canberra also suffered a setback in the mid-1990s with the loss of some 12 000 jobs from the federal public service.

Nor should other factors be overlooked. Each year, over half of all the immigrants that arrive in Australia settle in Sydney and Melbourne. This puts added pressure on lot and dwelling production. For these reasons, coupled with the running down of the surplus dwelling stock in Sydney and Melbourne, BIS-Shrapnel predict that house prices in Sydney and Melbourne will rise by nearly 40 per cent over the next three years (1997–2000).[30] Further, they forecast that this growth will be followed by Perth (26 per cent), Brisbane (22 per cent), Canberra (12 per cent), and Adelaide (9 per cent). In the case of Canberra and Adelaide, together with Hobart, after adjusting for inflation, median house prices may possibly be lower in real terms. Although other forecasters might take issue with the magnitude of the price rises predicted for Sydney and Melbourne, there is unlikely to be any disagreement about the respective ranking of the cities.

The keys to capital gains in the suburbs: timing and position

Spatially differentiated housing sub-markets *within* cities are 'as marked as, if not more marked than, the pattern of regional differences'.[31] Figure 7a shows the gradation in median house prices for sixteen sub-regions of Sydney in the first quarter of 1997. They range from a high of $600 000 for Neutral Bay–Spit in inner Sydney to a low of $131 000 for Penrith–Windsor in outer Sydney, a ratio of almost five to one.[32] Further, by ranking these same sixteen sub-regions (Figure 7b) according to the rates of growth in real house prices recorded for the two periods 1982–90 and 1990–96, it is possible to broadly identify which suburbs are on the way up and which are on the way down in Sydney's housing market. This is in a loose manner of speaking, of course, because technically the chart is comparing shifts in the rates of capital growth in the various sub-regions.

From Figure 7b it is evident that St George suburbs have moved up five places, Eastern Suburbs three places, Canterbury–Bankstown

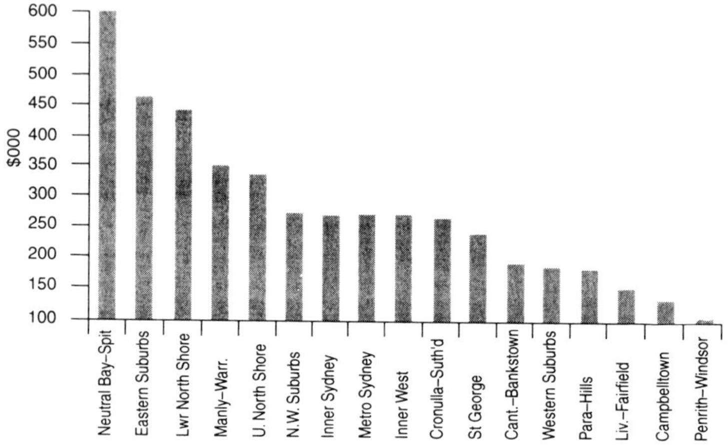

Source: Residex house price indices, Planning Resource Centre, University of Sydney.

Figure 7a: Median house prices, Sydney, 1997

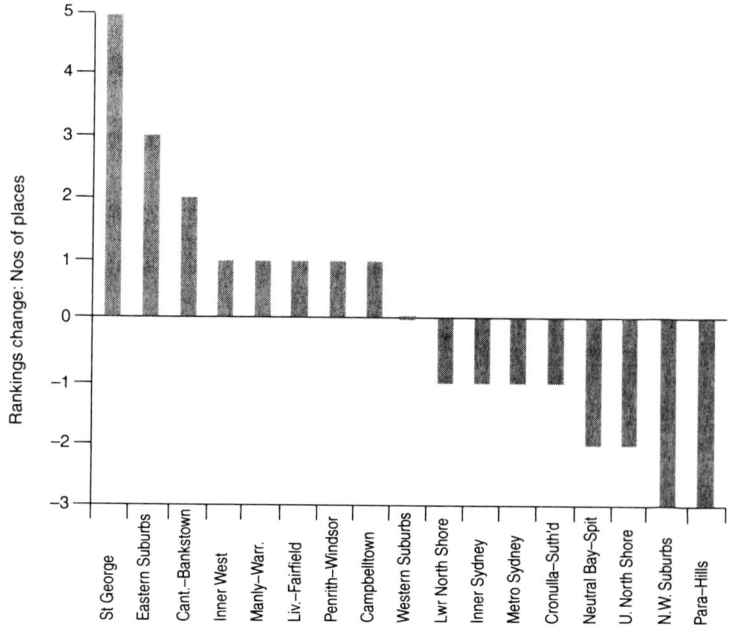

Source: Derived from Residex unit price indices; Planning Resource Centre, University of Sydney; Australian Bureau of Statistics, CPI series for Sydney.

Figure 7b: Change in the ranking of Sydney sub-regions according to real price growth (1982 compared with 1990)

two places and the Inner West, Manly–Warringah, Liverpool–Fairfield, Penrith–Windsor and Campbelltown one place each. Those that dropped back in ranking the most are the suburbs of Parramatta–Hills and the north-west suburbs (three places). They are followed by Neutral Bay–Spit and the Upper North Shore suburbs (two places). Then the suburbs making up the sub-regions of Lower North Shore, Inner Sydney, and Cronulla–Sutherland (one place each).

Viewed from the perspective of the metropolitan housing market as a whole, individual suburbs and their housing stock are like the interlocking pieces of a jigsaw puzzle. While the metropolitan pattern of supply and demand sets the broad framework within which price setting takes place at the local level, individual suburbs are subjected to the ebb and flow of urban development activity and the spill-over effects that this generates. As a consequence, suburban price levels are endlessly being reset as successive home buyers make their evaluation of the positive or negative features of an area.

This is seen at its best every Saturday of the year in Melbourne, the sale-by-auction capital of Australia. Buyers also factor in the quality and size, and perhaps the potential, of a house and land package. But, more often than not, these variables tend to be fairly uniform within any particular suburb. Since whole suburbs are subdivided and developed at about the same time, often by the one developer, it is not surprising that they take on a distinctive residential identity in the minds of house hunters.

Survey results obtained from 419 home owners living in eight Adelaide suburbs provide us with more detail on capital gains and losses in relation to timing and position.[33] The eight suburbs were selected to represent the upper, middle, and lower segments of Adelaide's housing market (Figure 8). This places North Adelaide, a gentrified inner-city suburb, at the top of the market along with Burnside and West Lakes. Burnside is a dress-circle suburb in the eastern foothills of the Mt Lofty Range. West Lakes, a comprehensively planned community—circa 1970s—close to Adelaide's foreshore, is a *nouveau riche* enclave in the western suburbs. Flinders Park is close to the middle in almost every respect—geographically, socio-economically, and demographically. Hallett Cove is a recent southern suburb settled by youngish families with commanding sea views, which places it in a stratum above most of the housing well to the south and north of the city centre. This leaves Birkenhead–Exeter, an old working-class suburb, with Christies Beach, close to the bottom of the market, which is represented by Elizabeth Park–Elizabeth Downs. These last two are outer-suburban dormitories that were developed by the South Australian Housing Trust in the 1950s and 1960s to be close to industry (Figure 8). Some of the workers bought their homes from the Trust under the rental-purchase scheme. These Trust tenants were able to pay off the house while paying the rent.

Estimates of the capital gains and losses by place of residence and date of purchase are set out in Table 3. They are based on actual property transactions and expressed in 1990 prices; however, no adjustment is made for the deposit, or outgoings like the mortgage bill, conveyancing, property rates, depreciation, and maintenance. Despite these deficiencies, and the reduced numbers of sales in some of the cells during the 1970s, the pattern of annual gains and losses according to where sellers lived, and when they sold in relation to the property cycle, is most informative.

To begin with, inner suburbs like North Adelaide and Burnside consistently register capital gains, while outer suburbs like Hallett Cove, Christies Beach, and Elizabeth Park–Elizabeth Downs appear to be losing ground in the market, or at best posting negligible gains. Reinvestment in the inner-zone housing market over the last twenty-five years has driven house prices upwards well beyond the consumer price index. Meanwhile, house prices in parts of the outermost suburbs have stagnated or even fallen in real terms. Many home buyers in the outer northern and southern suburbs of Adelaide, including some of the Housing Trust's rental-purchasers are probably unsuspecting casualties if the worth of housing is judged merely in terms of asset values and yields. By contrast, the upwardly mobile couples resettling Adelaide's inner suburbs have periodically engaged in concerted political action not only to secure the conditions for asset appreciation, but to defend their property investment where necessary.

Clearly, top suburbs like North Adelaide and Burnside, or West Lakes in the 1980s, have done much better in *absolute* terms than suburbs in the bottom of the market. But in some phases of the

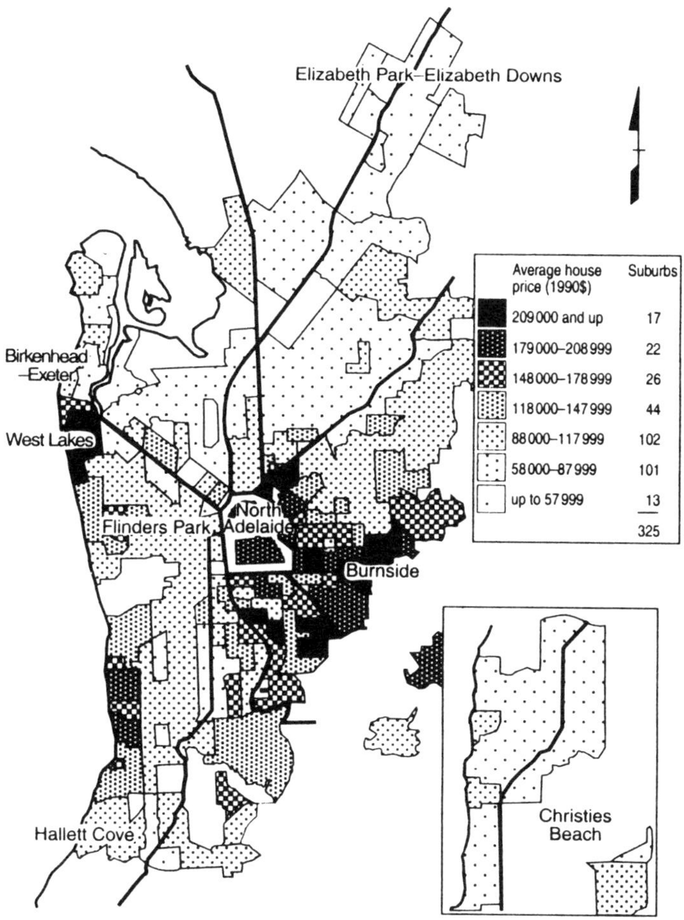

Source: South Australian Valuation Office.

Figure 8: Average house prices in metropolitan Adelaide, 1990

property cycle, the *yields* from this same gilt-edged real estate are not nearly as impressive (Table 3). Conversely, the experience of Birkenhead–Exeter vendors in 1988/89 seems to be at odds with its reputation as a run-down backwater. By the mid-1980s, this nineteenth-century mariners' settlement was beginning to attract

Table 3: Estimated gross returns, suburb and date of purchase of Adelaide home owners selling dwellings in 1988–89 (1990 prices)[a]

Gross returns	*Birkenhead –Exeter*	*Burnside*	*Christies Beach*	*Elizabeth Park– Elizabeth Downs*	*Flinders Park*	*Hallet Cove*	*North Adelaide*	*West Lake*
Total number	44	49	52	76	34	71	32	61
Average sale price	65 559	227 032	67 655	55 490	98 561	96 730	282 610	225 300
1971–73								
Number	–	5	3	4	3	–	1	2
Annual gain or loss	–	2 529	510	–548	1 451	–	10 809	–503
Yield[b]	–	1.7	0.8	–0.7	1.7	–	7.4	0.1
1974–76								
Number	3	4	4	11	4	3	1	5
Annual gain or loss	830	–1 396	–1 816	–1 154	–3	–881	2 707	78
Yield[b]	1.5	–0.6	–1.9	–1.4	0.0	–0.7	2.1	0.3
1977–79								
Number	4	4	7	9	4	6	1	2
Annual gain or loss	317	4 325	12	–276	241	–131	43 933	400
Yield[b]	0.6	4.4	0.7	–0.2	–0.1	–0.1	11.4	0.3
1980–82								
Number	4	4	10	12	10	20	6	16
Annual gain or loss	2 815	6 215	854	–245	3 191	1 905	12 442	5 666
Yield[b]	10.4	3.9	1.6	–0.3	3.6	2.5	5.2	3.2
1983–85								
Number	11	19	14	18	9	18	12	21
Annual gain or loss	1 353	5 490	–1 343	–3 369	–783	–476	6 887	6 442
Yield[b]	2.7	2.7	–1.5	–4.3	–0.3	0.1	5.4	3.7
1986–88								
Number	22	13	14	22	4	24	11	15
Annual gain or loss	7 215	24 213	2 069	–2 342	596	2 851	56 742	4 989
Yield[b]	15.3	10.9	2.8	–3.5	0.5	3.3	21.1	3.2

[a] Based on 1988/89 vendors who purchased in the suburb after 1970.
[b] Percentage return per year.

Source: South Australian Valuation Office, *Sales Report*.

young house hunters priced out of the inner-city renovation submarket, or wanting to live near the sea. Also, the redevelopment of nearby Port Adelaide, under way since the mid-1970s, and now Semaphore, has definitely had a positive impact upon yields (Table 3). Hence it looks as though changes in house prices and capital growth within metropolitan housing markets are not as clear-cut as some would have. The suggestion of a systemic class bias to the pattern of capital gains and losses might be intuitively appealing to old class warriors, but the facts do not always support it.

There is no doubt that the ongoing restructuring of cities plays an important role in shaping patterns of housing wealth. But the wealth effects of capital gains and losses do not normally hinge on the ownership of a single residence during a household's lifetime. Australians, along with Americans, are among the most mobile households in the world. By tracking movers, we can get a much better picture of how they build up their equity in housing in the process of shifting from suburb to suburb.

These *tracer studies* of consecutive shifts that home owners make in the course of a lifetime enable us to reconstruct the steps by which they acquired their housing wealth. They allow us to distinguish owners who have been consistent winners in the housing stakes, and the stratagems with respect to position and timing that have cumulatively helped along the way. The focus now shifts to the mixed fortunes of a selection of the 206 Adelaide owners who sold their homes in 1988–89. Some were winners, some marked time, and some had lost everything by the time mortgage interest rates finally eased in the early 1990s (Figure 5).

CHAPTER 2

Winners and Losers

Many kinds of home owners

WHO ARE THESE WINNERS enriched by home-owning, and who are the losers entrapped by their home purchase decisions? Is it even possible to answer this question in such a general form any longer? Can we really lump the 69 per cent of home-owning households in Australia into broad categories like winners and losers? Households are now so much more varied in their demographic and occupational make-up than they were a generation ago. Changes to the labour market and the structure of employment are altering the predictability of household earnings and the ability to repay housing loans.[1] As women rethink their expectations and role in the home,[2] the difference between the earnings of one-income and two-income households takes on a growing significance for the differential accumulation of housing wealth.[3]

Immigrants to Australia have brought with them quite different housing traditions to further complicate the picture.[4] Remarkably, those migrating from Europe in time to participate in the postwar prosperity currently enjoy higher levels of outright ownership (51.8 per cent) than their Australian-born counterparts (41.6 per cent).[5] Many of these same parents have also made a down-payment on second or third or fourth homes in the names of their children. This not only gives the young people a start in life, but it also avoids a capital gains tax on investment housing. By contrast, much higher proportions of the recent migrant intake from countries in South-East Asia (41.7 per cent), North-East Asia (41.9 per cent), and South and Central America (49 per cent) remain trapped in the rental sector. During the 1980s and 1990s there simply were not enough jobs to go round, which tends to consign newcomers to the bottom of the labour market.

At what point in their housing histories should we determine whether owners are winners or losers? As we will discover in Chapter 6, opportunities to amass housing wealth have been different for each of the postwar generations.[6] Anyone who has ever bought a house will recall that they were hardly in a position to make investment potential their top priority in selecting their first home. In contrast, changeover buyers have generally built up a sufficiently large nest-egg to give serious thought to the investment potential of their next home. Unlike cash-strapped first home buyers, established mortgagors and outright owners can usually meet the premiums commanded by promising or high-performance real estate.

During the course of a lifetime of buying and selling housing, it is more than likely that the same household could end up as both winner and loser on a string of house sales. From Chapter 1 it is apparent that the fluctuating fortunes of financial and property markets play a large part in determining the yields and opportunity costs associated with the biggest investment that most people ever make. The decades between 1960 and 1990 were characteristically times of higher inflation, higher interest rates, and higher capital gains. As the 1990s unfolded, a new regime of lower inflation, lower interest rates, and lower capital gains took over.

Whether or not there is much scope for playing the market to optimise returns to investment is a moot point. Superficially, first-time buyers have more latitude in relation to market conditions and expectations. They can opt to defer, or start looking for a home of their own if they think the market is right. But there have been occasions in the past, with land and house prices spiralling seemingly beyond reach, where first home buyers have been panicked into buying prematurely.[7] In the case of changeover buyers, the decision to sell could well be opportunistic in a pecuniary sense.

Equally, it could be pressured by events such as the arrival of a new child, an empty nest, or the need to keep a closer eye on a frail parent.

Some owners plan their intentional ascent of the housing escalator strategically, but for most people, this is much more a matter of luck. Others end up slipping down a 'snake' and have to return to the rental market until they are financially ready to put a foot on the bottom step of the 'ladder' once more.

For such reasons, then, we have to take the housing histories of home owners much more seriously. Ultimately their housing wealth accrues from the balance sheet of capital gains and losses. These are realised as households make their passage through the property market. The varied backgrounds and extraordinarily mixed experience of home owners with respect to housing wealth will become apparent later in this chapter when we explore the case histories of 206 Adelaide owners who sold their homes in 1988–89.

Equality and the distribution of housing wealth

Despite the diversity found among owner-occupiers, social and housing theorists have come up with four competing generalisations about how housing wealth is actually distributed among households from differing class backgrounds. The main point of this debate is to try to reach some agreement about the likely impact of wealth accruing from home ownership upon the structure of those societies with high levels of home ownership. Not only does housing wealth open options for consumption and inheritance (Chapter 3), but it also has a bearing upon the future shape of Australian society.

The battle lines are drawn between those who look to Marx for an understanding of property relations and the distribution of housing wealth, and those who feel that the extension of home ownership to ordinary citizens has helped to disperse wealth within the property-owning democracies. On one side are people like Mathew Edel and his colleagues in Massachusetts, who called their study of Boston home owners *Shaky Palaces*.[8] Surprisingly for social scientists working in the United States, they conclude that home ownership typically leads to the financial *entrapment* of working-class and lower-middle-class households. Among Australians writing about home ownership, Jim Kemeny probably comes closest to sympathising with the entrapment hypothesis.[9]

The British sociologist Peter Saunders is on the other side. He mounts a spirited defence of the enrichment hypothesis. In Britain 'millions of people have accumulated a substantial amount of wealth from their participation in the housing market'.[10] One of Australia's foremost thinkers, Hugh Stretton, has also expressed the opinion that home ownership has a more equalising effect within those societies that have promoted it above other tenures.[11] One of his papers from the mid-1980s proclaims, 'Housing—an investment for all', which it patently is not![12]

Supporters of the other two generalisations about the distribution of housing wealth sit uneasily somewhere between these two ends of the spectrum. A third position is taken by David Thorns,[13] a sociologist who has studied housing wealth in Britain and New Zealand, together with a group of British housing specialists headed by Ray Forrest.[14] They concede that some home owners are out of step with the majority. Retirees who are asset-rich but income-poor come to mind. But in their view, across society as a whole housing wealth is likely to be in tune with employment (or non-employment) histories. They maintain, then, that accumulation pans out to reinforce, rather than to break down, the existing concentration of private wealth in property-owning societies.

There is a fourth position that exhausts the possibilities. It can best be described as somewhat agnostic with respect to the distribution of housing wealth! Even though the link between the top salaries paid, the most expensive homes owned, and capital accumulation seems self-evident, both of your authors found themselves having to take sides with the agnostics after studying the housing markets in Canberra and Adelaide in the 1980s.[15] Better odds in the housing wealth stakes might appear to be linked with prime job prospects, but the outcome is by no means guaranteed. That is what we decided, along with a British housing specialist, when we first looked at the whole question. On the basis of his examination of house price trends in Britain and Europe, Simon Duncan concluded that short-term booms and slumps can distribute capital gains and losses erratically and, therefore, that 'redistribution is likely to be socially random'.[16]

It was only later, when we realised that housing wealth is accumulated not from the one-off house sale, but from the successive homes owned during the course of a lifetime, that we rejected this view.[17] It became clear to us, despite the sometimes unpredictable nature of the property market, that over the long term the distribution of housing wealth helps to perpetuate social inequality in Australia.

Let us look more closely, to begin with, at the earlier studies of Canberra and Adelaide home owners. In the case of Canberra, their experience proved to be quite mixed during the 20-year study (1961–82).[18] As a rule, the owners of expensive homes in top suburbs like Weetangera and Forrest collected the heftiest net gains. Yet these gains, while large in absolute dollar terms, did not necessarily translate into the highest rates of return. Market conditions at purchase and resale were far more important in deciding returns on investment than factors associated with the occupational rank of home owners. In particular, 1976 was a defining year for Canberra's property market. The credit squeeze in 1974 had precisely the effect intended by Treasury upon overheated capital city markets around Australia. Owners who sold before 1975 typically received annual returns on their initial capital outlay of 30 per cent; those who sold after that date suffered losses of 1 per cent. The 118 households who bought and sold between 1970 and 1973 during the boom, received an annual rate of return on equity, through their capital alone, of 62 per cent.[19]

Nor was the distribution of capital gains and returns to the 206 Adelaide home owners selling in 1988–89 as clear-cut as some would have it. Statistics that measure strength of relationship can help us out here.[20] For the purpose of the exercise, occupations are scored from high to low. A household with a sole wage-earner employed as a 'cleaner, waitress, orderly, etc.', receives a score of 6 on the occupational index. Those classified as 'managers, administrators or company directors' score 18, so if there are two earners with that status a household can receive a combined score of 36. Similarly, earnings from different sources—self-employed or employee, full-time or part-time, permanent or casual, statutory benefits (pensions etc.)—are combined to obtain an estimate of the income of households defined as having either one wage or two wages.

As you might expect, the price originally paid for the dwelling bears some relation to a measure of the *combined* occupational rank or earnings of workers in a household. This simply reflects the borrowing limit that home buyers run up against when they apply for a mortgage. Otherwise, there is no hint of a statistical connection in the Adelaide study between the *net gains* or *returns* on the houses sold in 1988–89 on the one hand, and the occupational background and earning capacity of the owners on the other. Even when the value of home improvement activity is deducted, the capitalisation of house values is too complicated for that.

Having said this, we have considered only one of possibly several dwellings owned by the household during the course of a lifetime. We must combine house price data for the dwelling sold in 1988–89 with information about a mixed sample of households, all of whom are at quite different stages of their housing career. In fact, each time owners buy and sell, the opportunity exists to adjust housing consumption so that it fits better with the earning capacity and savings of household members. In the case of the 206 Adelaide owners, there is a consistent strengthening of the relationship between the cost of the second, third, fourth, and fifth homes owned, and a household occupation index.[21] The value of housing owned generally rises in line with career advancement, higher wages, and the return of married women to paid employment. All the same, not all career moves, up or down, are accompanied by housing moves.

Occupational mobility and housing wealth

It seems obvious now, but any conclusions about housing wealth are likely to be suspect if they are based on the *sale of one dwelling*. Most of us, as home owners, buy and sell a number of places as needs change during our lifetime. Until we estimate the cumulative effect of the capital gains or losses on each dwelling owned, it is hard to be any more conclusive about the distribution of housing wealth in Australia. Consequently, we really have to investigate *lifetime ownership*.

This is borne out in Figure 9, which compares the improvement in asset values over the lifetime of home owners in eight Adelaide suburbs. These suburbs were chosen to reflect both the spread of property prices—from a low of $60 000 for Elizabeth homes to a high of $300 000 for North Adelaide homes—and social class in Adelaide (Figure 8). By adjusting house prices for inflation, it is possible to estimate what owners paid for their first home on average, and set that against the average value of the dwellings they sold in 1988–89. (In the following discussion, all sums of money have been converted to 1990 dollars.)

Figure 9 shows that home owners selling in suburbs with the cheapest housing stock—Elizabeth Park and Elizabeth Downs, Christies Beach, Birkenhead and Exeter—have the flattest trend lines between the 1930s and 1990. *On average*, they paid around $50 000 for their first homes, and by 1988–89 the last home they owned never realised more than $75 000, at the most, in current prices. Moreover, in the case of Housing Trust suburbs like Elizabeth Park–Elizabeth Downs and Christies Beach, where most of the first dwellings were bought under the rental-purchase scheme in the 1960s, the yields in real terms have been negligible. In some cases, because we are talking about the average, home owners from these poorer suburbs actually suffered losses in real terms over their lifetime.

By contrast, owners selling homes in suburbs that concentrate some of Adelaide's most expensive housing have the steepest trend lines. Households now residing in dress-circle suburbs like Burnside or North Adelaide have made spectacular gains in building up their housing assets. Examination of the individual records for owners reveal a series of step-wise moves to reach these desirable suburbs in the upper echelons of the metropolitan housing market. *On average*, they appear to have outlaid about $80 000 to $90 000 on their first home purchase, regardless of where that house actually was in Australia. By 1988–89, again *on average*, the

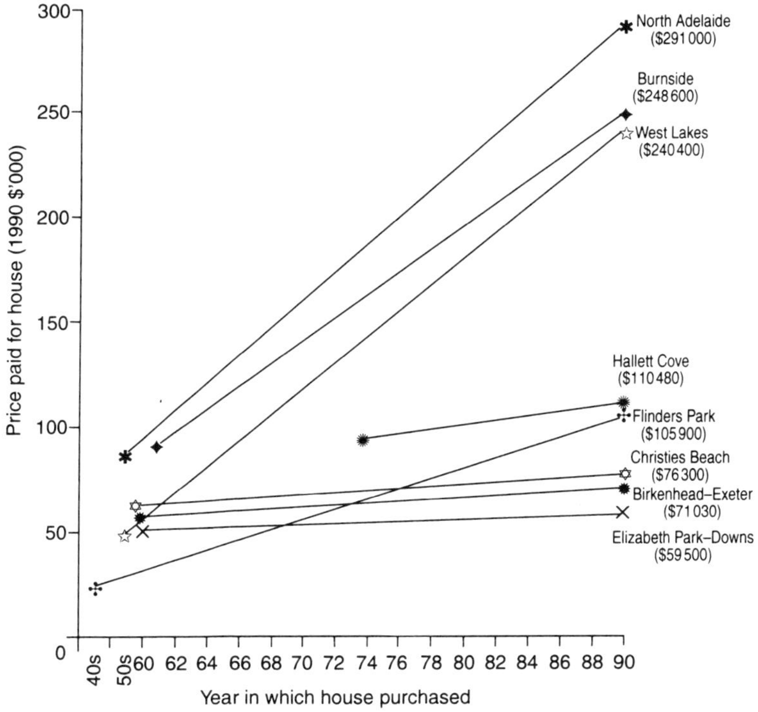

Source: Blair Badcock, 'Snakes or Ladders?: The Housing Market and Wealth Distribution in Australia'.

Figure 9: The upward progress of Adelaide home owners as measured by increasing house value
(amounts in brackets are average house prices in 1990 dollars)

housing sold by these same owners fetched about $248 000 and $290 000 in Burnside and North Adelaide respectively. West Lakes owners selling homes at an average of $240 000 in 1988–89 had bought their first homes mainly in the 1960s and 1970s for sums ranging from $50 000 to $100 000 in real terms.

This increase in asset values has two main sources: the increase in housing outlays, or trading-up, that frequently accompanies career advancement and/or access to a second income; or from the better-than-average rates of capital growth flowing to exclusive and well-located suburbs over the last two decades in all Australian cities (Figure 6a and 6b). Even allowing for the costs of moving, refinancing, loan repayments and normal overheads, these home owners can expect to significantly increase their equity after buying their first home.

In Figure 10 we have shown the working of these processes in Adelaide's housing market, graphing the housing wealth accruing (or not) to households against the occupational mobility of their working member(s). The estimates of change in housing wealth are the combined value of the capital gains and losses reported for each dwelling previously owned by a household. When these estimates are grouped, we find three outcomes: the majority of home owners, 53.6 per cent, saw a marked improvement in the value of their housing of more than $10 000 in real terms; the housing wealth of 32.9 per cent changed only moderately, with net gains or losses of $10 000; the remainder, 13.4 per cent, faced a marked deterioration in their housing equity during their housing career, losing more than $10 000.

Upward or downward occupational mobility is defined as a shift of three or more ranks on the occupational index. All told, 42 per cent of households contained members who together qualify as upwardly mobile; the occupational standing of 51.4 per cent of households remained unchanged; 6.6 per cent lost ground occupationally.

The way the bars are arrayed in Figure 10 is consistent with a general pattern of wealth accumulation by the majority of home owners over the years. But bear in mind that there is no record of any of the casualties among earlier home owners living in these eight Adelaide suburbs. The accrual of wealth is clearly linked as well with upward occupational mobility. This is especially pronounced in the case of households residing in the high-status suburbs. For example, more than half the households living in North Adelaide and Burnside had markedly improved their equity in housing along with advancing in the workplace. But even households with little occupational mobility have seen a marked improvement in the estimated value of their housing wealth through time.

The severest deterioration in housing equity occurred among home owners living in low-status suburbs like Elizabeth Park–Elizabeth Downs, Birkenhead–Exeter, and Christies Beach. Yet

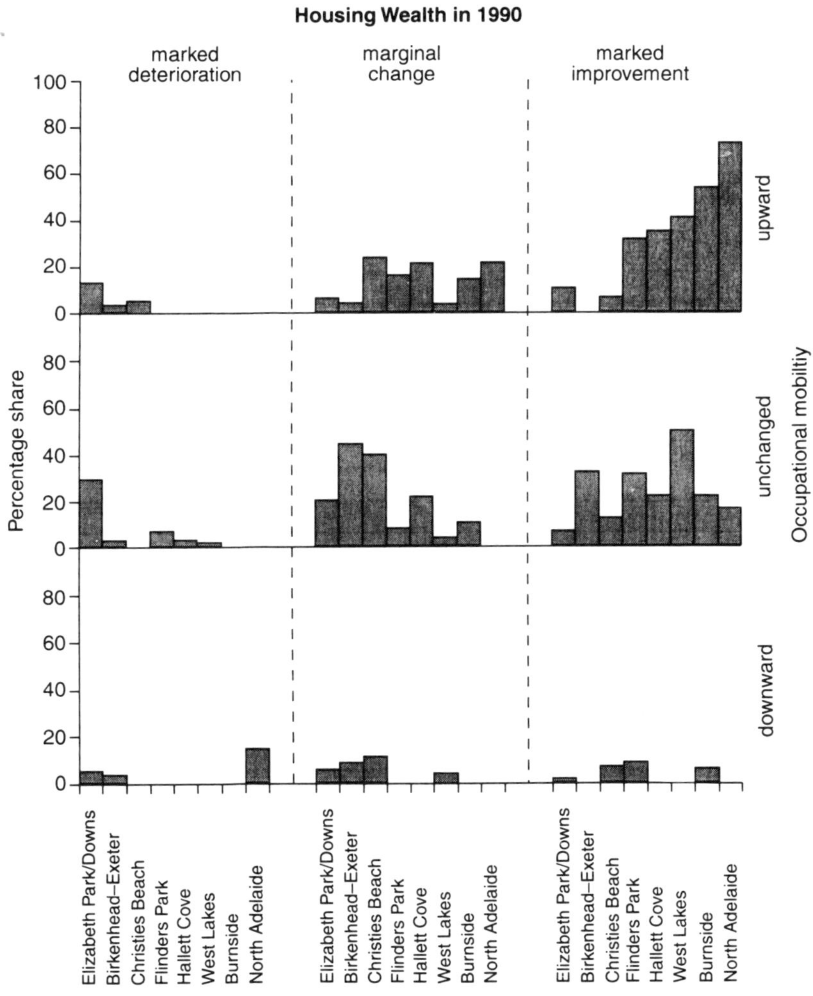

Source: Blair Badcock, 'Snakes or Ladders?: The Housing Market and Wealth Distribution in Australia'.

Figure 10: Correspondence between changes in housing wealth and occupational mobility of some Adelaide home owners

even in these suburbs, the proportion of households adversely affected seldom rose above more than 20 per cent of the vendors. And while home owners selling in Elizabeth Park–Elizabeth Downs suffered a disproportionate loss in their housing equity over time, many of the households from other low-status suburbs like

Christies Beach and Birkenhead–Exeter appear to have at least held their ground financially in the housing market.

'Identikit' winners and losers in the housing wealth stakes

There is much to be learned from a closer look at the experience of individual home owners. Some of the same 206 Adelaide home owners interviewed in 1988–89 were asked about their employment and housing histories. We believe we have captured much of the diversity of experience of Australian home owners—though no Aboriginal and Torres Strait Islanders—and that this can be represented by drawing a series of identikit portraits. This information was then matched with Valuation Department records documenting capital growth in the housing market over more than three decades. Importantly, the data were gathered at the beginning of the 1990s in conjunction with the onset of the recession that 'we had to have'.[22] Therefore the experience of all the identikit owners was shaped to some extent by economic events dominating the end of the 1980s.

A typology of winners and losers has been constructed from this interview material. Winning or losing in the housing wealth stakes is relative: regardless of the value of their homes, owners who *feel* they have prospered consider themselves winners. For the purposes of this exercise, we have applied rather more objective criteria to sort the winners from the losers. By what amount has the value of the successive homes owned increased in real terms? What is their current home worth? How far have they climbed or dropped on the housing ladder with each change of address? What other housing investments and assets do households possess? Do they expect to inherit, and how much? Losers tend to be the casualties, and this may even extend to financial entrapment in the worst case. In short, we want to know if owners have moved up the housing ladders, or down the snakes.

Home owners can be broadly separated into three types of *winners* and four types of *losers*. On the plus side of the housing wealth ledger are the Fortune Seekers, Squirrels, and Stayers respectively. Owners who have seen their housing wealth seriously depleted shake-out into Business-linked Casualties, Overwhelmed Battlers, Family Adjusters, and Castle Builders. While these broad groupings are akin to identikit characterisations, the descriptions of the distinctive housing histories that follow remain faithful to the information so generously provided by the interviewees.

Fortune Seekers

Fortune Seekers tend to be among the leading beneficiaries of capital accumulation in the housing market. They are rich in both assets and income. They are not necessarily two-income households: typically, they have reached mid-career, and they combine the salaries of senior public servants, high-level professionals or company directors with considerable business acumen. But this in itself does not make them fortune seekers. What sets these home owners apart is their strategic approach to home purchase and improvement as part of their overall investment planning. Often this is linked to business activity or professional earnings and involves an element of risk-taking. All the same, only a few of these Fortune Seekers are really hell-bent on climbing the housing ladder to the point where their housing wealth belies their occupational backgrounds.

Perhaps the most vigorous Fortune Seekers we came across are a Burnside couple in their early forties at the time with two teenage children; the husband is a financial planner with a degree, and the wife a freelance court reporter. They deliberately work the market. Since 1972 they have picked undercapitalised dwellings in inner suburbs on the move and renovated all seven of them. The crude estimates of yields from this history of trading up or trading down are set out in Table 4 as an illustration of one couple's housing history. By the mid-1980s, our compulsive up-graders had profited sufficiently to invest, as well, in a negatively geared apartment unit worth about $250 000. But they do not expect to inherit anything from their parents. Asked to comment on the impact of a capital gains tax introduced in 1985, the financial planner replied, 'the CGT did not change my policy of upgrading houses —I have always done it'.

Table 4: Housing history of a 'fortune-seeking' Adelaide household, 1972–91[a]

Date of purchase	*Suburb*	*Purchase price*	*Sale price 1990 $*	*Estimated gain or loss*[b]
1972	Unley	78 975	95 800	+16 825
1974	Parkside	79 035	90 860	+11 825
1975	Parkside	123 900	196 500	+72 600
1986	Adelaide City	87 770	124 450	+36 680
1986	Wattle Park	163 750	222 300 (minus capital improvements of $31 000)	+27 550
1988	Transfer to Sydney, NSW	199 500	212 000	+12 500
1991	Return to SA Netherby	195 000		
	plus apartment (negatively geared)	250 000		

[a] A finance planner and court reporter in their early forties with two children.
[b] These are crude estimates that do not deduct the value of home improvements, depreciation, transfer costs etc.

Source: Blair Badcock, Eight-Suburb Survey of Home Ownership, Adelaide, 1991.

Another Burnside couple with two children, though younger—in their mid-thirties—bought their first house, a modest interwar bungalow, in 1978. Then in their early twenties, the husband was a trainee draftsman and the wife a library assistant. They saved for three and a half years and paid $57 960 for it. Only ten years, but five houses, later, after a successful move into real estate on his part, their Mt Osmond home fetched $270 000.

A business couple in their early fifties, with personal assets worth in excess of $500 000, show how to make good use of the windfall gains bestowed by house price inflation in the late 1980s. In 1987 the husband made the move from corporate planner in a national firm, to managing director of their jointly owned and operated business. His wife is the firm's general manager. In 1989 they sold their North Adelaide home for $650 000 and bought into nearby, and equally well-heeled, Medindie for $280 000 (Figure 8).

This freed capital to spend on modernising the Medindie home and to plough back into the business, with enough remaining to negatively gear a block of flats they purchased for $200 000.

Some of the most conspicuous winners are home owners selling on the back of the rising market in *nouveau riche* West Lakes (Figure 8), where occupational background is not always such a good predictor of housing wealth! Take a couple in their early sixties without children. Both left school in their mid-teens without any formal qualifications. The husband moved from clerical positions to that of computer consultant, while the wife stuck with typing. Between 1953 and 1989 they owned ten homes. The first, a worker's cottage in Exeter, was worth $48 000. Now they are outright owners of a $240 000 home on the lakefront at West Lakes, and hold substantial equity in an investment flat ($130 000), and two farms valued at $300 000. They traded down in 1988 and lived briefly in a home unit purchased for $107 000, before trading up in 1991 against the tax advantage on the West Lakes place.

Similarly, a West Lakes couple in their early fifties, with three grown-up children, began married life as soldier and shop assistant. Soon after the first child arrived in 1963, they bought a $55 000, two-bedroom cottage well to the south of Adelaide in rural Reynella. In 1974 they moved into town, the Findon home costing $119 750. Following the husband's appointment to a company directorship in 1985, they sold Findon for $213 070 and moved to West Lakes. What with the landscaping and air-conditioning, that represented an outlay of $192 160. They sold for $251 450 in 1989 and moved up to a $505 000 West Lakes residence in order to take advantage of capital gains tax. They do not expect to inherit more than $25 000, but they also own a holiday house.

Lastly, there is the couple in their late forties who trained as chefs but are now joint owners of a restaurant with a take-home income of $60 000. The husband emigrated from the Netherlands in 1959, and the wife came from Sri Lanka in 1962. They have two adult children and one still at school. Their first home was bought in Edwardstown, an industrial suburb in the south-western sector of Adelaide, for $78 000 in 1965. Following two other moves upwards (1969, 1973), they purchased a show-home in

1981 at West Lakes on Delfin Island for $135 000. This residence was sold for $265 000 in 1989 in order to move into a $600 000 property on the seafront at Tennyson.

Squirrels

Squirrels are synonymous with the fulfilment of the Great Australian dream. Probably in the last decade of their working lives, or now retired, these owners are typical of comfortably-off nest builders from the era of the long boom. Industriousness and job security often went hand-in-hand with a long-term commitment to the neighbourhood in which the kids grew up. Home purchase was much less likely to be investment-driven. 'Safety first' has guided most housing decisions of Squirrels. Averse to risks and conscious of security, they have avoided the mistake of over-capitalising. With the property market peaking in Adelaide in the late 1980s, many long-time residents of sought-after suburbs like Burnside took the opportunity to cash in their substantial equity and move into lower-priced retirement housing. Some have modest additional wealth. Fewer could ever look forward to inheriting much from parents who never owned.

Squirrels include a retired Burnside couple in their mid-seventies, formerly owners of a caravan business, who built their own home in 1975 for $84 000. They sold it in 1989 for $245 000 in order to move into a townhouse costing $121 000. This released $124 000 for other purposes. Another retired couple, also in their seventies and both former teachers, sold their family home for $160 000, having lived in it since 1964 and paid $103 500 for it. Their move into the Lourdes Valley Retirement Home in Myrtlebank freed about $42 500 once they had paid for the unit. Another retired couple in their mid-sixties with an adult daughter bought their first home in 1952 for $57 000 in real terms, and traded it in 1980 for a new home in West Lakes for $114 500, on which they realised $365 000 in 1988. They are now renting in order to free some capital for retirement and 'help the family'.

Several widows in their sixties and seventies also withdrew equity worth between $40 000 and $60 000 in the process of moving from the family home into a home unit. The experience of two pensioners in their mid-sixties helps to illustrate the flexibility that home ownership provides to women living by themselves in their later years.[23] These cases also hint at the possible hardship that lies ahead for single women without the means to purchase on their own account.[24] The first lived on the land, working a small farm with her husband which they eventually owned. Two sons were born in 1951 and 1957. In 1982 when they sold up, her husband took out a war service loan ($12 000 at 3.75 per cent over thirty years) as part-payment on a place in West Lakes worth $176 000. When settling in, they spent about $2700 on improvements such as a pergola, security door, cupboards and outside blinds. The husband died unexpectedly after four years so in 1989 the widow put the house back on the market near the peak. The price she received ($222 560) enabled her to buy into a retirement village ($139 000), pay off the war service loan, and invest the balance (about $68 000).

Then there is a 65-year-old Englishwoman who arrived with her husband and two young sons in 1955. They rented a Housing Trust home until 1965, when they bought in Elizabeth Park, outlaying $58 960. It was financed through the Savings Bank of South Australia ($46 565 at 5 per cent over thirty years) and the South Australian Housing Trust ($7035 at 6.5 per cent over twenty-five years). A garage and some concrete paving added about $1600 in improvements. In 1967 her husband left her and she became the sole earner, working up from the line to become a supervisor in a local factory. In 1988 she retired, sold up for $59 945, and moved into a flat in another northern suburb 'to enjoy myself in my remaining years'. This left her with assets worth less than $50 000; and as neither parents or in-laws are alive, she has no access to an estate.

Once more there is a reminder that the munificence of property ownership does not entirely mirror occupational status. A Greek couple in their early fifties, with two grown-up children, saved for ten years before buying their first home in 1959 in Adelaide's inner west—working-class Mile End ($41 040). The husband began work in Australia as a fettler and farm labourer before moving to a job with British Tube Mills (ACTIL) in the north-western suburbs of Adelaide. The wife was employed as a shop assistant until 1970, when they decided to begin their own business, which they have run successfully ever since. In 1972, they moved to Woodville, paying $181 350 for the house. In 1980 they moved into a new home on the lake-front at West Lakes, which was sold for $319 200 in 1988 in order to refinance the business.

Stayers

There are also those who count as winners because they qualify as Stayers with respect to housing wealth—not necessarily just because they stayed put once they bought! For the most part, these are the battlers who have received modest capital gains, sometimes even against the odds. A 62-year-old English-born bachelor left school at fourteen years of age and worked as a builder's labourer before emigrating in 1950. By 1966 he had saved the down-payment on a small cottage in Taperoo, which cost him only $42 250. In 1977 he switched to commercial cleaning, moved to Birkenhead, and spent $99 224 on a home that he subsequently took a small loss on in real terms ($91 143). However, in the process of moving once more (in 1988), this time to the northern suburb of Elizabeth Vale, he was able to trade down and extract about $12 480 for other purposes. He puts his worth at between $50 000 and $100 000 and does not expect to inherit anything.

A couple in their fifties with a grown-up family is typical of those battlers who bought their Christies Beach homes from the Housing Trust under the rental-purchase scheme. Both are clerks, one a budget control officer and the other a secretary with a small distribution outlet. They emigrated in 1964 from England, where they owned their home, and bought a Trust house for $57 960. It had barely held its value when they sold in 1972, but it did allow the owners to make a cost-neutral move to another home in Christies Beach. After spending about $3200 on home improvements, they sold that place for $81 000 in 1989 and bought a roomier property costing $85 000 in Willunga township, an easy commute to the city (Figure 8).

Other battlers have managed to come out ahead by selling up in the city and moving to a country town. Two 47-year-old immigrants without children arrived from England in 1948, and

Uruguay in 1970. They met in Sydney in 1978, and then moved to Adelaide, where they bought their first home in Brighton for $82 000. In 1985 they sold for $79 500 and moved further out to a new house in Hallett Cove ($75 000). Then, in 1988, the opportunity arose to buy a shop-residence in Goolwa, a coastal holiday spot south of Adelaide. They were able to make a cash offer from the proceeds of their Hallett Cove sale ($84 000).

Business-linked Casualties

The timing of the study of Adelaide home owners exposed the potentially hazardous nature of home ownership. In the past the risks of mortgage defaulting and foreclosure had been remote, but deregulation of the financial system in 1986 changed all that. In the late 1980s a system of rationing was replaced by a free-for-all as newcomers to the mortgage finance scene jostled for market share. For a time, some banks were prepared to throw money at borrowers to get their account. With an expanding economy and the advent of the home equity loan, the owners of many small businesses were tempted to secure loans, at higher commercial rates, against the family home.

Thus when Treasurer Keating tried to apply the brakes to an overheated economy in 1988–89 (Figure 5), these family-owned and -operated companies felt the double whammy of escalating home mortgage *and* commercial interest rates.[25] Crippling interest rates take no prisoners. Between 1985/86 and 1991/92, the number of bankruptcies in Australia soared from 5581 to 16 803.[26] Small business is dogged by high failure rates in the first three years, but by 1991/92, Baby Boomers in their mid-thirties and forties dominated the declared bankruptcies, reflecting the failure of established businesses that had been trading for ten years or more. As well as bankrupting them, the high interest rates destroyed the housing wealth and life savings of prudent and well-off suburban families. They lost in every way. When asset prices tumbled, so did the value of their security. And when the banks foreclosed, they faced the prospect of having to sell in a buyer's market.[27]

Take the case of a Burnside family with four children, all of whom were enrolled in one of the highly regarded private schools that abound in the eastern suburbs of Adelaide. The parents had successfully run their own business since the mid-1970s, importing machine tooling equipment. The husband looked after procurement and supervised the installation, and the wife provided secretarial support. In the mid-1980s they borrowed against their home to enlarge the warehouse. But as manufacturers reduced their inventories and cut back production levels in the late 1980s, the forward orders dwindled to nothing for the first time in fifteen years. With revenue slowing to a trickle, the bank eventually stepped in, seized the assets, and forced the owners to place their spacious suburban bungalow on the market. Although it reached $216 000 at auction, by the time the owners had cleared all their debts they were faced with renting for the foreseeable future.

The building industry is notoriously cyclical. A builder in his late fifties, with a wife at home, paid $112 000 for a Burnside villa in 1979. Over the next seven or eight years he claims to have added the equivalent of $42 000 in sweat equity, which he then borrowed against to finance a business venture. Not long after, caught up in the interest rate spiral and economic downturn, he found himself in financial difficulties. He sold up without fully recovering the value of his home improvements, settled with the bank, and moved to rented accommodation in the growing coastal town of Victor Harbour where there is more building work.

An Elizabeth Park couple in their late forties, with an 18-year-old son at home, have owned five homes in the northern suburbs since 1974. By 1969, having trained as a motor mechanic, the husband was a service manager for a local garage. His wife worked as a shop assistant until the arrival of their son, but since then has run the home. They bought the Elizabeth Park place in 1985 for $60 420 because he 'liked its games room and the in-ground pool'. They borrowed 25 per cent against the dwelling's value for him to start out on his own account; since then they have been forced to sell to meet a tax liability. They lost money in real terms on the sale ($59 000), and are now renting a single-family dwelling in the Ardrossan countryside.

The trucking industry is so competitive that even in normal operating conditions owner-drivers are forced to shave margins to survive. The survey uncovered two truckies sailing close to the wind financially. A West Lakes couple in their late twenties, with two young children, built their first home in the area in 1983. It cost them $95 000 and at the time they qualified for a grant under the First Home Owners Scheme of $3000. They remortgaged to buy a new truck in the mid-1980s, but then they were forced to sell because they could no longer meet the interest repayments on the house and the truck. They are now renting from the Housing Trust in Salisbury East. The other case involves a pair of 40-year-olds with two grown-up children still at home. Their first jobs were in Sydney as a bank officer and an assistant to a chemist. With the move from Sydney in 1980, there was enough of a difference between Sydney and Adelaide house prices to make a down-payment on a new $76 000 home in Hallett Cove and start their own interstate trucking business. Facing business collapse in the late 1980s, they had to register as bankrupts and sell the Hallett Cove home. Although they more than recouped their initial investment in 1998 ($95 000), after clearing their debts they were forced to rent.

Overwhelmed Battlers

Politically speaking, skyrocketing interest rates in the late 1980s had the same effect as taking a knife to the soft underbelly of the mortgage belt.[28] Home owners who had discharged their mortgage were all right, and home buyers on reasonable incomes could tighten their belts and ride it out. But for first-time and marginal buyers without a cushion, the hike in mortgage rates was financially stressful. Ironically, many of the home buyers condemned to defaulting by punitive mortgage rates were the same low-income households who qualified for government assistance packages (including the state housing authorities' house sales programmes, and schemes like HomeFund, HomeStart, Capil, and First Home Owners Scheme). These are the families caricatured by posturing politicians as the 'little Aussie battlers'. In the Australian context, they are the home buyers who came to learn the meaning of *entrapment*.

Unprecedented mortgage rates in the late 1980s came on top of the freeing up of the labour market. Home buyers who pushed the limits of affordability also ran the risk, sooner or later, of losing the traditional protection of job security. Unreliable employment and deskilling are threats that thread their way through the common experience of the Overwhelmed Battlers. They form a second important group of losers, then, defeated by the vigorous restructuring of the labour, financial and housing markets in the 1980s. Not surprisingly, there is no shortage of cases to be found among buyers scattered through the working-class suburbs selected as part of the Adelaide study.[29] Only a handful of these buyers were ever likely to be thrown a life-line by a deceased relative in the form of a bequest. In these circumstances, the greater majority of those portrayed as Overwhelmed Battlers had lost their homes and life savings by the end of the 1980s.

Three former Elizabeth Downs families share this sense of being overwhelmed by these events in the late 1980s. A couple who emigrated from Britain in 1970, and now in their early fifties with four adult children still at home, began to buy their Trust home as a rental-purchase property in 1977, borrowing $63 000 at 5.5 per cent over forty years. At the time, the husband was a butcher by trade; the wife was a shorthand typist. They lost those jobs and were re-employed as a bus driver and a clerk. When the house was sold to avoid bankruptcy in 1988, they incurred a loss of $23 990 once capital improvements of $7250 are factored in. The Trust rehoused the family, further out, in a rental unit in Smithfield Plains (Figure 8).

A younger Elizabeth Downs couple with three small children are now renting after defaulting. They are both thirty-two years old. The husband worked at farm labouring jobs but then could not get work in the Mallee in Victoria where they bought their first home. The wife gave up her telephonist's job to raise the children. Their first place in Lameroo was financed with the help of a gift, which covered the 10 per cent deposit, and a grant of $5000 under the First Home Owners Scheme. They sold up in 1985 and moved to Elizabeth Downs, where they paid $75 700 for a project home. The Savings Bank of South Australia loaned them $45 000, but at 17.5 per cent in 1988 the monthly repayments eventually climbed to $550. They got only $58 140 for their Elizabeth Downs home, which represents a loss in real terms of $17 650, and are now renting in the Barossa Valley town of Nurioopta.

The last Elizabeth Downs couple left England in 1981 with their two young children. In their mid-thirties, with a boiler-maker's ticket and experience as a pharmacist's assistant, their prospects ought to have been good. They bought a modest home for $59 300 in 1983; but, after having to accept work as council handyman and a part-time cleaner, reluctantly sold up in 1988. Although they broke even, they are now back in the rental sub-market at Craigmore not far from the children's schools.

Other cases of Overwhelmed Battlers that came to light include a single Christies Beach male who was married when he purchased his first home in 1969. Forty-nine at the time, his career had taken him from machine technician to production planner when he was laid off in 1988. The second Christies Beach house, which he had paid $60 260 for in 1986, raised only $47 880 in 1988, a real loss of $12 380. He moved to a caravan at Mannum on the River Murray. Likewise, a Hallett Cove couple, both forty-eight years of age, sold the home they had bought for $78 210 in 1980 for $72 000. With two adult children, the wife had worked in the home. The husband switched from work as a fitter in aero-engineering to self-employment, and finally unemployment. Even though 60 per cent of the mortgage was paid off, with no work they had to default. He is converting an old bus to live in because 'we no longer want the hassle of owning a house'.

Lastly, two couples from Birkenhead–Exeter complete the picture. One couple, childless 32-year-olds, were forced to sell the Birkenhead home that they had spent $15 000 on renovating when the wife lost her job as an administrative officer. The husband is a fisherman with a variable income. As interest rates climbed during the second half of the 1980s, they had found the mortgage repayments increasingly burdensome. Not only did they barely break even, but they have been forced by events back to renting. The second couple in their early forties, with three teenagers at home, and both employed off and on as cleaners, decided to sell their basic cottage in 1988 because the mortgage payments were 'too much of a hassle'. They are currently living on the pension and renting a house in the Port Adelaide area (Figure 8).

Family Adjusters

Family adjustment is a euphemism for marriage break-up or the arrival of another mouth to feed. Either event has the potential to slash the family's earning power at a time in life when the financial drain on a household paying off a home is peaking. Matters were not helped by runaway mortgage repayments in the late 1980s. Where marriages were already shaky, the extra strain took them beyond breaking-point. And where the birth of a child stopped a mother earning, even if only for a short time, young families often had no option but to restructure the mortgage or sell. Thus, Family Adjusters suffer a financial setback as well as emotional trauma and may have to face the dislocation that goes with an enforced change of address and a move down-market.

Separation, followed by divorce, splits the household assets and wealth, whatever their value. Judged in housing wealth terms, divorcees are bound to be losers to some degree. Few have sufficient funds after settlement to remortgage and stay put. Others might have to settle for a home unit. But most are forced, for the time being at least, to rent. This range of outcomes emerges from the survey.

For example, a 44-year-old man, now living alone, left a wife and three teenage children in 1984–85. Their Wattle Park home in Burnside was sold for $242 000, and he is now slowly doing up a somewhat neglected, triple-fronted bungalow in Glenside that he paid $92 000 for in 1988. A bank manager, he figures that this is 'the only way I can afford to slowly expend money to improve living conditions with a house in a reasonable area which will show good capital appreciation'. But he places his current worth in a range between $100 000 and $250 000, and expects to inherit more than $100 000 from his parents' estate one day.

Another divorcee, in his mid-thirties, was eligible for a Defence Force home loan—$25 000 at 7.75 per cent over twenty-five years —when his North Adelaide residence was purchased in 1986. The second mortgage was with the State Bank ($70 000 at 14 per cent over twenty-five years). He left the army to take a job with a security firm on a salary of $50 000. The North Adelaide home was sold for $126 000 when his marriage broke up in 1988, representing an estimated gross gain of $28 000. His sixteen-year-old stayed with his former wife, and he bought a $53 000 home unit in Rose Park. He places the value of his assets at less than $50 000, and any inheritance would be minimal.

A branch supervisor aged thirty-seven years sold the Hallett Cove home purchased with a loan from an employer to pay out her ex-husband. Her half-share of the proceeds from the sale, with 60 per cent of the mortgage outstanding, came to about $17 000. With an annual income of $50 000, and no children, she is unlikely to strike problems with the mortgage repayments on her $64 000 home unit in Burnside. However, her estimated net worth is less than $50 000 and she does not expect to inherit anything.

Of the eleven one-parent households in the survey—six males, five females—the families all ended up in inferior accommodation. Another Hallett Cove 37-year-old divorcee, a male supporting two teenagers, bought that home in 1986 because the family wanted a larger place (with an en-suite bathroom, family room and separate dining room). With a purchase price of $106 000, it was mortgaged for $55 000 at 13.5 per cent over twenty years, which was the shortfall on the sale of the first family home in Happy Valley. It realised $130 000, just two years later, when the couple decided to separate. A financial manager on an annual salary of $43 000, he decided to rent a flat for himself and the two children, and use the equity he extracted from Hallett Cove to buy a third-share in a $90 000 house.

There were three female-headed households on supporting parent's benefits in their mid-forties who had been forced to sell homes in Elizabeth Downs. One moved with her seven-year-old son to live with her daughter and defacto husband, while the other two are renting. None of the three fully recovered a half-share of their initial investment because of the depressed state of the local housing market against the general trend in 1988–89. The mother who moved out to her daughter's 4-hectare block at Two Wells did so 'to give more of a better life style for my younger son'. She values her possessions at less than $50 000 and does not expect to inherit anything from her in-laws. One of the three women bought an Elizabeth Downs home in 1981 with a loan from the State Bank of South Australia ($25 000 at 7.5 per cent over thirty years), but lost $7000 at settlement. She has returned to further study while supporting two teenagers. Although she could eventually inherit between $75 000 and $100 000, currently her possessions are not worth much more than $50 000.

Only one of these solo parents is intent on buying again. An accounts clerk, she 'hated Elizabeth', even though the former home was close to family and friends: 'My house was broken into on at least three occasions. I was afraid to live there. I could not sleep at night.' With that behind her, 'I want to buy my own home again. I have applied for a HomeStart loan, but I don't have enough deposit. I need $4000 for the deposit.' She has less than $50 000 worth of assets. Her own parents are still alive, but she has lost touch with her in-laws, and has no expectation of inheriting on either side of the family.

The potential impact upon mortgage repayments of beginning a family is evident for a number of Hallett Cove households. This impact carries over onto housing wealth. Half a dozen couples in their thirties bought blocks of land at Hallett Cove and built their own homes in the first half of the 1980s while the wives were earning. But with the birth of a child and the loss of the second income, they were forced by a series of crippling interest rate hikes (Figure 5) to refinance and trade down. However, with the males occupying middle-rung positions—assistant manager, insurance supervisor, computer programmer, landscaping nursery manager, accountant—they were able to ride out the interest rate crisis that hit mortgage-belt suburbs like Hallett Cove particularly hard. Still, these owners are only losers in a relative sense because, despite their setback, they have every prospect of making up for their tumble down the housing ladder in the long term.

Castle Builders

Nothing is going to stop some people from building their very own castle. In spite of that, *over-capitalisation* is seldom the financial undoing of home owners. Castle Builders tend to put this to the back of their minds, but it does extract a price in housing wealth terms. Owners right across the market routinely plough money into home improvement for which they will get no positive return. What is more, many of them will be seriously out of pocket in real terms without realising it. Hence Castle Builders who over-capitalise, unwittingly or otherwise, also count among the losers in the housing wealth stakes. Having said that, there is no way of measuring the added pleasure and sense of satisfaction that some owners get from having everything that opens and shuts about the house.

This was the experience of a Burnside couple who moved from Melbourne in 1984 and bought a place in Stoneyfell which was overpriced to begin with, at $204 000. In their early forties, with two teenage children, these middle managers (manufacturing manager and child psychiatrist) could well afford to spend $28 600 on a new kitchen, a bathroom update, painting and wallpapering throughout, and new soft furnishings. But when he was transferred back to Melbourne in 1989, the Stoneyfell home realised only $160 500, which represents a capital loss of $72 100. To rub it in, they had to outlay an extra $40 125 to buy back into Melbourne's housing market.[30]

There are several instances from Flinders Park of young families overdoing the modernisation of their first homes. A qualified architect and his partner, a restaurant manager, paid $111 540 for a 1950s-style bungalow and spent an estimated $6650 on a new kitchen, interior paintwork, a pergola, paving and landscaping. They sold it in 1988 for $99 200, a capital loss exceeding $19 000. A second, slightly older Flinders Park couple in their mid-thirties, with two children, bought their first home for $124 600 with the help of a subsidised loan from their employer, the Commercial Bank of Australia ($35 000 at 5.75 per cent over twenty-five years). That was in 1981 along with his promotion to branch manager. Between 1982 and 1985 they redid the kitchen, added a spacious extension, and installed an in-ground pool. When they sold in 1988 to move to Fairview Park and buy a newsagency in expanding Golden Grove, they lost $27 760 in real terms on the Flinders Park property.

There are other stories as well of tenants who bought rental-purchase properties from the Housing Trust in Christies Beach and Elizabeth Downs–Elizabeth Park, spent too much on alterations and additions, and then found, when it came to selling, that house values in those suburbs were lagging badly (Figure 8). New kitchens, extensions, patios, swimming pools, and even a granny flat feature extensively in these stories. The estimates of real losses suffered range between $6180 and $28 485.

Housing wealth is unequally distributed and reinforces inequality

The study from which these case histories have been drawn is admittedly limited in scope—it does not pretend to represent all Adelaide, let alone Australian, home owners. It does lend some support to those researchers who claim that housing wealth is unequally distributed and reinforces existing inequality. Figures 9 and 10 are consistent with the proposition that housing wealth is progressively concentrated among those owners with the greatest opportunities for career advancement. For these Adelaide home owners, this took place in an era of high house price inflation coupled with high interest rates towards the end of the 1980s. Significantly, these results have caused us to revise our earlier agnosticism with respect to the debate about the distribution of housing wealth. Our research into *lifetime ownership* now compels us to side with those who assert that 'For the majority . . . housing wealth is likely to be in tune with employment (or non-employment) histories'.[31]

A later study of four Sydney suburbs (South Sydney, Ryde, Penrith, Campbelltown) and four Melbourne suburbs (City of Melbourne, Werribee, Box Hill, Berwick) reaches similar conclusions:

> capital gains and net housing benefits in real dollar terms in the property boom had a substantial class bias, favouring higher income groups substantially more than low income groups. Substituting interest rates, inflation and capital gains more akin to current conditions results in very few owner occupier families

being net losers from home ownership but does little to alter the bias of home ownership towards those with greatest economic wealth.[32]

Part of the underlying change that is taking place relates to the rising participation rates of women working outside the home. In order to become an owner-occupier, and to win from it, you need lifetime access to earnings and income, just as upward housing mobility relies for the most part on higher levels of remuneration during the working life. Although one income was enough in the past to repay a mortgage, women in the workforce who chose to live alone were routinely discriminated against in seeking to become owners.

That has changed for the better due to women's improved status and assertiveness, and more competition among mortgage providers, but there is no doubt that in today's world the best way for both men and women to acquire housing wealth is by being part of a couple.[33] In the past, it was said, a woman had to find her prince in order to get her palace;[34] these days it is increasingly necessary for men also to find their princess in order to acquire the keys of the castle and all that bestows in terms of housing wealth.

Of course, the rising social tide of singles choosing to live alone is working against this. Gay couples, on the other hand, can combine incomes but may still encounter discrimination in the housing system, despite the inroads that have been made by the gay lobby in recent years.

Low-wage, irregular, impermanent employment is increasing the economic necessity for coupledom, and this is certainly likely to be the case for entry to owner-occupation. Maybe this also has something to do with the falling rate of home ownership among those in their twenties and thirties. Unless they earn high incomes, as some young graduates in the professions do, it is much harder for singles to buy a home if they insist on living by themselves. The social and economic forces buffeting past, present, and future generations of Australian home owners are discussed further in Chapters 6 and 7, once we have shown how important home ownership and housing wealth are to the wider economy.

What happens to this unequally distributed housing wealth in old age, and then, ultimately, when it is passed on to the next generation? Will it further widen the gap between rich and poor, as many have assumed? Suppose every second household already owning in Australia stands to inherit the family home, or its cashed-up value. Is it the case that in absolute terms much more of this bequeathed housing wealth will flow to higher income households already in possession of considerable housing wealth? Or will enough of it disperse downwards to households with lower incomes and limited personal wealth to halt the widening wealth gap between the rich and poor in Australia? These are the kinds of questions that we mull over in the next chapter, which is devoted to the transfer of housing wealth between the generations.

CHAPTER 3

Bequeathing and Inheriting Housing Wealth

Lisel O'Dwyer

THE EXISTENCE FOR the first time of a generation of home-owning retirees in countries like Britain, the United States, and Australia marks a new stage in the chronicle of home ownership and housing wealth.[1] On reaching the end of their lives they will leave a great deal of their wealth in the form of bricks and mortar. A journalist writing in the *Business Review Weekly* suspects that 'Australia's middle-aged generation will get a stupendous windfall of inherited wealth in the next decade. Bequests will turn thousands of already comfortably established 40–55-year-olds into "common or garden millionaires"'.[2] Estimates for Australia based upon an actuarial study indicate that 94 000 homes were bequeathed on in 1996, and that this will rise to 168 000 dwellings in 2031.[3] This represents a potential transfer from one generation to the next of about $157 billion.

It is taken for granted that housing wealth has a substantial impact on the distribution of private wealth in property-owning democracies. The underlying logic maintains that a high level of home ownership, plus an ageing population, equals housing inheritance, which has significant impact on the distribution of wealth. But is this really the case? How large is the average bequest, and how much does housing wealth account for? Is it likely to materially affect the wealth of the beneficiaries? Patterns of housing inheritance reflect the strength of property traditions and primogeniture, even in a relaxed society like Australia's. Does this translate into a gender bias when it comes to housing inheritance?

And is it enough to make a real difference to the distribution of wealth?

There are those commentators who claim that housing inheritance will lead to greater wealth *polarisation*.[4] Others draw the opposite conclusion and assert that it will *equalise* the distribution.[5] With the help of South Australia's probate and title transfer records, together with a survey of inheritors, we hope to throw some new light on this debate. At the same time we ask two main questions. What does housing inheritance mean for the connections between wealth, housing and the sexes? And how does the geography of inherited housing and the background of its deceased owners influence the value, and thus the impact of housing inheritance? These questions formed the heart of a doctoral thesis on housing inheritance which was completed by the author in 1997.[6]

Inheritance as a process

Although inheritance is triggered by an abrupt event, it is better to regard it as the culmination of a chain of events that precede death (Figure 11). In turn, afterwards, housing inheritance may help to enlarge the pool of private rental stock, or add to an existing oversupply of dwellings, or inject funds into the economy if inheritors decide to spend the proceeds from an estate. In reality, housing inheritance may not always follow the steps outlined in Figure 11. Some home owners die young. Others fail to leave valid wills, and some may not have had children.

How much do home owners bequeath?

The dominance of housing in Australia's private wealth (Table 5) is partly linked to increasing longevity and appreciating asset values in the 1970s and 1980s. Wealth tends to increase with age, until the typical retirement age of sixty or sixty-five. But the most striking aspect of Table 5 is the amounts by which the wealth of the middle-aged groups exceeds that of the oldest groups. These

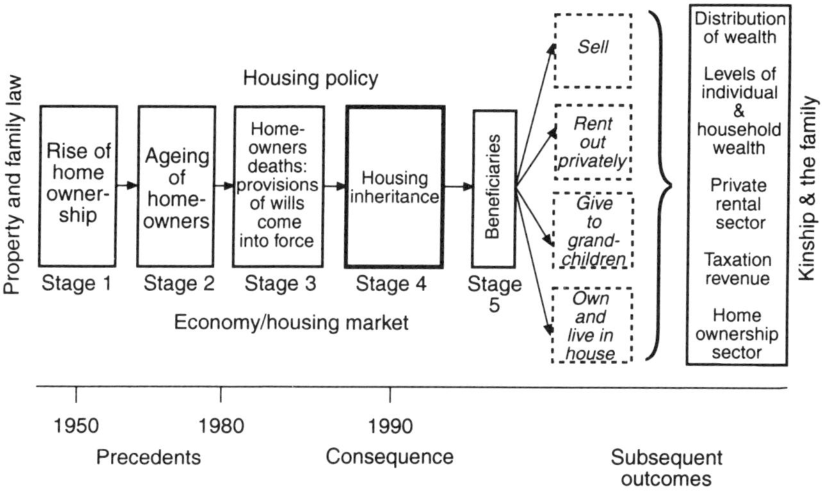

Source: Lisel O'Dwyer, Housing Wealth and the Inheritance Factor.

Figure 11: The housing inheritance process

are the two generations most caught up in the transfer of housing wealth, since there is still a strong tradition for inheritances to pass from parent to child rather than skipping a generation.

Even though the estimates are for all households, not just home owners, Table 5 contains the first clue that the size of bequests falls somewhat short of popular belief. What we need to find out is the proportion of deceased estates containing property, the value of those estates—both in sum and for individual home owners—and the number of people who inherit that wealth. It is reasonable to expect that the ratio of estates that include a housing asset should reflect home ownership rates among the older age groups. But this is not so. Even though the home ownership rate amongst elderly South Australian households was about 74 per cent in 1991,[7] only about 50 per cent of the 5000 estates subject to probate in 1990 contained property. This is because a surviving partner holds on to the family home.

Approximately 2500 estates containing housing assets were registered in 1990 in South Australia. The significance of these

Table 5: Forms of household wealth held by age group, Australia, 1986 ($000)

Age group	*Total*	*House*	*Equities*	*Interest*	*Other*
0–19	1	0	0	0	1
20–29	13	8	2	2	1
30–39	57	42	10	3	2
40–49	99	67	21	6	5
50–54	113	74	24	9	6
55–59	103	72	13	9	9
60–64	118	71	21	17	9
65–69	93	63	12	14	4
70–74	74	48	11	11	4
75+	81	54	9	14	4

Source: A. W. Dilnot, 'The Distribution and Composition of Personal Sector Wealth in Australia'.

estates depends on what they were worth, and on how many people shared in the transfer of this wealth. How much wealth did these home owners leave when they died? The probate records show that these 2500 estates were worth a total of $200 million.[8] About 80 per cent comprised housing assets, so the term 'housing inheritance' is certainly accurate.

Although $200 million sounds a reasonably large sum, compared with other forms of capital it pales into insignificance. South Australia's gross domestic product was $25.7 billion in 1990/91, the value of bank deposits was $12.1 billion, the value of exports was $3.5 billion, while the value of tourism was $1.8 billion. Clearly, the value of housing wealth left by dead home owners is a minor capital item in the wider economy.

How much were estates worth? The median value of total estates was only $77 500, while the housing wealth in those estates was on average around $76 500.[9] Interestingly, at the time this figure fell short of the median value of all housing in South Australia ($89 000). How does this difference arise? In order to answer that we have to turn to the housing careers of those owners dying in the 1990s.

Not only is the value of most deceased estates quite modest, therefore, but they show less variation than the variation in house values found across the Adelaide metropolitan area as a whole. In other words, the houses owned by these people, who were mainly elderly, are not representative of the housing stock in general. Most would have been bought with the one income either in the Depression and war years, or in the postwar boom years. Building materials were often difficult to obtain, especially during the housing crisis of the 1950s. Not only are the dwellings of poorer quality, but they are mostly located in the older areas of Adelaide. This pattern is also tied geographically to the industries that were important when these home owners were in the labour force. As might be expected, the occupational profile of elderly persons dying in 1990 reflects the traditional dominance of manufacturing in the South Australian economy.

Maintenance and upkeep tend to lapse with the onset of old age for physical and financial reasons. Without maintenance, poor-quality housing tends to deteriorate quickly as it ages.[10] Also, when the upkeep finally gets too much the frail aged often trade down to smaller and less expensive housing in the neighbourhood. It is not uncommon, then, for these inherited houses to be worth less than the surrounding dwelling stock. This point is usually overlooked.

The $200 million in probate registered in South Australia in 1990 was shared among 4500 people.[11] This is less than 0.5 per cent of South Australia's population. So, clearly, the impact upon the distribution of wealth is likely to be slight in the short term. Further, the more people getting a piece of the pie, the smaller each piece is. And because completed families tended to be larger in the 1950s and 1960s, the average number of beneficiaries per estate in South Australia worked out at three, with each inheriting about $39 000. The amounts inheritors receive can vary greatly depending upon the wish of the deceased, but in this South Australian study 78 per cent of inheritances were divided equally between beneficiaries. No clear relationship emerged between value of estate and number of inheritors, as observed in Britain.[12]

So we are not yet in a position to say anything conclusive about the impact of housing inheritance on the distribution of wealth. It depends somewhat on how much wealth a beneficiary already has, and what difference the $39 000 makes to their financial situation. This leads on then to an examination of the inheritors.

Who are the inheritors?

The meek may inherit the earth, but do they inherit much housing wealth? Do the rich get richer through inheritance, or do the poor catch up? Most Australian writing on the distributive effects of housing inheritance tends to assume that it contributes to greater *polarisation* of wealth. This makes sense—logically, the only way for housing inheritance to equalise wealth would be for the poor to inherit more than the rich. Unless the poor all have rich elderly relatives who like to play fairy godmother, this is not about to happen. It would also imply an *inverse* relationship between the wealth positions of parents and their children.

In fact, there tends to be significant upward inter-generational mobility in Australia, and South Australia is no exception.[13] So a tendency toward equalisation of wealth through housing inheritance is unlikely. But does the reverse situation hold? That is, do the rich always inherit more than the poor? Table 6 suggests that it is a bit of both. Although the average tenant inherited more than the poorest home owners, it is quite clear from Table 6 that the average size of the bequest does rise in line with the amount of housing owned by the beneficiaries.[14]

Table 6: Average value of bequest according to tenure and wealth of inheritors

Tenure	*Number of cases*	*Average value $*
Tenant	55	39 097
Value of owner-occupiers' housing		
0–$50 000	25	24 752
$50 001–$100 000	132	37 923
$100 001–$150 000	73	51 413
$150 001–$200 000	33	64 799
+$200 000	38	61 929
Total owner-occupiers	301	53 242
Total sample	660	50 928

Source: Lisel O'Dwyer, Housing Wealth and the Inheritance Factor.

Obviously an inheritance worth $39 000 is likely to represent a significant addition to the wealth of tenants. Interestingly, the average age of inheriting tenants does not differ at all from inheriting owner-occupiers,[15] even though normally there is a strong relationship between age and tenurial status (that is, there tend to be many more young people renting privately than older or middle-aged people).[16]

Another way of examining the pattern of wealth flows via housing inheritance is to consider the amounts inherited by occupational grouping. This provides a reliable indicator of the socio-economic status of inheritors. At first sight in Table 7 it appears that the higher-status groups do indeed receive larger inheritances. But in absolute terms the difference, at only $15 000, is not so great. In relative terms, the wealth positions of beneficiaries actually *improve*. The lowest occupational group initially owned 58 per cent of the wealth of the top group. After inheriting, they own 61 per cent.

So to summarise: it is true to say that the rich do get richer, but the less wealthy also profit in the process. What we ultimately make of this depends on whether or not an improvement of three percentage points in relative terms—or $5000—is enough to make any real difference, either to individuals, or to the distribution of wealth in society in general. Although the impact is cumulative across the generations, because of the inordinately long timespan it is difficult to see how the present pattern of inheritance could upset the distribution of private wealth in Australia.

The timing of inheritance and its overwhelmingly inter-generational nature is also important. The younger the beneficiaries are when they inherit, the more time they will have to enjoy it; the more likely it is that they still do not have all the material possessions they want; and the more impact there is on their life chances. Even a modest sum could assist earlier entry to home ownership, with all the benefits that home ownership then bestows. Nevertheless, given that most deceased home owners are elderly and that they are more likely to bequeath to their children than to anyone else, most beneficiaries are middle-aged when they inherit. In South Australia in 1990 the average age of housing inheritors was forty-seven years. At that age, directions in life have already been set; though, admittedly, there is still time enough to change course.

Table 7: Average value of bequest by inheritor's occupation and house value

Occupation	*Mean value of bequest* $	*Mean house value* $	*Median house value* $	*Bequest as % of existing housing wealth*	*Per cent owner-occupiers*	*n*
Managers, Administrators, Professionals	47 291	153 192	124 500	30.7	97	94
Paraprofessionals	47 148	115 884	108 888	40.1	88	37
Tradespersons	35 135	139 211	88 500	25.2	91	46
Clerks, Sales, Personal Services	37 170	110 800	104 500	33.3	79	37
Machine Operators, Drivers, Labourers	32 181	90 291	77 500	35.6	69	45
Not in labour force	36 904	111 789	92 000	32.1	85	79
Total	41 138	129 285	99 000	31.8	84	346

Source: Lisel O'Dwyer, Housing Wealth and the Inheritance Factor.

The case of Ms B and her brother illustrates the importance of tenure when beneficiaries are of a similar age. She was in her late forties, working as a cleaner, when she and her brother (a mechanic) inherited their father's house. The house was in very poor condition and located in a modest middle suburb, so it did not fetch much at auction. Ms B and her brother each received about $35 000. This was enough money to enable Ms B to buy a unit in a similar area, leaving her with a very modest mortgage. If it had not been for the inheritance, she would still be renting. On the other hand, the brother, also in his forties, already owned his own home and for him the money was a pleasing windfall. He did not do anything in particular with it, spending it on consumer goods like a new car and washing machine.

Wealth and tenure are strongly related. Because they are middle-aged when they inherit, beneficiaries are likely be home owners themselves and so probably have already amassed some wealth.[17] In fact, 84 per cent of the beneficiaries in the South Australian study were home owners, which exceeds the general level of home ownership. Furthermore, their own housing was worth around $100 000.

Feminist theory traces inequality between men and women to an array of social processes.[18] To what extent does the process of housing inheritance actually contribute to unequal ownership and wealth between the sexes, given the traditionally gendered nature of inheritance?[19] To begin with, has disadvantage in the housing market worked against women? British research indicates that women leave smaller estates than men.[20] But this is not borne out by the South Australian results: the median value of women's estates was $79 700, compared with $75 200 for men. Maybe women have more wealth at death than men simply because they live longer. The male spouse is more likely to die first, and the wealth of the two partners is combined in the hands of the widow. But this does not explain why the *houses* owned by women were more valuable than those of men. Is it possible that the wealth position of the surveyed women is influencing their marital and tenure status, rather than the other way round, which is the usual case for most women?[21]

Men and women may also have different attitudes regarding the division of their estates. Yet both men and women willed their estates to their spouse or children. Also, childless men and women all willed their estates to nieces, nephews, siblings and charity in similar proportions. The fact that wealth remains in the family does not mean that the distribution of wealth becomes more concentrated. The crucial determinant of the impact of inheritance on wealth is the wealth position of inheritors, not their family connections to the person who died. In other words, family relationships are very important in determining whether someone inherits anything at all, but not in determining the distribution of wealth in society as a whole.

Nor do males and females appear to favour beneficiaries of a particular gender. There were signs that there might have been some kind of a bias operating in 13 per cent of the 891 bequests surveyed, but even in these cases just over half of the bequests went to female beneficiaries. This pattern is indicative of the changes in family inheritance and transfer law and in societal attitudes (which do have a reciprocal relationship).

A different picture emerges, though, if we consider bequests specifically related to the fate of the testator's house. The inclusion of specific directions for the house was in fact unusual, accounting for 26 per cent of wills, and most of these did not single out any particular gender. But when they did, males clearly won. Thirty-seven houses went to a male beneficiary, while only twenty went to a female beneficiary. Though the numbers are small, the pattern is intriguing because it suggests that a vestige of the traditional relationship between property, gender and inheritance remains. What is noteworthy is that testators of *both* genders made the bequests favouring males. This would suggest that it is not just men who perpetuate patriarchy. Although the role of culture was not addressed in the original research, it may well be a factor asserting some influence here. It must be stressed, however, that the vast majority of inheritances were *not* based on gender and that divisions were made equally.

Effects of a bequest on the inheritors

Inherited wealth is welcome, but it is usually not enough to change people's lives. Answers to the questions, 'Did your inheritance have any significant effect on your lifestyle?' and 'Did it enable you to do something you wouldn't have been able to do otherwise?' were answered in the following terms:

> No, not really, life went on just the same. [Mrs K, widow aged 67.]

> Well, we bought a caravan and a few things but otherwise no. [Mr A, electrical maintenance worker, aged 51.]

> No ... well, we probably wouldn't have got our own holiday house ... but no. [Mr G, a retired panel-beater in his early fifties. The Gs also explained that they already had the use of a holiday house even before Mr G's mother died.]

> No. But we wouldn't have bought the other rental property if we hadn't rented out my parents' house. [Mrs R, student aged 45. In

this particular case, the initial ease of renting out the inherited house led the Rs to invest in another rental property. But eventually problems with tenants prompted them to sell the second house and use the inherited house as a holiday home. It was a modest 1950s-era dwelling located near the beach, while the Rs lived in the more distant Adelaide Hills.]

No. Nothing's changed. [Mr D, real estate manager aged 50.]

We used the money to buy a place at Middleton—a popular weekend holiday destination in South Australia—but we were looking down there anyway. We would have bought it irrespective of the inheritance. [Mr M, middle level manager aged 46. Mr M was retrenched shortly before he was interviewed in early 1996 and acknowledged that the balance of the bequest had provided something to fall back on.]

Inheritors who used the bequest to buy consumer goods stressed that they would eventually have got the equivalent of the new car on their wish list. As Mr Z, a retired university lecturer aged 60, pointed out, 'It just enabled us to get it a bit sooner'. Bequests came as windfall gains to most people. The main exceptions, of course, are young people or those who were not home owners at the time—and, as we have seen, these inheritors were in a minority.

The experience of Mr L illustrates how unsettling a bequest can prove to be in the life of a young person. Mr L was only eighteen and unemployed when he inherited his grandfather's modest house in an outer suburb. The inheritance was a major event in Mr L's life. Never before had he been compelled to budget for electricity or telephone bills or council rates. In fact, this event marked the beginning of his adult life, because he was forced to seek a job in order to fix the house up. He willingly admitted that if he had not inherited the house, he would still be partying with his mates—most of whom were either still living with their parents or renting flats in the private sector. This is not to say that Mr. L gave up partying! He and his friends seized on the place as the ideal venue for holding some very wild parties. Now somewhat older and wiser, Mr L is in the process of repairing the additional damage to the house caused during the parties, mainly in the form of cigarette burns and unidentifiable stains in the carpet.

At an age where many of his peers are struggling to save a deposit, Mr L already has a possibly precarious foot on the housing ladder—only time will tell. But his is an unusual case, because only about 2 per cent of bequests pass to grandchildren or other third-generation family members. Not only is it rare for young people to inherit, but only a quarter of all housing inheritances go to a sole beneficiary (this excludes transfers to surviving spouses, which are not really inheritances in the true sense of the word). It is even more unusual to be so young *and* the only beneficiary. Thus Mr L was one of very few people to receive a significant inheritance at the right time.

Although the impact of a bequest on wealth was hardly noticeable, the inheritances occasionally affected personal lives in quite unexpected ways. Several inheritors specifically mentioned, without any prompting at all, that although their financial position was much the same, the bequest had dire effects on their family and marital relationships. Mr T, a butcher aged forty-six, and his sister and brother were no longer on speaking terms after the sister and brother challenged the will in which everything was bequeathed to him. In the end, after the court decision that the estate should be redistributed more evenly and paying lawyers' fees, Mr T found himself worse off than before!

Mrs W, a forty-year-old hairdresser running her own small business, inherited her father's house while her brother was bequeathed a token legacy. Her brother also contested the will. According to Mrs W, her brother behaved as if the way the estate had been divided was her fault: 'I couldn't believe it . . . it was really upsetting, he never even spoke to me all during the business with the court'. Mrs W's brother became more cordial after the case was resolved (he had been awarded a larger share of the estate), but Mrs W felt that 'it just goes to show what money can do to people, even people you wouldn't think'. Her experience led her to take steps to make sure there was no fighting among her family in the division of her own estate.

Mr D attributed his divorce partly to his inheritance: 'All the money just sitting there just puts pressure on you . . . I didn't want to spend it, I wanted it as security . . . but she wanted to spend it. It caused a lot of problems and then eventually—well . . .'. The behaviour of Mr K's siblings after the death of their father represents the most extreme case of emotional hardship encountered. According to Mr K, a 23-year-old storeman, 'The day he died they were round there taking things, they were like vultures. My brother even took one of the doors off its hinges! I couldn't believe it! Dad would have had a fit the way they were carrying on.' Mr K clearly felt very deeply about his whole experience and was upset by his brother and sisters' behaviour at the time of their inheritance. He was interested to know whether his experience was common among other families settling an estate.

Finally, we wondered whether Australians are at all conscious of the extent to which housing dominates the formation of wealth and its transfer between the generations in our society. Few South Australian inheritors saw their bequest as special in any way. For example, no one mentioned that it represented the embodiment of their parents' labour, or the fulfilment of the Great Australian Dream. Accordingly, there was no sense of obligation to use the home bequeathed to them in a particular way, or with particular care. Only one inheritor, Mrs W kept her parents' house and rented it out because she could not bear to part with it. It held too many memories of her parents. It was a large, old house, which meant that it was a considerable burden to maintain, not to mention all the problems Mrs W had with tenants. Mrs W confided that inheriting her father's house has been a financial burden but still she cannot bear to sell it. So sometimes beneficiaries do have an emotional attachment to their inherited houses but, more often than not, the material value from selling the house outweighs any sentimental value. Even when sentimental value does outweigh the material value, there may still be *use* value—Mrs W was able to reap rent from her inherited house.

Housing inheritance—much ado about nothing?

Housing may indeed form the vast majority of wealth at death, but apparently this means little to the beneficiaries of deceased home owners. It is just a realisable asset. Without the institution of home ownership it would not otherwise have existed; but even so, it is still not much money by the time most beneficiaries get to inherit. Indeed, a fair amount of housing wealth actually gets dissipated in the process of transferring it to the next generation.

The popular view that high levels of home ownership amongst the aged will translate into high levels (and values) of inheritance[22] clearly overstates the *present* position if the results from this South Australian study are anything to go by. Similarly, the idea that the housing bequests from the first postwar generation of home owners could shift the distribution of wealth also seems somewhat far-fetched. It is true that never before have so many people stood to inherit.[23] But by the time they reach the end of their lives, the value of the housing owned reflects the modest start that most home owners made after the war, together with the tendency for fewer women of that generation to return to paid work. Of course, we must not forget that the value of bequests is bound to be more impressive in cities like Sydney, and parts of Melbourne, where house prices are now stratospheric by Australian standards.

Given the presently modest overall levels of housing inheritance, there is not much scope for greatly modifying wealth inequalities in Australia as has sometimes been argued.[24] But by comparison, the mounting housing wealth of the baby-boom generation promises to have a regressive impact upon private wealth in Australia if the property and tax laws and structures of provision allow it. If the distribution of housing wealth continues to become more unequal, as it obviously did in Sydney, Melbourne, Brisbane, Adelaide, and Perth during the 1990s (Figure 6a and 6b), then future governments will have to think much more seriously about taxing housing inheritance.

There is no doubting the multiplicity of ends that housing wealth may serve. But perhaps it has taken on greater symbolic value than is warranted in the minds of sociologists writing on the meaning of home ownership.[25] It has been virtually reified. Yet once inherited, housing wealth is treated by South Australian beneficiaries in the same way as any other kind of asset, liquid or otherwise. It appears not to be the sacred cow that has so far thwarted the half-hearted attempts of political parties to levy an impost upon the inheritance windfall—remembering that part of this accrues as betterment generated by social investment (Chapter 1). This is one of the policy issues that we return to in the postscript, which looks at measures for fairer shares of housing wealth for Australians.

CHAPTER 4

Housing: An Investment for All?

'THE RAPID EXPANSION of home ownership in the immediate post-war period and the continuing stability of the overall home ownership rate at approximately 70 per cent since 1961 has led to owner-occupation playing a central role in housing the Australian population.'[1] Admittedly the plateau on which the home ownership level has sat since 1961 disguises an underlying shift in housing preferences and access—since the mid-1970s the home purchase rate has fallen by 10 per cent (Figure 13)—but the Great Australian Dream still shapes the long-term plans of most Australians.

Even though young Australians are now deferring home purchase, the majority undoubtedly still aspire to own their own home in the distant future. The strength and power of this affection among Australians for home ownership has been reflected in numerous government policy reviews[2] and in the platforms of the major political parties. At the same time, our national infatuation with home ownership is just as likely to reflect other, economic factors. High on the list are the tax incentives and the inherent attraction of being able to combine housing consumption with investment. Until very recently, most Australians regarded the stock and bond markets as too complicated and risky as alternatives.

Surprisingly little attention has been paid to one of the prime consequences of a sustained high level of home ownership. As home buyers eventually become owners, and as house price inflation pushes up the value of housing assets, the pool of housing wealth within the economy grows in size. Admittedly it fluctuates somewhat, depending upon the duration of the periodic property booms that have been such a pronounced feature of the Australian economy.

As a consequence, housing wealth represents a substantial concentration of national assets. Almost 60 per cent of all private wealth in Australia is housing.[3] This is 50 per cent greater than in Britain, twice the rate in France and almost three times the percentage in the United States.[4] Moreover, this is a long-established pattern. From the 1920s one-third of all investment in Australia has gone into housing.[5] The concentration of wealth holdings in residential property raises important questions. Why do Australians hold so much of their wealth in housing? What effect has this concentration had on our economy, and how has it influenced the way we live, do business, save, recreate and associate?

How much wealth?

In June 1990 Australia's net private sector wealth stood at $1269 billion in market prices and some $1245 billion at replacement costs. This was equivalent to $74 400 per capita and 340 per cent of gross domestic product.[6] Land and housing is the single most important type of asset in Australia, outstripping all others by a huge margin. In 1995 housing represented 59 per cent of all private sector wealth in Australia. As such it was double the proportion of wealth in business capital (28 per cent), and roughly ten times the wealth held either in consumer durables or government securities. By comparison, they only represented 6 per cent of Australian private sector assets. The remaining 1 per cent of wealth was held as cash.[7]

By international standards Australians have a large proportion of their wealth locked up in bricks and mortar. Dwellings (net of mortgage debt) now represent 40 per cent of personal wealth in Britain.[8] This compares with 30 per cent in France in 1979 and approximately 20 per cent in the United States.[9] Australia does not lead the world in this respect, as 70 per cent of wealth in Japan is held as housing.[10] But it is among a group of nations in which housing dominates wealth composition. There is also evidence that other developed nations are becoming more like Australia, as there has been substantial growth in the proportion of wealth held as housing. In Britain it has risen from 21 per cent in 1971 to 36 per cent in the 1990s, a two-thirds increase in twenty-five years. Regardless of developments elsewhere, there can be no doubt that Australians have been willing to back their commitment to the Great Australian Dream with substantial investment. It is important to ask why Australia outstrips most other developed nations in this regard.

Statistical error is one possible reason why Australia appears to have a greater percentage of wealth in housing. The old adage of 'lies, damn lies and statistics' applies as much to housing as other areas of life. Perhaps the definitions of wealth and housing used by researchers and the various national authorities charged with estimating wealth explain Australia's divergence from the normal pattern for developed economies. For example, the estimate of personal sector wealth for Australia in 1993–94 calculated by Anthony King and Hans Baekgaard is based on the household expenditure survey by the Australian Bureau of Statistics (ABS) and differs markedly from Treasury estimates.[11] They put housing wealth at 52 per cent of all assets and 66 per cent of household wealth if superannuation is excluded. This is at odds by some seven percentage points with the Treasury's official estimate. Consequently, the different technical assumptions made by economists may be one possible source of confusion about the magnitude of housing wealth in Australia.

Yet, by definition estimates are just that. We expect some variation to occur. This may be due to perturbation within the overall economy, a decline in the housing market relative to the stock market at that particular point in time, or vice versa. In fact, in a later piece of work designed to update his own estimates, Hans Baekgaard calculates that by 1998 the value of owner-occupied dwellings (without superannuation) had fallen to 58 per cent of total household wealth.[12] Thus between 1993 and 1998 the value of the family home in the aggregate picture fell due to the growth in the proportion of assets now held as equities (12 per cent) and in superannuation (24 per cent).

But regardless of the underlying causes for these disparities, estimates produced for Australia generally fall within the range of

52 to 59 per cent.[13] This places even the lowest end of the range substantially above Britain, the United States, or most of Europe. It seems, therefore, that we need to look for other reasons for the prominence of housing in the make-up of private wealth in Australia.

The long-established *preference for owner-occupation* in Australia has contributed to the high percentage of wealth held as housing. At the 1996 Census 69 per cent of households were owner-occupiers. This is a high rate by international standards, but Australia no longer really stands out among property-owning democracies (Table 1). This is due to a general trend which has seen an increase in this tenure in most advanced economies. Because of the size of the owner-occupied sector in these countries, house prices are set by the market, rather than by a government bureau. Housing is liable to be undervalued where a substantial portion of the stock is publicly owned or held as other social housing. The rapid escalation in house prices—and housing wealth—in Britain during the 1980s was caused partly by the transfer of council houses from social to private ownership. Once these dwellings were tradeable, they were revalued in a rising property market.

On balance, the level of outright ownership is more significant than owner-occupation rates as an explanation of the high proportion of wealth held as housing. Australia has a long history of home ownership, with owner-occupancy rates rising rapidly from 1945 and peaking in 1966, over thirty years ago. Because of this, many owner-occupiers are now outright home owners. In fact, outright owners increased their share of owner-occupation throughout the 1980s and 1990s (Figure 13). Many retrenched workers used their severance and lump-sum payments to discharge their mortgages at a time when home interest rates soared.

Such a high level of outright home ownership has a bearing on monetary policy because these households own their dwelling free of liabilities. The whole value of the house is owned domestically, whereas dwellings with outstanding mortgages may be partly financed from overseas borrowings.

The pattern of urban development in Australia has also played an important role in boosting the value of housing assets relative to other forms of investment. Australia's population is highly concentrated in the capital cities: 42 per cent live in either Sydney or Melbourne; 60 per cent live in one of the state capitals, and this percentage rises to 62 per cent when Canberra and Darwin are included.[14] Unlike many other nations, Australia does not have a sizeable rural population or large proportion living in small towns and regional cities.[15]

Therefore, most of the nation's housing is bought and sold in the big-city property markets where demand is most acute and pressures are greatest. Housing is simply worth more in the large cities. Hence the stock of housing has a greater asset value than if the population was more decentralised. Sydney and Melbourne, which between them account for almost half of the Australian population, are some of the most expensive markets in which to buy, with only Canberra challenging Melbourne for the second highest average price. According to ABS data, in the December quarter of 1998 the median house prices in Sydney and Melbourne were $262 400 and $196 000 respectively.[16]

The nature and functioning of the Australian economy plays a role in the pre-eminence of housing wealth within the nation's assets. Unlike most other advanced economies, Australia remains heavily dependent on resources to pay its way in the world. Tourism is now Australia's single largest export earner, although in aggregate terms traditional resource-based industries such as coal, gold, alumina, iron ore and wheat still account for most national exports.[17] Despite recent growth in manufacturing exports—especially in the category of goods referred to as elaborately transformed manufactures—Australia still imports more manufactured goods than it exports. In addition, the penetration of imported manufactures into the economy has been growing over the last decade.[18] By comparison, Australia lacks the level of investment in factories, hotels and other income-producing assets that other advanced economies have. Thus the housing sector has greater overall importance within the Australian economy.

Foreign ownership of assets, and in particular income-producing assets, has also contributed to the concentration of Australia's wealth in housing. By world standards, Australia has a very high level of foreign ownership in key income-generating sectors, such as manufacturing, mining and agriculture. Australian governments have encouraged the integration of the Australian economy into the world economy by promoting foreign investment while urging Australian firms both to invest overseas and to enter world markets. During the 1980s, and again in the latter part of the 1990s, there was a high level of foreign investment in commercial property—especially office accommodation in the major capital cities. In 1988/89 almost $15 billion was invested by foreigners in Australia's commercial real estate markets, representing 46 per cent of all foreign investment in that year.[19]

Foreign ownership has had a pronounced impact on the assets of Australians. The value of foreign claims on Australian businesses grew by 13 per cent per annum between 1958 and 1975.[20] By the mid-1970s, some 37 per cent of business assets were in foreign hands. The pace of foreign investment increased through the 1980s, rising by 34 per cent per annum between 1983/84 and 1988/89, from $81 billion to $222.9 billion. This inflow of funds was concentrated in the financial services sector, where foreign investment grew by 89 per cent per annum, but investment in manufacturing also grew by 29 per cent each year.[21]

The nature of economic activity in Australia has had a twofold effect on the proportion of housing held as wealth. The smaller size of the capital-intensive industries, such as manufacturing and knowledge-based enterprises, relative to resource-based activities makes housing appear more prominent; at the same time, the 40 per cent of business assets in foreign hands gives the impression that businesses are much less important relative to the nation's stock of assets than they really are. Housing, which is domestically owned to an overwhelming degree, fills the vacuum.

Australia's high inflation rates during the 1970s and 1980s encouraged investment in assets that could hold their real value. Throughout this period inflation was higher in Australia than in its major trading partners. For twenty years, Australia's economy functioned within a high-inflation environment. Investment strategies that struggled to keep pace with inflation were discarded, while those that were insulated grew in popularity. Housing was particularly privileged because house prices generally held their own against inflation, while inflation eroded the real value of the outstanding mortgage.

Both the taxation and financial systems have played a role in the high proportion of Australian wealth in housing. The Australian taxation system confers tax advantages on owner-occupation and, most importantly, on high levels of equity and outright ownership. Because tax benefits are capitalised into the price of housing, they raise housing prices and elevate the wealth of home owners.[22] Owner-occupation has been the most rational investment for households in Australia, whatever their income level. Although the incentives differ for each income group, economic analysis is unanimous in its verdict that the Australian taxation system —through the failure to tax imputed rent, the use of negative gearing by landlords, and the application of progressive income tax schedules—steers households into the residential property market. The deregulated financial system has also played a part as various institutions have sought to release the wealth stored in the housing stock via home equity loans.

Australia's low level of domestic savings is the final factor to be mentioned. Australians save a tiny proportion of their incomes compared with households in other advanced economies. This has increased Australia's reliance on foreign capital. For this reason, the Keating Labor government introduced the superannuation guarantee levy to encourage a greater national savings effort. In the past, Australians have preferred to save for their futures by investing in their housing rather than establishing equity through the stock market or bank and other deposits. Therefore, home purchase has played a crucial role in the savings strategies of most Australian households, and for many it has been the only significant form of saving and investment.

Who are the major holders of housing wealth?

Over two-thirds of Australian households are owner-occupiers and hold some housing wealth. However, the possession of housing wealth presents a more complicated picture than that. It depends very much on the value of the house and the size of the outstanding mortgage. In addition, a relatively small number of households hold additional wealth in the form of dwellings that they rent out privately.

As is to be expected, most housing wealth is held by older persons. Households with heads aged forty years or more have the greatest housing wealth. They have had longer to pay off their mortgages and they are likely to live closer to the central business district where they benefit from higher house prices. Contrast this with the younger households who commenced home purchase in the 1980s. They incurred higher interest rates (Figure 5) and much greater purchase costs. In addition, many were forced to borrow more, or choose a less valuable house, than they would have ten or twenty years previously. Average mortgages rose significantly between 1985/86 and 1993/94, with the greatest increase in value falling upon the youngest households.[23]

Ownership of private rental property is one strategy used by some households to increase their wealth. A 1993 survey of rental investors by the ABS[24] found that just over 752 000 persons, or 6 per cent of the adult population, owned at least one rental property as an investment. Men slightly outnumber women investors in a ratio of five to four. Of these investors, 78 per cent owned one property only, 13 per cent owned two properties, and 4 per cent owned five or more.[25] These 26 300 landlords with five or more rental properties constitute a small core of quasi-commercial operators in the private rental sector.

Ownership of rental housing forms a considered part of the wealth-creation strategy of these investors, especially those owning five or more dwellings. They have much in common with owner-occupiers with very expensive homes. People aged 45–54 years represent just over one-quarter of these investors and are the largest single group. Together with the 35–44 age group they accounted for 54 per cent of all investors. Only 8 per cent of landlords were over sixty-five years.

The ABS survey of investors in rental dwellings provides a detailed profile. The median income of investors from all sources was in the modest range of $25 000 to $30 000, and only 20 per cent earned $50 000 or more per annum. Some 51 per cent of landlords were wage and salary earners. Small business people made up 25 per cent of rental investors, but only 10 per cent of wage and salary earners. Just under 13 per cent of investors received the major portion of their income from their investments, while 8.4 per cent received most income in the form of a government pension or benefit.[26] Clearly, there is considerable diversity among landlords with respect to their sources of income, and it is equally clear that investors generally use private rental housing as a supplementary, rather than a primary, source of income. Of those receiving most of their income from investments, the majority are older persons living off their rental property and other capital.

Overall, older persons have the greatest housing wealth, both in owner-occupation and in investment properties. Persons aged over sixty-five are likely to have substantial housing wealth in the form of owner-occupation, but are unlikely to be rental investors. The value of housing wealth among younger households is reduced by their much higher mortgages. Location is also a significant determinant of the value of housing wealth held by a household (Chapter 1).

Wealth creation, negative gearing and landlords

The broader dynamics of housing wealth in Australia are crucial to understanding why individuals become investors. From the early 1970s through to the first years of the 1990s real house prices outstripped the general inflation rate in every capital city in Australia, with the possible exception of Hobart. Once inflation is taken into account, a household purchasing an average-priced dwelling in Sydney in 1979 paid $151 000 in 1992 dollars. By 1992, the average price had risen to $225 000—a 50 per cent increase in real capital over thirteen years.[27] In Melbourne the average price in 1979 was $93 700, and this rose to $123 700 in 1992. During these years rising real house prices offered property owners —whether landlords or owner-occupiers—attractive returns.

Residential property was made even more attractive by the relatively high rates of general inflation within the economy. With the traditional approach to financing housing in Australia, which is called the *credit foncier* system, the capital owed to a lending institution is not adjusted for inflation. Instead, higher inflation rates flow through as higher nominal interest rates. Significantly, although the cost of servicing the mortgage rises, those able to carry the higher cost are likely to receive a greater nominal return on their capital because both the real rise in house prices and the general inflation rate contribute to the difference between purchase and resale price. This set of arrangements can operate to the advantage both of owner-occupiers and private landlords; but, as explained below, certain aspects of the tax laws in Australia make rental housing a very attractive investment for some high-income individuals.

Investment in private rental property has been affected by a raft of changes in taxation laws since the early 1980s.[28] A tax on capital gains was introduced in 1983 to stop wealthy individuals avoiding taxation by diverting income into capital-generating schemes. In 1986 negative gearing[29] was quarantined by the federal government so that net losses incurred in purchasing a rental dwelling could not be used to reduce other taxable income. A depreciation allowance was introduced at the same time for new properties. Taxation laws remain important, not the least because some high-income households chose to keep negatively geared property during the 1990s.[30] Under conditions of expanding incomes for many professional workers, rising real house prices and buoyant economic conditions generally, young and middle-aged high-income households were able to reduce their immediate taxation liabilities while generating the potential for capital gains in excess of the returns on other investments.

In the 1990s, it was mainly high-income earners earning more than $50 000 who incurred the capital gains tax. This raised about $2.1 billion of revenue in 1996/97.[31] However, if the federal government exempts 50 per cent of capital gains from any tax as it currently plans to do, this could breathe new life into the very rorts that the reform of 1983 was designed to discourage. Subdued inflation in the years ahead might act to reduce the overall attractiveness of property compared with shares, but any change in taxation on capital gains is likely to have an important bearing on the supply of rental housing and the housing market generally.

The 1993 survey of rental investors undertaken by the ABS asked landlords why they purchased properties for rent. The single most significant response, with over half of the total, was the perception that rental housing offered a secure long-term investment. Other important reasons included the income received from rent, the ability to reduce taxable income by negative gearing, and the prospect of a capital gain. Other factors relate to the investor's life course, including the possible use of the investment property as a home, and the landlord's return to the property at some future date.

Three points emerge from the survey. Firstly, the ability of private rental housing to offer a secure long-term investment is the dominant motive for investment. This is partly the product of a well-established assumption amongst Australians that bricks and mortar are the best forms of investment; however, it also reflects both the boosterism and the reality of Australian residential property markets. In some periods, investment in housing has provided rates of return that exceed all alternatives.[32] In all periods the real estate industry has keenly promoted housing as an investment.[33] Secondly, landlords are drawn from all income groups. There are almost twice as many landlords in the lowest income group as in the highest, and this is partly a function of the age of investors. Many retired people supplement their pensions with rental income. Those on high incomes are over-represented relative to their share of the population. But it is apparent that rental housing is an investment pursued by all strata of Australian society. Thirdly, individuals invest in rental housing for disparate reasons. Some are saving for their retirement; some are reducing their taxable income; others rent out their house while they live elsewhere.

The rental investors survey found that, although the secure long-term investment offered by rental properties was important for all income groups, the income received from rent was most important for those on low incomes, and the ability to engage in negative gearing was prominent for those on high incomes. Further insights into investment decisions were obtained through a question asking landlords which factors were considered prior to committing their funds. Negative gearing and capital gains were by far the most commonly considered issues. Once again, the prospect of capital gains and negative gearing was more important for those on higher incomes. Finally, it is worth considering the attractiveness of rental investment. Landlords were asked to estimate their rental income from their dwelling net of mortgage and other costs. Over one-third of all landlords and 40 per cent of those with mortgages did not have a clear idea whether their investment generated a profit or not. Those with a mortgage were more likely to receive a negative return, with almost one-third reporting a loss. These landlords were engaged in negative gearing regardless of whether or not that was their intention in purchasing their rental property. It is also reasonable to assume that at least half of the 'don't know' category (and probably substantially more) also incurred losses. The ABS also found that investors with incomes in excess of $720 per week were more likely to make a net loss on their investment.[34]

This survey by the ABS presents valuable insights into the behaviour and intentions of rental investors in Australia. It is clear that individuals become investors for a range of reasons. Some inherit their properties, some are planning for their retirement, some are consciously using strategies to reduce their current taxable income, while others appear to place a degree of blind faith in the 'security' of property. Rental investors are therefore a differentiated group, but there are some important common elements in their intentions and actions. The expectation of capital gains and the ability to write off rental losses against other income is fundamental to the participation of many landlords. Fundamentally, investors view the generation of wealth through the housing market as the most attractive of several alternatives. With at least 40 per cent of landlords negatively geared, this form of investment is favoured because of the combination of taxation benefits and appreciating house prices—both real and nominal. Together these factors attracted investment in rental properties and associated housing wealth worth $80 to $90 billion in 1996.

Have Australians over-invested in housing?

Have Australians over-invested in housing? This is one of the most hotly debated questions in housing policy circles.[35] Economists routinely argue that the financial advantages of home ownership have almost certainly encouraged Australians to invest far too much in housing. The concern is that this crowds out, or diverts, capital which might otherwise flow to more productive investment.[36] An embellishment is to claim that Australia now has more bedrooms in its housing stock than people.[37] However, this argument treats housing simply as a consumption good and dismisses the stimulus to productive activity and job creation that comes with the demand for building materials, whitegoods, furniture, and the like.[38] Besides, most home owners buy their household goods from local rather than foreign producers. When all is said and done, there can be no guarantee that funds directed away from the housing sector will find their way into Australia's exporting or import-replacing industries.

In 1991, Bernie Fraser, then governor of the Reserve Bank, pointed out that Australia does not spend significantly more on housing than other OECD nations, and that occupancy rates are only slightly below the OECD average.[39] In fact, dwelling investment in Australia has averaged between 5 and 5.5 per cent over the last twenty years. Moreover, during the 1980s and 1990s the pattern of dwelling investment has shifted towards home renovation and away from new construction.[40]

Part of the difficulty in settling the argument is that simple comparisons between nations are singularly unhelpful as there is no agreed standard or benchmark on the *appropriate* level of investment in housing.[41] Furthermore, what constitutes an appropriate level of investment depends in large part on the tax and financial arrangements in each nation. As these arrangements change, so too does the appropriate level of investment. The conventional formulation of the over-investment thesis needs rethinking. Instead of asking whether the nation as a whole is over-investing in housing, we should ask whether individuals are devoting too high a proportion of their capital to bricks and mortar. Tax arrangements lie at the core of this debate, a point neatly summarised by Issues Paper No. 3 of the National Housing Strategy:

> some critics have claimed that tax expenditures are inefficient at a macro-economic level because they lead to over-investment in housing. This argument is based on claims that tax expenditures

have led to an expansion of the housing sector at the expense of other sectors of the economy and that, as the productivity growth in the housing sector is relatively low, this has a detrimental effect on the long-run growth of the economy.[42]

It is crucial therefore to examine taxation arrangements and how they interact with owner-occupation and wealth creation. Four key attributes of the tax system in relation to wealth are relevant to this discussion. To begin with, personal income taxation has been highly progressive in Australia—that is, tax rates have been much higher for those on greater incomes. Secondly, unlike the United States, taxation is directed to individuals rather than households. Thirdly, owner-occupied housing is treated as a consumption good rather than an investment. Finally, owner-occupied housing is exempt from capital gains tax. The significance of each of these attributes is considered in turn.

The highly progressive nature of income taxation in Australia is a prime suspect.[43] Currently the highest rate of personal income tax is effectively 48.7 cents in the dollar for incomes in excess of $50 000. This is 7 cents in the dollar more than the company tax rate. Tax rates were even more progressive in the past. In the early 1980s the highest tax schedule was as much as 60 cents in the dollar. These marginal tax rates are much higher than in the United States and effectively reduce the incentive to earn additional *taxable* income. Under this tax regime, high-income earners are encouraged to consume disposable income or seek investments that minimise their taxable income. This effect is further compounded by the direction of income tax to individuals rather than households. In the United States, high-income earners can split their income with partners who are outside the paid workforce or in lower-paying jobs, and thereby reduce their tax liabilities, but Australians cannot do this. Hitherto, there has been no incentive for high-income earners in Australia to invest in speculative capital, stock or financial markets.

The failure to tax capital gains associated with owner-occupied housing is a significant feature of taxation in Australia. Capital gains tax was applied to all assets from September 1993 as part of wider reform of the taxation system; however, owner-occupied housing was exempted. This encourages high-income earners in particular to invest in expensive owner-occupied housing. Any capital gain on the property is free of tax. Better still, under the right conditions home ownership may offer higher rates of return than those available in alternative investments. Finally, the treatment of housing as a consumption good by the tax system produces distortions. Unlike the United States, and to a more limited extent Britain until the 1999/2000 budget, mortgage repayments are not tax deductible in Australia. This encourages households to be owner-occupiers, and if at all possible to be outright owners. The net effect of these tax arrangements should not be underestimated. An individual or a household in the highest tax bracket has a strong incentive to purchase a home and add to their equity in their dwelling as quickly as possible. They can do so via enforced savings, or through the use of 'mortgage offset' accounts that simultaneously reduce their interest burden, add to the principal repaid and avoid tax.[44]

As a consequence, taxation arrangements have played an unambiguous role in the high proportion of wealth in Australia held as housing. In many respects, high-income earners would be foolish to invest elsewhere! However, there are equally compelling reasons for households on lower incomes to invest in home purchase. In the past, housing loans in Australia have been effectively subsidised by a system of regulation in which depositors have received meagre returns, and the banks have passed on the lower borrowing costs to home purchasers.[45] This has provided a strong incentive for low-income households to borrow money for housing rather than build up their savings. Also, in Australia their welfare is enhanced in retirement so long as they can hang onto their position on the housing escalator—even if it is on the bottom step!

The National Housing Strategy commissioned two studies that investigated the issue of over-investment. They come to different conclusions: one argues that investment in owner-occupation is justified because it contributes to increased income equality;[46] the other argues that taxation arrangements provide an unfair advantage to housing investors, and thereby restrain national economic performance.[47] In large part the conclusion you draw depends on your values. Those who believe a more efficient economy will be beneficial for all will side with the latter. Those who are sceptical of the ability of greater efficiency to meet the needs of all citizens will opt for the former. Either way, at the level of the individual household, sinking savings into housing is entirely rational, although changes introduced to the taxation system in 1989 and followed up in subsequent budgets will partly erode the privileged position of owner-occupied housing. Investments such as franked dividends which pay tax at the corporate rate of 39 cents in the dollar, and the expansion of superannuation are generating new and more flexible investment opportunities, and home ownership may no longer claim such a central place in the investment strategies of Australians.[48]

Conclusion

Australians have built up their housing wealth for good reasons. In a period of high inflation it offered a secure, tax-advantaged investment that also provided significant welfare benefits in old age. The benefits of this strategy for individuals are obvious, but as a nation we may have erred in hoarding all our wealth in housing as it created an economic environment in which a significant proportion of our productive capacity is owned by foreigners. No nation can sustain itself by buying and selling real estate. As a wealth-creation strategy, it is vulnerable to change—the economic environment of the late 1990s is very different from that of the previous quarter of a century. In the future far fewer households, especially the middle class, can expect to achieve a comfortable level of wealth as a consequence of their participation in the housing market. The wealth-generating processes outlined in Chapter 1 are likely to be far more restricted to particular locations within certain cities, and within defined socio-economic groups.[49] Housing will remain an investment for all, but it should no longer be the only investment. The new millennium will require new investment strategies and a new role for housing wealth.

CHAPTER 5

Housing Wealth within Australia's Economy

UNTANGLING THE IMPACT of housing wealth on the Australian economy is a difficult task. Should we view Australia's substantial housing wealth as ballast in the financial system, adding stability and security to an otherwise volatile sector? Or has there been excessive investment in the housing sector, creating misallocation within the economy? Have we been throwing good money after bad? Would Australians enjoy higher living standards if these resources were not being diverted into a non-productive asset?

These are strategically important concerns for those managing the economy. But to date, economic managers have dwelt more on the short- to medium-term implications of fluctuating housing commencements, at the expense of understanding the long-term impacts of Australia's housing wealth. Until 1993, Reserve Bank regulations discouraged the use of equity in housing for other purposes.[1] For the most part, housing wealth remained a growing but idle asset. Deregulation of the financial system in the mid-1980s changed all that. There is growing evidence that this change in the status of housing wealth contributed to the expansion of mortgage debt through the 1990s.

These developments are part of the broader impact of housing wealth upon the economy to which we now turn. What is the cost to governments of the existing arrangements that shape the structure of housing provision in Australia? How does drawing upon home equity affect the general well-being of the economy? Two case studies are instructive in this regard. Events in Britain in conjunction with the phenomenon of negative equity,[2] and the sequel to the 'Massachusetts boom',[3] both help to deepen our understanding of the potential significance of housing wealth within the economy.

The cost to governments of housing wealth

Housing wealth comes at a cost to governments. This cost is largely hidden from view because, unlike public housing grants or rental allowance schemes, the subsidies provided to home owners and home purchasers are not normally entered in annual federal or state budgets. For example, the full range of subsidies flowing to each tenure in Australia was worth an estimated $8.7 billion in 1990/91.[4] Contrary to normal belief, public tenants are not the largest recipients of benefits. They received $1.038 billion, but they were overshadowed by private tenants with $1.187 billion, home purchasers with $1.641 billion, and outright owners with a massive $4.653 billion in subsidies. Community housing made up the difference, with $250 million in subsidies. There are two important questions associated with this distribution of benefits. What are the subsidies flowing to owner-occupiers and home purchasers? And on a household basis, which tenure or tenures receives the greatest assistance?

Owner-occupiers and home purchasers are chiefly subsidised through the capital gains tax exemption for owner-occupied housing and through the failure to tax imputed rent. The imputed rent is the rent home owners would pay if they were renting the dwelling they own; or, to put it another way, the amount an owner would receive if their home was rented out. Landlords are taxed on the rent they receive from letting their dwellings, and it can be argued on equity grounds that owner-occupiers should also pay tax on their housing services.[5] There is a historical precedent, as imputed rent was taxed in Australia between 1915 and 1923.[6] The non-taxation of imputed rent accounts for the lion's share of the subsidy to home owners and purchasers because outright owners in particular tend to occupy valuable dwellings. As a consequence of these tax arrangements, each owner household received

$2000 per annum in subsidies, compared with $1000 for purchasers, $990 for private tenants and $3020 for public tenants.[7] Thus Australia's substantial stock of housing wealth has been underpinned by government subsidies. These taxation benefits have been capitalised into house prices and have further encouraged households to enter home ownership and then remain in that tenure.

Housing and macro-economic management

Even though dwelling investment in Australia has held at around 5 to 5.5 per cent of gross domestic product over the last twenty years or so,[8] from time to time the housing sector has been used to regulate the rate of growth within the economy.[9] We need only recall the words of the governor of the Reserve Bank who, at the time, was advocating a role for housing in pulling Australia out of recession in the early 1990s:

> it is the cyclical sector par excellence ... Given their amplitude these fluctuations can have a significant effect on aggregate economic activity. In the current year, for example, private dwelling investment is forecast to decline by around 10 per cent but to increase in 1991/92. Such a turnaround would make a useful contribution to recovery in the economy as a whole.[10]

Both monetary and fiscal policies have been used to stimulate housing production and thereby the economy. Much of the funding provided to the states by the Hawke Labor government in 1983/84 under first the Wage Pause Programme, and later the Community Employment Programme, was used to boost housing construction and thereby 'prime the pump' of local economies. This practice was particularly evident in South Australia. Similarly, with the economy slowing in the early 1990s, the federal government increased its spending on public housing by using capital otherwise earmarked for future years.

Monetary policies determine the cost of borrowing money, and therefore interest rates. Although the Reserve Bank of Australia has control of interest rates, the federal government is influential through its appointment of the governor and by engaging the bank in a broad dialogue on the directions for monetary policy. The federal government has become much more reliant on monetary policy since financial deregulation in the mid-1980s. Nominal interest rates peaked in 1982, 1986 and 1989 (Figure 5), reaching 8.5, 9.8 and 12.5 per cent in real terms. Dwelling commencements generally fall with higher interest rates, and increase when monetary policy is loosened and interest rates decline. Commencements tend to lag behind movements in interest rates,[11] but the link is pronounced, and appeared immutable throughout the 1980s. Only in the mid-1990s has any variation in this relationship appeared, with continued high numbers of dwelling commencements despite rising interest rates.

But the impact of housing construction on the economy is not a true measure of how housing wealth can affect national economic performance. Dwelling starts account for less than 2 per cent of the housing stock in most years and most housing wealth is located in established dwellings. The ABS estimated that in 1989 dwelling construction was worth $3.7 billion.[12] This is less than 1 per cent of the $537 billion in housing wealth in Australia estimated for 1988/89.[13] Therefore housing construction is just a tiny part of housing wealth. This raises questions about the contribution of housing wealth in other ways to the quality of life of Australians—especially given the fact that wealth tied up in a dwelling cannot be applied in a straightforward fashion to the purchase of consumer goods or the payment of bills.

Britain and the United States

Some clues as to the role of housing wealth in the broader economy emerged following the economic boom in Britain in the late 1980s. Owner-occupation rates surged in Britain from the late 1970s to reach 67.4 per cent by 1994 (Table 1). A number of factors played a part in this: the British economy was on the boil throughout the 1980s; the private rental sector continued its long-term decline; financial deregulation led to the introduction of a range of home loan products; but most importantly, more than 1.4 million council houses were sold to sitting tenants under right-to-buy provisions introduced by the Thatcher governments.[14] As a result, real house prices in Britain surged through the 1980s, especially in the booming economy of south-east England. This expanded the wealth of individual households which, in turn, fed the boom until 1988. 'The boom was fuelled to a large extent by increasing housing credit. The amount lent on mortgages increased substantially during the late 1980s, and rapidly rising house prices encouraged households to withdraw equity to fuel consumption.'[15]

Estimates reveal just how much equity British home owners withdrew or borrowed against for each year from 1970 to 1990.[16] Those withdrawing equity included the elderly leaving the housing market, other last-time sales, and persons trading down. Then there are those who remained in their house while making use of the equity they had built up through owner-occupation. The equity withdrawn by this latter category increased more than sixfold from £1.191 billion in 1980 to £12.36 billion in 1988! The cash injected into the economy from housing wealth fuelled a consumption boom that eventually hampered the government's attempts to regulate the economy.[17] Measures to slow economic growth in the last half of the 1980s failed as households continued to buy consumer goods generally, especially foreign imports, on the strength of their housing wealth. According to Will Hutton, now editor of the *Observer*, 'people were eating their own seed-corn'.[18]

The expanding housing wealth that fed economic growth in Britain in the latter half of the 1980s then had the opposite effect in the first years of the 1990s as many households in the south-east of England were left with negative equity:[19] the outstanding debt on the mortgage exceeded the resale value of their home. Almost 75 000 British homes were repossessed in 1991, up from 3000 in 1980. Even more people would have lost their homes if mortgagees could have got an acceptable price. But with so many households in difficulty, wholesale repossession made no commercial sense. This overhanging housing debt—or negative wealth—helped push the British economy into recession in the early 1990s, and set back the government's plan to stimulate growth.

Whereas equity withdrawal in the 1980s contributed to high levels of consumption while interest rates were rising, in the 1990s the accumulated debt in housing dragged down the economy and dampened domestic consumption. The impact of housing wealth on the British economy over the last fifteen years is not to be underestimated. The government was forced to revise its economic models to take better account of housing market dynamics and the flow of housing wealth into other sectors of the economy.

Clearly, then, housing wealth can exert a significant influence on economic cycles. There are also long-term impacts.[20] Personal savings in Britain fell from around 12 per cent of income in the early 1980s to under 4.5 per cent in 1988. Almost 80 per cent of wealth withdrawn from the housing sector in the 1980s was used to finance the purchase of non-durable goods. This figure is almost exactly equal to the decline in household savings. By drawing on their housing wealth to purchase luxury goods such as holidays, whitegoods or other items, households cut back their saving and thereby reduced the national savings effort. Also, in small open economies like Britain's, equity withdrawal is often financed by foreign funds and thereby contributes to a decline in the terms of trade.[21]

The 'Massachusetts boom', 1988–91, provides a second example of enhanced cyclical volatility caused by equity withdrawn from the housing market. During the early and mid-1980s the Massachusetts economy fared well: it had a diverse industrial base; unemployment rates were low; and economic growth rates were modest, but steady. From 1984 house prices increased rapidly, which saw household assets increase by an average of $US57 300 between 1983 and 1986.[22] The increase in home equity accounted for virtually all of this rise, as cash assets remained unchanged and household debt increased by $10 300 on average. In fact, 'It is likely that the additional home equity changed household saving and spending patterns. Some borrowed against home equity, while others simply saved less, or spent some of their previous savings.'[23]

House prices rose until 1988, when they began to fall in real terms. The overall effect on the Massachusetts economy was catastrophic. Rising house prices fuelled a construction boom, which in turn created a shortage of labour. This subsequently pushed up prices. At the same time, higher house prices in the region made it more difficult for corporations to attract skilled workers. As well as suffering the distortion of boom-time conditions, Massachusetts had to bear the long-term costs of a loss in competitiveness. The withdrawal of housing wealth 'amplified the business cycle significantly, both on the way up and on the way down'.[24] Many of the lending institutions which wrote these home equity loans were left with bad debts when the housing market crashed. In turn, they were either bought out by other institutions or placed under the surveillance of regulatory agencies.

Australia

Australia has been spared an economic boom and recession fuelled by wealth extracted from housing. Nevertheless, the Australian banks soon realised as they wrote off the bad debt that followed the lending binge in the 1980s[25] that those least damaged by the episode had lent proportionally more funds for housing. Others with greater exposure to corporate or small business lending had deeper wounds to lick. And of those, where the family home had also provided the collateral on loans for small businesses, the exposure of the banks was much more limited. As well as absorbing those lessons, since the early 1990s home lending has been the scene for fierce competition between the banks and a range of new lenders.

The Australian financial system has been transformed in the last few decades and it is still evolving. Prior to 1956 private banks were essentially trading banks. The Commonwealth Bank and savings banks owned by state governments were the only banks offering retail accounts and lending for home loans. In 1956 governments and their banks advanced 56 per cent of all finance for home ownership in Australia. Building societies, trading banks and other bodies made up the remainder. Private savings banks were created under the *Banking Act 1945–53*. By 1972 they had 31 per cent of all home loans and have dominated lending ever since.[26]

The financial sector was reformed in the early 1980s following the Campbell and Martin reports.[27] Controls on bank deposits were removed, and controls on interest rates on home loans taken out after April 1986 were abolished. Regulation of bank assets was relaxed. This sparked a wave of corporate restructuring and bank mergers that extended into the 1990s. Small regional banks were swallowed up, as were many of the permanent building societies. They had prospered in the 1970s and early 1980s by offering cheaper housing loans than the banks, but lost this competitive advantage in the wake of financial deregulation.

Prior to that, the availability of bank finance was partly governed by a fairly complex subsidy system that passbook holders knew little about. Effectively, the low interest rates paid to small depositors subsidised home loans, which were set at a percentage point or two below the true market rate. In turn, the banks rationed their funds by limiting an advance to 70 or 75 per cent of the bank valuation; and made loans only to those customers who had a history of saving with them. To a certain extent, it was a turn-and-turnabout system: only depositors who never took out a home loan missed out on the benefits. The business sector generally benefited from this set of arrangements: although commercial rates were higher than home lending rates, the corporate sector relied on household savings to provide capital for investment purposes.[28] Crucially, home purchase, and a prior history of saving, were central to the structure of the financial system. This all changed in the mid-1980s when the banks lowered the deposit requirement to 5–10 per cent, and domestic savings could no longer fully meet the capital needs of an overheated economy. Household savings were replaced by foreign capital as a source of funds for business, although households in total continued to save more than they spent or invested.[29]

The recession of the early 1990s exposed the stupidity that followed deregulation and highlighted the strategic importance of advances for housing. Of the big four banks, the National Australia Bank and the Commonwealth Bank were relatively untroubled by economic crisis because a high proportion of their loans were advances for owner-occupation. Of the other two, both the ANZ and Westpac Banks faced substantial difficulties because they lent more to small businesses and other enterprises. The State Bank of Victoria and the State Bank of South Australia were among the great losers within the financial system because they were over-exposed to the high end of town—office towers in the central business district. Significantly, both the ANZ and most especially Westpac sought to increase their lending for housing as part of their recovery from the tumult of the early 1990s.

What has made lending for housing such an attractive outlet for funds for banks and other lenders? Firstly, as the axiom 'as safe as houses' suggests, a home loan is very secure. The level of mortgage default in Australia is normally low, although in the 1990s high interest rates and recession dinted that reputation somewhat. In any event, those borrowers at greatest risk are required to insure their loan with the Housing Loan Insurance Corporation or other agency. In 1996 the home loan market in Australia was worth $175 billion.[30] At the same time the level of arrears was just under 1 per cent, which was twice the rate of two years earlier. Even this is tolerable for lenders, given the buffer of mortgage insurance.

The profitability of home loans is the second factor that explains the attractiveness of lending for housing. Deregulation in the 1980s allowed the market to set interest rates, yet *real* interest rates charged by mortgage lenders have remained high compared with alternative investments. Usually a spread of two percentage points provides sufficient profit for commercial loans, but during the late 1980s and 1990s the difference between the cost of capital to the banks and the rate charged to home loan mortgagors widened to five or six percentage points.[31]

The security and profitability of the home mortgage business has seen banks expand their operations and new, non-bank institutions enter the field. Specialist mortgage providers, such as RAMS, Aussie Home Loans, FAI First Mortgage and Australia Mortgage Corp, now compete with the banks by offering cheaper no-frills loans. Unlike bank loans, there is usually no capacity to offset mortgage payments or repay the loan early, but interest rates have been significantly lower—initially by one to two percentage points. This can represent the difference between being able to buy a home or not. Competition between banks has been sufficient to create a boom in housing credit: the financial pages of Australian newspapers display headlines such as 'NAB declares home loan war' or 'Banks launch mortgage war'.[32] By the end of 1996, the refinancing of home loans represented 30 per cent of the market, almost three times their share in 1994.[33] Linked with this has been an overall rise in indebtedness. In the five years to June 1995, lending for owner-occupation doubled to nearly $114 billion. This increased the total indebtedness of Australian households from 50–52 per cent of disposable income in 1980–82, to 68 per cent in 1995.

To the extent that borrowing continues to exceed savings, this indirectly puts added pressure on the current account deficit. Home equity loans are partly responsible for this. Prior to 1993, under Reserve Bank rules, personal and small business loans were rated at twice the risk of home loans, and therefore were double the cost to a bank's balance sheet.[34] With a relaxation of this requirement, banks re-entered the market for personal finance and began to lend against housing equity in a fashion that parallels developments in Britain in the late 1980s.

There is some evidence to suggest that equity withdrawal may have supported the Australian economy during 1994–95, when official interest rates were raised but home lending and consumer spending remained unchanged. However, it is most unlikely in the foreseeable future that Australia will repeat the sort of boom-bust cycle led by housing wealth that destabilised the British economy in the late 1980s. For one thing, there has been less innovation in Australia's housing finance markets than in Britain's. There are a number of banking products in the Australian market which allow households to draw upon their housing equity, but the rate of take-up has been much lower than in Britain. For another, Australian financial regulators have been far more heavy-handed in the monitoring of monetary policy than the British. The Reserve Bank has used interest rates both to check the rate of economic growth and to limit the current account deficit. As one bank official wryly notes, the Reserve Bank does not loosen its grip on monetary policy until there is 'blood on the floor'.[35]

The British government played the role of financial regulator until the election of the Blair government in 1997, when an independent regulator of monetary policy was appointed. Previously, monetary policy tended to be less stringently applied than in Australia because governments directly responsible for setting interest rates are reluctant to face the public odium of a prolonged interest rate squeeze. Finally, negative equity has been an uncommon phenomenon in Australia—though costly for the households affected. In the first years of the 1990s, negative equity selectively penalised home owners on the edges of Sydney and Canberra, and more generally in south-east Queensland. But even then, only those owners seeking to sell at the time faced a shortfall on the outstanding mortgage.

Housing wealth undeniably plays a part in shaping the wider economy. It is supported by substantial government expenditure —or revenue forgone—in the form of non-taxation of imputed rent, capital gains tax exemptions, negative gearing for landlords, and other subsidies. It affects the functioning of the financial system. The large fund of housing wealth in Australia indirectly contributes both to the stability of the major financial institutions and to the level of overall demand within the economy. Since 1993 home equity loans have unlocked the value stored in housing. Then, after the age of sixty, 'net dis-saving' begins as wealth accumulated by owners during their working years is gradually consumed after retirement. Housing wealth released at this stage also contributes to demand, as does the housing inheritance (Chapter 3). Although most persons receiving a bequest gain a relatively modest sum, the inheritance windfall is usually spent buying goods and services rather than lifting investment levels or savings. Inheritance therefore also adds to the level of demand within the economy.

Housing and the welfare regime

Lastly, there is an even broader respect in which housing is significant for the management of the economy. Although often overlooked, the structure of housing provision, erected as it is around owner-occupation, is one of the pillars of the Australian welfare system.[36] As part of the postwar social compact upheld by successive federal governments, Australian voters opted for owner-occupation instead of a universal and well-funded system of income support.[37] Our social security system might not be as generous as those developed in much of Western Europe, but vulnerable groups such as the aged in Australia have enjoyed an income offset in the form of high rates of home ownership which have been supported by government subsidies for owner-occupiers.

Welfare provision tends to be parsimonious in Australia. The federal government makes various types of payments to persons without income or on low incomes—such as the unemployed, the disabled and the aged. In addition, it provides a social wage, such as support for general health care, child care, and pharmaceuticals, as well as financial assistance to low-income households renting privately. In 1995/96, 35 per cent of federal government outlays ($45.3 billion) was spent on income support.[38] Direct income support and social wage expenditures may represent a significant proportion of total public sector outlays, but by international standards Australian governments are meagre providers of benefits. In 1990 Australia spent 13 per cent of gross domestic product on social security payments, compared with an average of 26 per cent for all Europe and 15 per cent for the United States.[39]

The income support and social security system in Australia differs from arrangements in other countries in a number of important ways. In the first instance, most forms of assistance are tightly targeted, with strict eligibility criteria with respect to income and assets. A second distinguishing feature is that social security payments are funded from general government revenue rather than from the contributions of individuals. Thirdly, federal governments have included tax arrangements in their welfare policies, arguing that progressive income taxes reduce inequality and ensure that the burden of meeting the cost of government programmes is carried by those most able.[40] The interaction between welfare polices and home ownership is most clearly seen when we consider the position of the aged.

In common with many other developed nations, Australia has an ageing population[41] and many people rely entirely or principally on the aged pension for income. Until the 1980s there was an extremely low take-up of private or workplace-based superannuation among low-income households. Only about 20 per cent of all households had superannuation in the early 1980s. For more than a decade the aged pension had been set at approximately

25 per cent of average weekly earnings, and prior to 1983 it was allowed to slip below that rate. This is a modest income; the level of income replacement in retirement is much lower in Australia than other developed nations, especially those in continental Europe.[42] Retired Australians receive much lower incomes than similar households in Western Europe, where 'social policy provision is built around notions of contribution and earnings-replacement'.[43] Retired Australians therefore receive low incomes relative both to Australians in the workforce and to their peers in other advanced economies. However, these households do not face absolute deprivation because government-provided health services, pharmaceuticals and other benefits substantially lift their final income.[44]

Home ownership makes an equally substantial contribution to the real incomes of retired people, lifting many above the poverty line.[45] An estimated 85 per cent of Australian households pass through home ownership at some stage, and owner-occupation rates are as high as 90 per cent among some of the older cohorts.[46] There is a distinctly Australian, egalitarian dimension to this phenomenon as a high proportion of households from all income groups are owners.[47] When compared with the admittedly small number of nations for which comparative data was available—Canada, Luxembourg and Britain—'Australia has the highest level of completed home purchase in all quintiles of the income distribution both in the general population and amongst older people'.[48]

This evidence on incomes and home ownership has been used to argue that Australians have traded a comprehensive, universal income support system for high levels of home ownership.[49] This trade-off operates to the benefit of home owners because they are able to secure both a significant asset, and greater security in old age or in the event of misfortune. It works to the advantage of governments because much of the burden of providing for those outside the formal labour force is shouldered by individual households—who have purchased their home—rather than the community. Some European nations are now struggling to finance their pension and other welfare obligations.[50] Australian governments, by contrast, do not have to fully provide for older citizens who are principally outright home owners and this grants Australian governments somewhat greater discretion in their fiscal policies. Although the emphasis on a high level of owner-occupation has created winners, there are also losers. Those who do not own a home and have little prospect of doing so are undeniably disadvantaged.

The high levels of housing wealth in Australia have allowed governments to spend less on welfare provision and related services. This is an important conclusion for the wider discussion of the role of housing wealth within the economy. Australia is the second lowest-taxed nation in the OECD. The tax burden is less than in the United States and only exceeds Turkey. A lower level of home ownership would almost certainly result in a greater welfare bill and a higher tax burden overall. This would significantly reshape the Australian economy. It emphasises the multiple functions that housing wealth can play as an asset for small business formation or enhanced consumption, as a lifetime store of savings, or as a strategy for minimising living costs later in life.

Conclusion

The high level of housing wealth in Australia has helped boost the popularity of owner-occupation, added considerable stability to the financial system, and influenced the decisions of households seeking to generate additional wealth through investment. The wealth generated from owner-occupation has lifted many elderly households out of poverty and has almost certainly influenced the nature of the Australian welfare system. Households who invest in owner-occupation effectively provide for their own retirement by reducing their housing costs later in life and establishing an asset that can be used in a multitude of ways.

The impact of housing wealth on the economy is rarely discussed either in the popular press or in academic forums. Yet most Australians appreciate how it contributes their individual well-being, and this keeps their aspirations alive—even those households for whom it is a receding dream. There are, however, disadvantages arising out of a national concentration of savings effort in bricks and mortar. It makes for a higher level of foreign ownership of productive capital, which reduces the ability of Australians to control their own destiny. Therefore the level of investment in housing has been beneficial for individual households, but may run counter to national interests.

Tax reform may reshape investment behaviour, but it is unlikely to have much impact in the short term, and even then households are still well advised to purchase their own housing. We are mindful, given the express focus of this chapter, that Australians who do not own their own homes have not received much attention thus far. Tenants are typically low-income and low-wealth households and do not qualify for the tax benefits and other subsidies enjoyed by owner-occupiers. They miss out on the imputed rental income so long as they remain in the private rental sector. If they cannot build up other assets over time, they will not have the equity that owners possess to fall back on in times of crisis. Denied access to what has been a bountiful fund of housing wealth, many Australian families face a grim prospect in a welfare system that still places considerable reliance on self-provision.

CHAPTER 6

Housing Wealth in the Lives of Three Generations of Home Owners

HOUSING PLAYS A MAJOR ROLE in determining the living standards and personal fulfilment of every one of us. Indeed, there are those, especially later on in life, who fabricate their very existence around the home. But this reality is often so taken for granted as to be overlooked. In his otherwise splendid book on the postwar generations,[1] Hugh Mackay makes little mention of the contribution that home ownership, let alone housing wealth, makes to material well-being, social mores, and popular culture.

Each generation carries with it into the future life-conditioning experiences which influence expectations and the ability to adjust. Let us focus, then, on some of the differences that home ownership and housing wealth have made to the lives of each generation of Australians during the second half of the twentieth century. Then we will wind the clock forward in the next chapter to consider what Australia's housing system could look like in 2030. We do not pretend to be able to identify an exact moment in time when one generation ends and another begins. Demographers usually space generations about fifteen years apart, which is the case with the Baby Boomers (1946–61). For argument's sake, we take some liberties with this definition. Nor are we suggesting that everyone's experience conforms to our broad characterisation of generational differences.

Roughly speaking, we delineate four groups: the Safe and Sound generation of owners from the 1950s and 1960s; the Baby Boomers, who dictated housing provision between 1970 and 1985 as 25–40-year-olds; Generation X, who were beginning to make their mark as prospective home buyers in the mid-1980s when deregulation freed up Australia's financial, labour and housing markets; and the generation of Keating's Children born in the 1990s, and taking shape as we write.

One of the key points of difference between these home-owning generations relates to a general feeling that currently an important generational shift is taking place. If these developments are sustained, the 1990s may be seen as a watershed for the Australian housing system. For despite the apparently undiminished enthusiasm that Australians express towards home ownership in surveys,[2] there are growing signs that the present generation is rethinking where it fits into the overall scheme of things.

Although household formation rates in Australia are holding up reasonably well as young people leave home and find partners, this is no longer automatically translating into demand for a building block in a new suburb—certainly not as it used to a generation ago. The affordability index—the price of a standard house relative to average earnings—reached an all-time low by the end of the 1990s. Yet growing numbers of those now aged in their twenties and thirties will never be able to afford to buy. Some will delay home purchase; of those who do become owners, many will have to settle for much less housing than they originally set their hearts on.

As to the future, Paul Keating can hardly be held responsible for the actions of the generation that will be consuming housing in the 2010s. But as Treasurer in the 1980s and Prime Minister into the 1990s, he set directions and forced the pace of change within the Australian political economy for decades to come. More than any other generation, Keating's Children have suffered competition policy let loose on every sector of their lives from kindergarten to job placement. We can only speculate about what housing wealth futures hold for this next generation. To be on the safe side, we leave that final part of the history of housing wealth in Australia until we fast-forward into the future in Chapter 7. In the process of putting some flesh on these bones we will profile one or two households that help convey the essential differences between the postwar generations of home owners in Australia.

Safe and Sound

The first mass generation of home owners emerged in Australia in the 1950s and 1960s. They were born in the 1920s and 1930s. Readers may recollect that home ownership climbed from 52.6 per cent in 1947 to a peak of 71 per cent in 1966.[3] After the trauma of the war years, state-supported housing assistance was fashioned as an element of cradle-to-grave social security in welfare state societies like Australia. Certainly there was a housing shortfall of some 300 000 dwellings after the war;[4] but once housed they were safe and sound, and that has been an expectation they have carried with them as a generation into old age:

> By the time I was ready to look for a job, employment was easy. I was able to afford to buy a house and lead a far more comfortable life than my parents could ever have imagined. I feel as if I have lived like a king in the world—a nice little three-bedroom cottage with a garden, and a feeling of security which my parents never had.[5]

Safe and Sound home owners came through the war, or grew up during the war years. Soldiers returning from overseas service and displaced families arriving in Australia in the late 1940s and 1950s had experienced hardship and discomfort. Survivors understand what it means to make do and pull together in adversity. Assisted migrants from the British Isles and Northern Europe, together with Southern Europeans who left poor towns and villages, fell for the allure of the so-called lucky country. With so much disruption in their lives, little wonder this generation places such a premium on security and stability. Not only did the quarter-acre block provide a protective haven in which to raise a family, but as privately owned property it could not be taken away from them.

These same impulses after the war laid the foundations for a rough-and-ready public ethos that was more collectivist than libertarian. Universalism, the cornerstone of the postwar welfare state, made for much greater reliance upon governments to fund schooling, housing provision, health care, public transport, and pensions for the elderly. By 1950, and throughout the next decade or so, Australia, along with New Zealand, was constructing more housing for owner-occupation than any other industrialised country. Three developments lie below this great upsurge in house building—two of them were government programmes. The War Services Homes Scheme helped returning soldiers with advice and finance. Nearly 72 000 homes in New South Wales were financed and built under the scheme by the early 1960s.[6] Secondly, amendments to the Commonwealth–State Housing Agreement in 1956 diverted government housing funds to a Home Builders Account to support low-income buyers. Further amendments to the agreement paved the way for the sale of public housing units constructed with programme funds. Between 1945/46 and 1968/69, almost 90 000 of these dwellings were sold Australia-wide, with New South Wales and Victoria accounting for nearly two-thirds of the total.[7]

The other option for couples who were fed up with living with parents in the 1950s was to buy a cheap house block far out in Woop-woop. Known as 'owner-builders', they could live there in a caravan or a shed until they could afford to begin building. Up to one in every three dwellings during the 1950s was built by owner-builders, who assembled their homes bit by bit as savings and availability of scarce building materials allowed. You can still see some jerry-built housing in the vicinity of railway suburbs like Merrylands and Wentworthville in Sydney, Essendon and Oakleigh in Melbourne, and Albert Park and Woodville in Adelaide.

For twenty-five years or so after World War II, government housing programmes ensured that home ownership expanded in line with a fairer distribution of earnings for all Australian households. Unemployment was low and stable, and did not rise above 3 per cent until the mid-1970s. Together with the bounty of centralised wage fixing, this gave home buyers the confidence to enter into the long-term financial commitment that a mortgage entails. Once the downturn in the early 1960s was past, a tradesman working full time, earning award rates plus skill-based margins and a bit of overtime, could usually manage the repayments, the furniture bill, and maybe a car on hire purchase.[8]

Assistance for home owners was fashioned around implicit assumptions about the suburban bungalow on a quarter-acre

Safe and Sound owners: Tom and Jean

Tom and Jean are classic Safe and Sound home owners—the one home, the one car! Tom started work as a tool setter in 1941 with Horwood–Bagshaw in Adelaide, who used to make farm machinery. He met Jean, who worked near by at the G-H woollen mills in Hindmarsh, and before they married in 1946 they paid £135 for a block of land 'out in the sticks' between the city and the beach. When the Commonwealth government lifted the ban on house building after World War II, they signed up with a builder, and moved in towards the end of 1948. Jean stopped work to start a family, and they managed to pay off the mortgage (£842.18.6d) in just eight years, with Tom spending his Saturdays gardening for a doctor in North Adelaide. While Jean raised five children over the next three decades, Tom had a series of promotions that culminated in a supervisory position with Horwood–Bagshaw, and peace of mind for them both in their twilight years.

Safe and Sound owners: Heather and Joe

Heather and Joe are typical of the Safe and Sound generation, having lived at the same address in the eastern suburbs of Melbourne for the last thirty-six years. Three sons grew up in this home, one of whom still occasionally returns for short stays between sharing with other flatmates. Heather spent her childhood in Shepparton, Victoria, and along with plenty of other kids from the country moved to the 'big smoke' when she left school to look for her first job. Joe came out to Australia from Croatia as a young man, and met Heather. Together they built up a business, paid off the family home, then bought a beach shack—all in the space of two busy decades. This is the success story that helped to earn Australia, with such a high rate of ownership amongst postwar immigrants, its reputation as the Lucky Country.

Baby Boomer owner: David—now without Anne—with sons, Mat and James, and their friends

Baby Boomer David, who now lives alone in a townhouse fronting the beach in Brighton on Melbourne's Port Phillip Bay, married Anne in 1968. Like David, Anne had trained as a teacher, and within five years had given birth to two children and returned to her position on a part-time basis. That enabled them to save the deposit for their first home—a tiny bungalow built between the world wars and by 1974 badly in need of renovating. A combination of sweat equity and house price inflation during the 1970s provided the platform for the next move—in 1979—into a more spacious home closer to good state schools. Fifteen years later, with the boys no longer living at home and a big property to maintain, David and Anne joined other Baby Boomers making their next lifestyle move—this time, to sun, sand and surf. With each move, these upwardly mobile Baby Boomers saw the real value of their housing grow: from $110 000 in 1974, to $152 200 in 1979, to $385 000 in 1995 (all in 1990 prices).

Baby Boomer owners: Robert and Karen, with Rebecca and Alice

Raising a family and building a nest-egg went hand-in-hand for a couple of Baby Boomers like Robert and Karen of Canberra. Both were born in the first half of the 1950s, and with good tertiary qualifications behind them they are now enjoying the fruits of well-paid careers—Robert as a software designer and Karen as a senior public servant. They moved to Canberra in the early 1980s when it was one of the fastest-growing regions in Australia. At first they rented a three-bedroom house in Monash on the outskirts of Canberra. With a strict savings regime, and by putting off children, they saved the deposit on a three-bedroom home in the suburb of Waramanga, which is more central. The arrival of their first child—Rebecca—prompted a move to a bigger house in the neighbouring suburb of Stirling. The latest move to the prestigious and central suburb of Red Hill coincided with the start of school for Alice, their youngest daughter.

Generation X buyers: Sarah and Christopher, with Emma

Sarah and Christopher were born in the late 1960s, placing them at the very end of Generation X. Their experience and prospects—now that they have a toe-hold in Sydney's eastern suburbs housing market—show starkly how Sydney house prices have outstripped other parts of the country. This couple married in their late twenties, and baby Emma didn't arrive until they were in their early thirties. Both these events took place a lot later than they did in their parents' generation. Sarah is a lawyer, Christopher is an electrical engineer. They are buying a two-bedroom unit on the fourth floor of an apartment block without a lift, but overlooking Bondi Beach. Costing $252 000 in 1994, it was recently valued at $325 000 (in 1990 prices). Without the double income of highly paid professionals, the alternative is some combination of a less desirable location, a pokier unit, or a life beyond reach of central Sydney.

Generation X buyers: Jon and Rachel, with Penny

Jon and Rachel were born at opposite ends of the 1960s decade and they typify Generation X couples attracted to an alternative, less materialistic lifestyle. Following his withdrawal from a science degree in the early 1980s, Jon was employed as a lab technician, helped to build and renovate houses, then worked his way around Australia picking up contract work on rural properties. Jon and Rachel met in 1986. Eight years later, with help from relatives, they paid $85 000 for their secluded block in the Adelaide Hills (in 1990 prices). Their aim is to be self-sufficient, so in between finishing off his degree and taking on casual work, Jon has built a large workshop and a garage, and established an orchard. When Penny arrived, he added a bedroom and a studio to the original fibro cottage. Rachel manages the vegetable patch as well as the free-range chooks and ducks.

Generation X buyers: Paul and Christine, with James (Batman), Olivia (Princess) and Alistair (*in utero*)

Onwards and upwards is the housing wealth strategy for Paul and Christine. Over the last thirteen years they have moved seven times. Some of these changes have been long-distance moves, from Brisbane to Rockhampton to Adelaide to Darwin and back to Adelaide, but they have traded up within each city. Their ride up the housing wealth escalator has been assisted by two factors—a booming housing market through the late 1990s and Christine's talent as a professional interior designer. They are battle-hardened renovators: in twelve months they converted this non-descript 1950s brick house to something that should appear in a fashion magazine. Along the way they added 70 per cent to the value of the property.

Keating's Children: Jamie and Delmarie, with their parents, Jacobus and Olive

Jamie and Delmarie are examples of the housing difficulties facing the generation born in the 1970s. The whole family immigrated from South Africa to Sydney in the 1980s—a shift that saw a substantial fall in the family's wealth and position within society. South African government-imposed limits on the value of capital to be taken out of the country and the low value of the Rand slashed the value of their assets and made them a much less affluent family in Australia than in South Africa. Although he has moved out of home several times, Jamie, twenty-eight, continues to live in the family home while he studies part-time and picks up casual work. Delmarie, twenty-six, has just moved back into the family home after living and working in Darwin for two years. She expects to stay for at least six months while she finds a new job and arranges somewhere to rent. Jamie and Delmarie are typical of a generation that has struggled to find permanent, well-paid employment and they therefore need to draw upon the housing wealth of their parents rather than establishing their own.

block as the ideal environs in which to raise a healthy and happy family. During these years the patrilinear, family-centred household went pretty much unchallenged. Marriage rates among 20–24-year-old women almost doubled after the Depression years, to reach nearly 60 per cent by 1954. The relative stability of the economy, the structure of housing provision, and the favourable housing costs helped sustain the domestic subservience of women in the postwar era. Table 8, which again draws upon the survey of Adelaide home owners, reveals this as the dominant pattern in the 1950s and 1960s. In cases where the first home was bought before 1959, 82 per cent of wives reported 'home duties' as their employment status at the time.

The memories of parents painfully coping with debt in the aftermath of the Great Depression instilled the virtue of savings and life insurance to protect against premature death. Yet this is also 'the generation who willingly embraced the mortgage as a way of dramatically increasing the rate of home ownership in the Australian community'.[9] Despite queues for housing finance throughout the 1960s, in real terms mortgage repayments were no more than 3 or 4 per cent, allowing for the underlying rate of inflation.[10] As a result of this rationing, school leavers had to work longer before they got to the head of the home loan queue (fourteen years prior to 1959, and sixteen years during the 1960s), and married couples were often not in their own homes until for some years after the arrival of the first child (Table 8).

On the other hand, the situation was much more frustrating for working women living by themselves and wanting to buy in the 1950s and 1960s. They faced two hurdles. As well as the discriminatory lending criteria, they were generally disqualified from buying a home during these years because of the lower wage rates paid to women.[11] Thus elderly single women who are now owners tend to have acquired their homes following the death of their husband. Currently, 30.4 per cent of single females over sixty-four years do not own their homes compared with 23.3 per cent of males in the same age group.[12] These undoubtedly include some of the women who might otherwise have been able to buy homes in the 1950s.

Table 8: Experience of Adelaide homebuyers purchasing before 1959, in the 1960s, 1970s, and in the 1980s

Household attributes (averages unless otherwise stated)	*Year in which first home purchased*			
	before 1959	*1960–69*	*1970–79*	*1980–89*
First Home				
No. of buyers	34	44	69	52
Age at purchase				
— Single person	29.5 yrs	31.5 yrs	31.2 yrs	38.1 yrs
n =	13	13	19	7
— Couples	28.5 yrs	31 yrs	28 yrs	25.6 yrs
n =	21	30	50	44
Years worked before purchase[a]	14 yrs	16 yrs	13.7 yrs	10.4 yrs
Timing of first child (years before/after purchase)	–1.4 yrs	–4.5 yrs	0.7 yrs	1.5 yrs
n =	20	33	56	26
Employment status				
— One full-time earner	82%	58%	33.8%	32.6%
— Two full-time earners	9%	39.5%	53%	59.2%
— One full-time/one part-time	9%	2.5%	11.8%	8.2%
Home Sold in 1988–89				
Age of owner(s)	67.1 yrs	58.6 yrs	43.6 yrs	37.8 yrs
No. of homes owned	3.2	3.4	3.0	2.1
Household included				
— Pensioner(s)	75.8%	36.4%	10.3%	8.5%
— Unemployed worker	–	12.1%	–	8.5%
— Overseas migrant(s)	21%	66%	56%	46.8%
Sale price ($1990)	$174 994	$145 983	$121 007	$106 568
Estimated equity	96%	73%	65%	43%
Capital gain/loss p.a. ($1990)	$2 353	$1 559	$2 541	$3 449
Return p.a.	2.1%	1.2%	1.9%	3.0%
Estimated gross worth				
— <$50 000	24%	14%	24%	28%
— $50 000–99 999	17%	19%	21%	53%
— $100 000–249 999	31%	43%	38%	15%
— >$250 000	28%	24%	17%	4%
Expected inheritance				
— Nothing	94%	68%	37%	30%
— $50 000	3%	25%	37%	35%
— $50 000–99 999	–	4.5%	16.5%	18.5%
— $100 000	3%	2.5%	9%	10%

[a] The time elapsed, calculated for the eldest wage earner in the household, between leaving school and buying the first home.

Source: Blair Badcock, Eight-Suburb Survey of Home Ownership, Adelaide, 1991.

The material privation and delays to home ownership that this generation encountered after the war were more than made up for in retirement by the wealth dividend delivered by inflation in house prices in the 1970s and 1980s. By this stage of their lives they had bought and sold three or four homes in the course of thirty to forty years. This is not a particularly high rate of turnover by today's standards. Almost all of the owners from the 1950s, and three-quarters of those from the 1960s, owned their homes outright by 1988–89 (Table 8). On average, the 67-year-olds who had bought their first home before 1959 received \$175 000 for the house sold in 1988–89 (in 1990 prices). This represents a capital gain of \$2353 per annum, boosting the estimated gross worth of one in four of these pensioners to over \$250 000 (Table 8). While this is well above the average of \$77 500 obtained from the study of probate in South Australia, there is likely to be a considerable draw-down of this housing wealth in the remaining years as old people gradually become more dependent upon intensive residential care.

Baby Boomers

Baby Boomers were born over a fifteen-year period after World War II. Their parents wanted a better start in life for their children than they had had themselves. It was this prospect that persuaded many adult migrants to settle in Australia with their young children in the 1950s and 1960s. Young Baby Boomers were goaded into progressing beyond high school, which many of their parents had never completed. If a trade certificate was emblematic of their parents' educational attainment, a teaching diploma is the educational hallmark of the Baby Boom generation. At teachers' college or university they were exposed to meritocratic values and grew used to well-funded state education and health systems. The absence of fees, and the availability of student stipends, enabled tertiary students to make the break and live away from home in their late teens.

Compared with their careful parents, Baby Boomers were not prepared to defer consumption while they saved. As the generation in search of instant gratification, they attracted the disapproval of their parents and the disrespect of their children in equal measure.[13] Abundant job opportunities for graduates and apprentices alike in the 1970s, together with the assurance of permanent, full-time work, removed any fears about living beyond their means or future indebtedness. In the normal course of events, their meal ticket led to a secure and well-paid job and a middle-class lifestyle in the suburbs. Unreasonable or not, they wanted bigger and better homes than their parents, and the neighbourhood trappings to match. Without an apparent care in the world, they committed to loan repayments on the house and extensions, cars, the children's education, a pool and overseas travel. All this was reasonably manageable on two incomes until the marriage started to come apart—Baby Boomers have earned a reputation as 'our most-divorced generation'[14]—and employment became unreliable in the 1980s and 1990s.

As a result of abnormally high fertility rates between 1945 and 1959, the sheer weight of Baby Boom numbers has been a potent social and political force for change in the postwar era. With each new milestone in their lives, Baby Boomers collectively upped the ante in terms of the demands they placed on the state for goods and services. By 1970, those born immediately after the war were in their mid-twenties and beginning to put pressure on the housing industry and service providers in the outer suburbs. General inflation in the 1970s spilled over into the residential land market and kept pushing up house prices, albeit in fits and starts, to the end of the 1980s. The inflation rate as measured by the consumer price index averaged about 7 per cent during the 1970s and 1980s, but house prices ran a couple of percentage points ahead. In the longer run, though, between 1960 and 1990 house prices only rose by about 0.5 per cent above inflation.[15]

Despite this, inflationary expectations had become a powerful driving force in the property market by the time Baby Boomers were buying their first homes. 'Baby Boomers have inflated expectations of property because they are the generation which inflated property prices.'[16] This often encouraged Baby Boomers to stretch themselves to the limit to borrow as much as they could possibly repay in those early years. That was fine in the 1970s, as long as home interest rates were pegged a percentage point or two beneath the prime bank rate. In fact, mortgage interest rates were negative in real terms for a short time in 1973/74. With *credit foncier* home loans, Baby Boomers were the chief beneficiaries of the government policy in the 1960s and 1970s. The years of the Fraser government in the late 1970s were marked by the arrival of the first affordability programmes for new home buyers. And under Hawke in 1983, the First Home Owners Scheme paid a rebate to those mostly lower-middle-class buyers struggling to bridge the deposit gap. Then in 1986, the concessional rate for home buyers came to an end when the financial system was deregulated. This was about the time that the youngest of the Baby Boom generation were buying their first home as 25–30-year-olds.

If there were two wage earners in those early years when young couples were starting out and beginning to pay off a house, so much the better. In 1972, 83 per cent of females were married by the time they reached their twenty-fifth birthday.[17] For the first time, the contraceptive pill prevented the complication of an unplanned child in those early years of marriage. Nevertheless, two-thirds of women had had a child by twenty-five years of age. Whereas only one in two women worked after marrying before the mid-1950s, by the 1970s this ratio had climbed to about two in three.[18] This reduced the saving and waiting time before working couples from the Baby Boom cohorts could buy their first home (Table 8). But equally, it meant that they could make much greater inroads into the mortgage before starting a family. This applies especially to career-oriented couples born between 1951 and 1955. With the acceleration of inflation in house prices in the early 1970s, there was a noticeable increase in the proportion buying at an earlier age. These career couples turn out to be a select group even among fortunate Baby Boomers. Not only did they get a head start in the housing market compared with others of their generation, but they also reaped disproportionate gains during bursts of house price inflation.

While the Safe and Sound and Baby Boom generations are chalk and cheese in many respects, until the 1990s, Baby Boomers held the same deep-felt convictions about the comparative safety of real estate as their parents. But Baby Boomers are not so keen on planning. Most have saved little for their retirement, assuming their real estate will somehow 'take care of it'.[19] With life expectancy for men and women gaining an extra ten years between 1947 and 1995, governments are looking for ways to unlock these savings to fund the care that pushy Baby Boomers will seek through the ballot-box in their old age. In societies like Australia, by the age of seventy per capita health care expenditure is twice the average; and from eighty-five upwards, the cost has climbed to approximately eight times the adult average.

'As safe as houses' is part of the aura that surrounds the traditional attachment to bricks and mortar as a vehicle for household savings. A steady 20 to 30 per cent of household savings went into real estate during the 1960s, 1970s, and 1980s.[20] Preference for shares never rose above 10 per cent during these decades. According to Phil Ruthven, who runs IBIS Research, 'Until the end of the 1970s, the most well-off households in Australia were those people who owned a small business—a service station, a milk bar, a plumbing business'. Ruthven's point is that they were never pioneers when it came to investing profits.[21] Although real estate is a fixed asset, it is readily convertible, and for a long time in the 1970s and 1980s offered reliable, and sometimes spectacular, returns to investors.

What distinguishes Baby Boomers from their parents in the housing wealth stakes, however, is the greater prospect of inheriting a share of the proceeds—no matter how modest—from the settlement of the family estate. Although we questioned the relative importance of this bequest in Chapter 3, there is no denying that Baby Boomers will be the first generation to benefit from the wealth accumulated from home ownership at close to saturation levels—about 70 per cent—for the first time in history.

> As the baby-boomers' parents age and die over the next two decades, they will be bequeathing to the children a wealth of assets—assets built up in a bygone era of stable employment, high inflation and real estate booms. And the baby-boomers, who will have reached at least their mid-fifties by then, will inherit that windfall at an age when most are already 'comfortably' well-off with a home and other assets of their own . . .[22]

As likely as not, then, many Baby Boomers will inherit as full owners in their own right and probably spend the windfall on non-essential consumption or more housing, or diversify their share portfolio. As a consequence, the case for death or estate duties will become more compelling on the grounds of intergenerational equity.

Generation X

Now we are in a position to look back, it is becoming clearer that the middle of the 1970s represents a crossroad in economic and social terms. The 1950s and 1960s were a time of comparative economic stability, reliable work, and family-centred households. This was the comforting and self-satisfied society that Donald Horne exposed in *The Lucky Country*. But all this began to break down in the second half of the 1970s, and increasingly Australians came to be buffeted by unsettling changes in the workplace, in community life, and within the household.

The first members of Generation X were coming to adulthood by the beginning of the 1980s. Growing up, 'their experience of impermanence and unpredictability has taught them one big, central lesson: *keep your options open*'.[23] And in the meantime, live for the present. This is the defining motif of what Hugh Mackay prefers to call the Options Generation. But let us be clear what we understand by this. On current trends, economic restructuring is going to expand the options of the fortunate few who can pick and choose between the top jobs—Robert's Reich's 'symbolic analysts'[24]—while shutting off options for those with unwanted skills or insufficient schooling. If a trade certificate lifted their grandfathers above the ruck, and a teaching diploma sufficed for their mums and dads, the pace-setters in this Brave New World need an MBA. Consequently, Generation X lines up at the starting gate with much more unequal life chances than their grandparents or parents.

The economic and social disruptions to daily life in the 1980s and 1990s owes as much to the undoing of the existing political culture in Australia as it does to the forces of globalisation. A sea-change has taken place in the values that underpin economic life and make for a good society. A competitive instinct, freedom of choice in the market place, and self-reliance are virtues to be lauded above all else in the 1990s. Governments everywhere have been retreating from tasks that were previously taken to be a legitimate part of their public duty. These tasks are being handed back to private providers ruled by the profit motive. Intentionally or otherwise, precious social capital is being destroyed at all levels within the community. Competition policy and deregulation began to shake up all the old arrangements for managing the markets for labour, finance and housing; and now social services have been added to the list.

None of us is immune to this newly imposed value system, but Generation X is the cohort that has to cope with, and adjust to, these sweeping changes at an age when previous generations have been settling down to establish a home and have children. Those that have grown up as part of Generation X are making quite different choices in relation to domestic living arrangements. At the same time they have had to come to terms with greater uncertainty in almost every other aspect of their lives as well.

On the work front, permanent full-time employment is rapidly becoming a thing of the past. Of the 1.4 million new jobs created by the Australian economy between 1980 and 1993, 60 per cent were part-time, and three-quarters of these part-time jobs were filled by mothers in their forties returning to the workplace after their children entered school.[25]

The current generation of home buyers face the prospect of short-term employment contracts, and much greater geographical mobility if they are to be where the work is. In the case of the first members of Generation X, their ultimate intentions are hedged in doubt: 'I don't think I will ever achieve the same level of prosperity as my mum and dad, and it doesn't really worry me. I'm not inclined to get on that treadmill . . . the ability to change from one thing to another is more important to me than settling into the grind of a mortgage and one career in one job.'[26]

Ironically, home purchase is now more affordable than it has been for a generation yet many of these young people could not care less. A new breed of customer-oriented mortgage providers like Aussie Home Loans has shaken up a staid banking industry. Borrowers are reaping the benefits of an unprecedented range of lenders' products. For their part, the federal and state governments have probably pushed subsidies for marginal home buyers to the limit.

Although financial deregulation has made it easier and quicker to access home finance, labour market flexibility has reduced the numbers of households who *can be sure* that they can maintain the repayments on a mortgage. This depends increasingly on the presence of more than one wage earner and the mix of full-time and part-time work secured by Generation X partners. It also has a lot to do with the security of these jobs in the long-term. According to a recent estimate, 'around one in five Australian employees work variable hours and do not have security of employment or leave entitlements'.[27]

For these reasons, a life-shaping gap is now opening up between households with one wage earner at best, and those lucky enough to be able to pool earnings from a variety of sources. We spoke figuratively in Chapter 2 about the equal need these days for a 'prince' to find his 'princess' in order to get into the housing market. But at the very time when traditional gender-based dependencies are being overturned, fewer young adults are prepared to enter into this kind of contractual arrangement to buy a house.

By the mid-1990s, as they approached thirty years of age, half the males and one-third of the women in those cohorts were still unmarried. Estimates suggest that 44 per cent of young Australian males may never marry, compared with 25 per cent a generation ago. In the case of younger women, it is likely that 42 per cent will never marry.[28] The effect of these changes to Australian society is to place more women outside the household unit that has most favoured status within the prevailing economic system. Even though they are much less likely to be members of Generation X, when sole parents, widows, and divorcees are also included, this trend appears to be unstoppable for the foreseeable future. For example, the sole-parent family, which is headed by women in 91 per cent of cases, is now the fastest-growing family type in

Australia. Between 1986 and 1992, the numbers of one-parent families with female heads grew by 29.6 per cent and they now account for over 7 per cent of families in Australia.[29]

The upshot of these changing attitudes is that many young adults have no immediate desire to buy. Between 1975 and 1994, 'the home ownership rate for households under 35 decreased noticeably, with the most significant decline from 68.8 per cent to 55.2 per cent occurring for those in the 30–34-year-old age group'.[30] Then there are the older single people and one-parent families who, much more reluctantly, have abandoned any hope of ever owning their own home. In the late 1990s, they have also been joined by increasing numbers in their late thirties who managed to buy, but are now being forced to return to the private rental market. About 16 per cent of all the reported moves between owner-occupation and renting in the nine months to August 1997 were of this kind,[31] although these return moves appear to be linked with marriage breakdown as much as employment difficulties.

In a 1988–90 survey of first home buyers in Australia, 54 per cent were aged between twenty-five and thirty-four years.[32] Since 1976, the proportion of buyers, as opposed to owning outright, has fallen from 36 to 28 per cent in 1994. As is to be expected, there has been a corresponding increase in the proportion of households in the 25–34-year-old group who are renting—up from 36 per cent in 1976 to 43 per cent in 1994. Evidence from the Australian Life Course Survey suggests that low-skilled and low-paid households are increasingly unlikely to ever own a home if they have not bought by the time they reach thirty-five years.[33]

The dramatic decline in the purchase rate can be traced to several shifts in the life experience of the up and coming Generation X. Firstly, the number of 20–34-year-olds fell by two-thirds between the beginning of the 1980s and the middle of the 1990s. More young people are staying at home while they complete their studies, or simply because they cannot be financially independent without a job. Because of this, the percentage of 20–34-year-olds living with parents rose from 16.1 to 19.3 per cent between 1981 and 1991.[34] Further, for the first time in the late 1990s, graduates leaving university had incurred a substantial liability for their fees.

This could range from $12 000 to $30 000 for a first degree and an up-front payment of $5000 to $9000 per year for a second or higher degree. As well as this, all were obliged to contribute to a superannuation fund, even when in part-time work or a poorly paid entry level position.[35] Even the best-paid graduates of their generation will take five years to clear themselves of debt, which will delay entry into owner-occupation and increase reliance on the private rental market.

Projections of home ownership over the period 1986–2006, which coincides with the years in which Generation X households are most likely to buy, warn of a continuing deterioration in rates of home ownership among 25–34-year-olds.[36] By 2001–06, the proportion of households who were *capable of meeting the home ownership thresholds* varied widely. Among households with two adult earners it was one in four or one in five; among households with one earner it was one in forty or one in fifty.[37]

As well as these obstacles that are helping to delay home purchase by some members of Generation X, other investment opportunities have emerged in the 1990s that now compete with bricks and mortar. Even though home owners are still storing up significant real wealth in a climate of low inflation and low interest rates, the slowing of capital growth in the housing sector together with the growth of compulsory superannuation and equity markets in Australia has seen a flight of savings from home ownership in the 1990s.

Such has been the enthusiasm for the stock market that the rate of share ownership by Australians has almost caught up with the US rate of 43 per cent. More than 40 per cent of household assets in Australia are now in circulation in the stock market, though predominantly in the form of superannuation and managed funds.[38] Figure 12 charts the changing attitudes of investors to real estate, bank deposits, and shares over a ten-year period. From the time of the 1987 crash, confidence in the stock market recovered to the point where those investors surveyed by the Melbourne Institute in 1999 believed it was a better earner than real estate.[39]

During the 1990s the biggest block of shareholders has been getting younger, so that the over-fifties, who dominated share

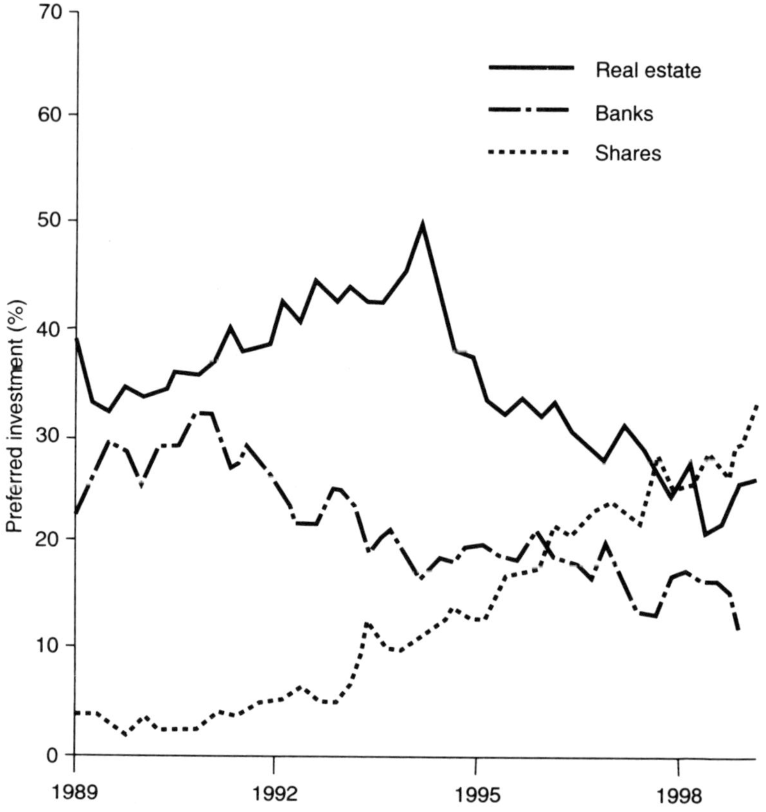

Source: Melbourne Institute Surveys, 1989–99.

Figure 12: Changing attitudes of Australians to investment and savings, 1989–99

ownership at the beginning of the decade, are now being overtaken by those aged in their mid-thirties to mid-forties. Even experts in the investment and financial services sector are 'not quite sure where this will head at the end of the day but the first thing is ... people are now putting their capital into wealth-creating assets as opposed to bricks and mortar'.[40] It is true, though, that when the All Ordinaries index broke through the 3000 barrier in the first quarter of 1999, some nervous investors cashed up and moved their takings back into property.

On present indications, therefore, Generation X is not as committed to home ownership as their grandparents and parents before them. At the very least, as a generation they are delaying home purchase by up to a decade. The reasons are many and varied, as we have shown, but there is no doubt that one effect of a more flexible labour market has been to cast a huge shadow over future housing intentions. The federal Private Rental Assistance Scheme, which was greatly expanded during the second half of the 1990s, is helping to assuage the disappointment and cushion the burden of tenants who seem destined to rent for the foreseeable future. Also renting are Generation X workers who command some of the best jobs in information technology and financial services and are opting in the 1990s to invest in assets other than a home of their own. Eventually, even if they remain single, they will probably purchase some property as a way of diversifying their portfolio.

We began this chapter by suggesting that the 1990s might be viewed as a watershed so far as the traditionally favoured status of home ownership in Australia is concerned. All these tendencies are bound to make for much more unequal housing wealth outcomes as Generation X approaches retirement age. If anything, this break with established norms on the part of Generation X is likely to make the gulf between winners and losers in the housing stakes even deeper than it has been in the past. In the next chapter we stick our necks out, and suggest what the distribution of housing wealth in Australia might look like by 2030 as a consequence of present trends and policies.

CHAPTER 7

Fast Forward: Home Ownership and Housing Wealth in 2030

SOME WOULD SAY THAT leaping forward a generation to envisage the future of home ownership and housing wealth in Australia is foolhardy. But this chapter is also intended as a provocation because it teases out the longer-term implications of present economic trends and government policies for the housing sector. Despite the economic setbacks in Asia and the former Soviet Union as we enter the new century, some futurists speculate that the global economy is on the cusp of a new wave of economic growth based on advances in information technology, cybernetics, biotechnology and the like.[1] Assuming they are correct, and if the Australian economy was properly positioned to make the most of these new technologies, this could usher in a phase of economic prosperity for the next generation. Indeed, Alan Greenspan, the chairman of the Federal Reserve Bank in the United States, has attributed the 'truly phenomenal' performance of the US economy in the late 1990s to the information technology revolution.[2]

But prosperity for whom? Although millions of new jobs have been created in information technology and the services sector in the United States, reducing unemployment to a postwar low of 4.5 per cent, many of these jobs are poorly paid, part-time, and casual. They are not to be compared in quality or security with the predominantly full-time and permanent jobs that Australian workers took for granted during the long boom. Nor are they backed up any longer in the United States, or in Australia, by an adequate welfare safety-net. Although the second Clinton Administration put 'an end to welfare as we know it', for its part the Howard government in its second term is pursuing a 'modern brand of conservatism'. The longer the Howard government is in office, the more far-reaching are the implications for government policy, 'especially in the extension of "mutual obligation" throughout the welfare system, and also the application of competition to an ever-greater range of government services'.[3] A radical shift is being engineered away from state provision in favour of private providers in education, health, employment services, and housing.

If these trends and policies are embedded over the next three decades, Australian society will become even more deeply divided. Although it is convenient to talk broadly in terms of winners and losers, it must be emphasised that we do not mean to imply such a superficial two-tier model of society. In the case of labour and housing market participation, for example, household needs continually evolve, and fortunes can wax and wane during the course of a lifetime.[4]

Housing wealth in 2030

By 2030 the pattern of housing wealth in Australia had changed markedly. It no longer accounted for the same share of national assets as twenty or even thirty years ago, and its distribution had become much more uneven. The property market played a key part in the change. The continual massing of people, houses and economic activity into Brisbane, Melbourne, Perth, and most especially Sydney, added fuel to asset prices that were already escalating. The inner cities and other desirable areas gained most, while property values in the smaller capitals and non-metropolitan regions languished. People on the metropolitan fringe did not do too well either. Across a swathe of new growth areas, falling levels of investment in roads, schools, urban rail systems and other infrastructure worked to further deepen the sense of suburban blandness that was a hallmark of urban development in Australia during the second half of the twentieth century.

Location, the mantra of real estate agents, remained a powerful discriminator of people and their homes, their types of jobs and work experience, their migration patterns, and their demography. The decline of the nuclear family and once conventional modes of life generated winners and losers: the cashed-up who never had children and empty-nesters who swarmed back into the inner city; the families struggling to keep their toehold in middle-class suburbs; those whose families broke up, with many banished forever from home ownership and access to housing wealth.

Just how housing wealth changed in the period 1990 to 2030 makes an interesting story. In 1990 the gross value of the housing stock in Australia was approximately $475 billion.[5] Some 86 per cent of that total was in owner occupation and 85 per cent of the asset pool was owned outright. That left loans for home purchase and rental housing accounting for $67 billion.

Over the next forty years the real value of housing rose slowly but steadily. While there were peaks and troughs within the housing market, the average long-term gain across the nation—adjusted for inflation—was 2 per cent a year. By 2030 Australia's gross housing wealth exceeded $1 trillion for the first time in the nation's history. Housing was still a substantial asset, but it was no longer as dominant as it had once been. Its share of the nation's assets fell from about 60 per cent in the 1980s and 1990s to about 40 per cent by 2030. This decline simply reflected the fact that other sectors of the economy grew more rapidly than the stock of housing assets. The distribution of housing assets also changed. About a quarter of the value of the housing stock now lay within the rental sector. Not only were there fewer households among home owners, but the public rental dwelling stock had been progressively sold off. As a result of the sale of publicly owned housing, which was completed by 2010, it now counted as private wealth.[6] However, the value of private rental housing still did not quite match its overall importance in the housing market of the 2030s, because rental dwellings remained relatively less expensive than those lived in by owners.

The decline in mortgage debt was the second major shift to affect the pattern of housing wealth. Loans on housing fell to approximately 10 per cent of the stock of assets—about $100 billion. Thus in the first three decades of the twenty-first century the home mortgage market continued to grow, even though its share of the total stock of assets fell.

The amount of housing wealth a home owner held by 2030 depended very much upon where the house was located. The gap that was evident at the turn of the century, between those who lived in the major metropolitan areas and those resident elsewhere, had become a chasm by 2030. In 1995 the national median house price was $141 000, but there was significant variation according to location. The median for Sydney was $210 000, Melbourne $165 000, Canberra $163 000, Brisbane $150 000, Perth $146 000, Adelaide $109 000 and Hobart $98 000.[7] Clearly, Sydney led the pack and there was an appreciable gap between it and the others. Adelaide and Hobart brought up the rear among the capital cities and were in danger of being surpassed by some of the more expensive tourism-oriented regional centres. With Sydney, Brisbane and Perth attracting the lion's share of population and economic growth over the next thirty years, these differences were bound to widen. The Greater Brisbane area exceeded the population of Melbourne by 2020, but Melbourne managed to cling onto its economic standing within the urban system.[8] Advances in communications technology could not compensate sufficiently for the geographical handicap of Adelaide and Hobart, and they slipped further behind the other capitals. The real value of houses grew annually by an average of 3 per cent in Sydney, Brisbane and Perth, 2 per cent in Canberra and Melbourne, and just 1 per cent in Adelaide and Hobart. Consequently, by 2030 the median price for home purchase—in 1995 terms—reached $440 000 in Sydney, $340 000 in Brisbane and $334 000 in Perth. In Melbourne and Canberra, median house prices climbed to $287 000 and $283 000. The 'backmarker' capitals, Adelaide and Hobart, delivered much more modest capital gains to home owners. Over the thirty years the median real price rose to just $152 000 in Adelaide and $130 000 in Hobart.

Of course, these figures represent broad aggregates only, and housing in the inner city and other sought-after localities—such as the North Shore and eastern suburbs in Sydney, and the eastern suburbs of Melbourne and Adelaide—was much more expensive. To some extent this was accompanied by a move to higher-density living, with fully 55 per cent of Sydneysiders living in a dwelling other than a detached house by 2030. The attractions of inner-city living had become so pronounced by 2012 that a new 'cone of wealth' formed, volcano-like, at the centre of Australia's capital cities.[9] That is to say, as more and more highly paid office workers opted for luxury, downtown apartment living, the land-price gradient in Australian cities got steeper and steeper. These tendencies built upon patterns of income and wealth concentration that emerged in the 1980s and 1990s, along with the opening up of the Australian economy to the forces of globalisation.[10]

Taxing goods and services

The re-election of the Howard coalition government at the 1996 federal election was to have a profound effect upon the composition of future housing wealth in Australia.[11] A goods and services tax (GST) of 10 per cent was imposed on virtually all transactions.[12] The GST reshaped the financial landscape of Australia as wholesale taxes were abolished, some state taxes were removed, and the relative attractiveness of various investments changed.

Housing wealth was affected by the GST in three primary ways. Firstly, there was a one-off boost to the value of existing housing of approximately 8.5 per cent. Secondly, the GST diminished the attractiveness of rental investment and eventually pushed up rents. Thirdly, other investments became more attractive. The GST encouraged savings through the share markets, commercial property, bonds and fixed interest, but made both superannuation and rental housing less attractive avenues for generating wealth. Each of these will be discussed in turn because they helped change the composition of housing wealth in Australia. Without the GST and associated tax reforms, Australia's housing wealth would have looked very different by 2030.

The implementation of the Howard government's tax reform package immediately boosted house prices by approximately 8.5 per cent in all markets across Australia.[13] The housing industry was not exempt from the GST and the cost of all inputs for new housing construction rose. Virtually everything cost more as building materials like timber, cement, and bricks, along with design work and fittings, went from a 2 per cent wholesale tax to the GST's flat 10 per cent. This added $16 000 to the cost of a mortgage—or $29 per month at prevailing interest rates—on an average new house and land package worth $194 000.[14] Owners of existing homes enjoyed the flow-on when the price effect of the GST filtered into other segments of the housing market. This was compounded in the period leading up to July 2001 as middle-class home owners and buyers, well aware of the implications of the new tax system, renovated, extended and traded up. The federal government's compensation package of $7000 for first-time buyers was quickly nullified by the market as the additional spending power of this group of purchasers simply pushed up house prices.

The GST and associated taxation changes made life harder for landlords. The smart ones seized on the opportunity to sell on the back of the GST-induced price hike in the early years of the twenty-first century and banked the profits. Otherwise, investors with a long-term stake in rental housing faced added costs on all their inputs—maintenance and repairs, agent's fees, etc. But unlike businesses, for example, which could claim a quarterly tax rebate on their purchases, landlords did not qualify for GST credits.[15]

Thus housing lost some of its attractiveness as an investment vehicle. The situation was not helped by other elements of the tax reform package. State governments surrendered some ten taxes in 2001 in exchange for the income from the GST. Stamp duty was removed from all forms of property *except residential property*. So the states continued to collect a hefty sum from home buyers and rental investors every time they bought housing. Owner-occupiers thought twice about trading up as opposed to staying put, and ploughing their money back into additions and alterations. Investors, on the other hand, thought more carefully about buying rental properties, as the high entry and exit costs were unattractive when compared with the alternatives. Inevitably, rents rose in real (inflation-adjusted) terms.[16] Tenants simply had to pay a higher percentage of their income in rents, which in turn adversely affected their capacity to save to enter home ownership. Of course it added to the woes of the federal government also, as higher rents meant higher rent assistance payments and a blow-out in the budget.[17]

The growing appeal of other investment opportunities was the third development to undermine housing market and rental investment (Figure 12).[18] The Howard government reshaped the tax scales—mainly to compensate for the impact of income tax 'bracket creep' over the previous three decades—so that 80 per cent of taxpayers were now paying a marginal tax rate of just 30 cents in the dollar. Those earning more than $50 000 were taxed at 42 cents in the dollar and there was a marginal rate of 47 cents in the dollar for incomes in excess of $60 000.[19] The shift in the tax brackets meant that a substantial number of middle-class workers previously paying the highest marginal rate were no longer in that situation, and the temptation to look for negative gearing was much reduced. In addition, people who saved rather than consumed their incomes did not pay the GST, and their average tax rate was reduced. Company tax rates fell to 30 per cent, which raised after-tax profits and made franked dividends especially attractive. Under some circumstances it was also possible for company losses to be passed down to investors, effectively minimising and delaying tax liabilities. Those who invested in shares, commercial property, bonds and other relatively liquid assets did well under the new financial regime.[20] Rental investment now had to compete with these alternative investments, which offered significantly greener pastures than previously.

The combined impact of the Howard government's tax reforms left some wondering whether the government had actually decided to deter investment in housing. After all, from the early 1980s onwards, there were powerful voices in Treasury and in other public policy forums arguing that Australia invested too much in housing.[21] These tax changes made new investment in housing less attractive and saw a flow of funds into the stock and property trust markets.

Winners and losers

It was those who managed to hold onto permanent full-time employment, and in turn reap some of the biggest benefits from the housing market, who had the widest smiles by 2030. As far back as the late 1990s the changing pattern of paid work was beginning to seriously affect the ability of many households to remain home owners.[22] The ranks of both the white-collar and blue-collar workforce were thinned by public sector and corporate downsizing. Those who turned to self-employment—as consultants or service providers, or in home businesses—found their new working environment offered greater freedom but no guarantee of a steady income. Many struggled to meet their mortgage repayments because the short-term nature of their contracts, or the gaps between contracts, made for patchy earnings. For the first time, white-collar households found that graduate qualifications no longer guaranteed well-paid employment for life. Even salaried staff in middle management grew to accept that no job was protected in a world where the pay-packet of senior executives includes performance bonuses and a parcel of the company's stock.

Casual and part-time workers found it much harder to save the deposit for a down-payment on a home. In a world of *precarious* work, those who did manage to get over this hurdle then lived with the threat of reduced earnings, almost at a moment's notice. Those retrenched were more likely to become unemployed again.[23] Yet some members of the traditional working class did very well for themselves, holding manufacturing, mining and construction jobs that were better paid than many middle-class occupations. Shift work and overtime ensured additional income when needed, and helped create conditions that secured home ownership and a stake in the pool of housing wealth.

Others, of course, may have had the skills and qualifications to enter these occupations but were never given the opportunity to secure full-time work. Besides the pecking order of the labour market, luck or life circumstances continued to prevent some workers in depressed areas, or with children at home, from obtaining reliable employment. For them, home purchase was out of the question. Thus during the years 1989 to 2011 a class of working poor emerged with low hourly rates and take-home pay, who had little hope of home ownership.

On the other hand, most of those with professional degrees in the last decades of the twentieth century were able to sit pretty in both the workplace and the housing market. Their incomes were high and access to home ownership was relatively straightforward. After all, lawyers and engineers who were married or cohabiting could afford to buy a home in the 1980s and 1990s. But circumstances changed around the turn of the century. As noted in Chapter 6, graduates began leaving universities carrying substantial debts, with superannuation contributions to fund, and with little hope of buying a home within those first five years.

In view of this, we must not lose sight of the fact that there were winners. Households that negotiated their way through the minefield of the labour market and kept one—or, better still, two—secure incomes could build their housing wealth and extend it into other areas. With the creation of a whole new generation of mortgage-related products, middle-class and wealthy households were suddenly presented with an enticing array of options for building further wealth. Unlike previous generations, they could choose to repay their mortgages at an accelerated rate without financial penalty. They could also draw down their housing equity to finance forays into the stock market and could link their salary or wages to their mortgage which in turn was linked to their credit cards—all with the aim of making the most effective use of their capital. Before long the standard 25-year mortgage had become a historical curiosity—at least for many households on generous incomes. By building their housing wealth through home ownership and at the same time using their housing equity to develop a portfolio of other investments, winners could have their cake and eat it too.

Falling home ownership rates

Overall, home ownership rates gradually drifted downwards, falling from about 70 per cent of households in 1996 (Figure 13) to just under 60 per cent by 2031. There were a number of reasons for this decline. Even in the 1990s it was evident that access to home purchase was falling: in 1975 almost 70 per cent of persons aged under thirty-five owned or were buying their home, but by 1994 this had declined to 55 per cent.[24] Well into the twenty-first century owner-occupation rates remained higher than they might otherwise have been due to the high ownership levels of a progressively ageing population. Unlike their parents, the generation coming of age in the 1990s and in the first decade of the twenty-first century were conservative borrowers. They were also willing to entertain lifestyle choices that made for flexible working and domestic arrangements. The number of persons in their late twenties living with their parents had already increased by the 1990s, but in the first decades of the twenty-first century it looked as though some offspring would probably never leave home. As a result, the number of thirty- and forty-year-olds in the family home rose dramatically. This was a reversion to past living arrangements whereby unmarried women lived with their parents, or the children of postwar migrants stayed with their parents until marrying. The difference was that this time it had more to do with the axing of income support for young people out of work.

The pattern was not the same everywhere in Australia. By 2031, the pressure on housing costs in Sydney had opened up a gap of ten percentage points in the home ownership rate—52 per cent for Sydney and 63 per cent for the rest of Australia. In Sydney, home ownership progressively became 'the domain of

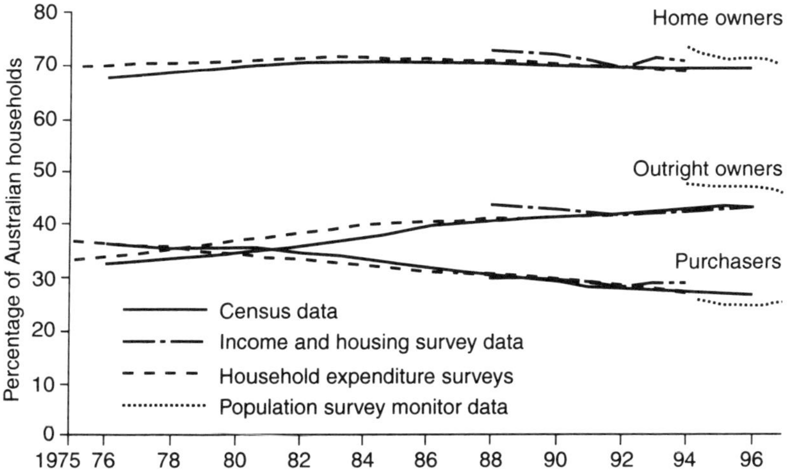

Source: J. Yates, 'Is Australia's Home Ownership Rate Really Stable?'

Figure 13: Changing home ownership rates in Australia, 1975–97

those with sufficient wealth to own their homes outright' and 'a luxury for those who face the uncertainties and volatility of a global economy'.[25] Those priced out of the market helped to swell the size of Sydney's private rental sector, which by 2031 had topped 40 per cent. Home ownership continued to remain accessible in Hobart, Adelaide, Perth, Brisbane and Melbourne to households on middling incomes; in the non-metropolitan areas, the same factors ensured that it remained the dominant tenure. In part this reflected the continuing difficulty of finding investors willing to invest in rental housing outside the capitals.

Such reliance upon an otherwise unresponsive tenure like owner-occupation created difficulties in rural areas which got caught up in global markets (such as regions growing wine and cotton). But in the small, slowly growing capitals and in regional Australia there was the opportunity to build a modest housing asset. Thus by 2020 the distribution of housing wealth was distinctly bi-polar with respect to location and value. Quite possibly, households with prime real estate in the largest cities also owned a second, holiday home. After all, having paid $1.5 million for a house in Sydney, why not use that equity to buy a weekender on the coast? The remaining home owners held a much more modest stake of housing wealth. They lived in the smaller cities and in the regions beyond the capitals; and while some were outright owners, many were mortgagors.

The decline of owner-occupied housing in Australia created the conditions which gave rise to long-term tenancies and a new class of rental landlord. For a comparatively short time in the second half of the twentieth century, private rental housing—and public rental to a lesser degree—served as a springboard for young couples aspiring to home ownership. But by the 1990s, tenants renting for ten years or more had increased to 40 per cent of all tenants in the private sector.[26] Forty years on, with governments still disinclined to offer the tax breaks needed to make rental investment attractive to life offices and pension funds, private renting remained the Cinderella tenure of the Australian housing system.

For their part, landlords continued to be small-scale operators, even though rental returns came to feature in the investment equation after the year 2000. Middle-class households double-dipped into the pool of housing wealth, and many established substantial equity by investing in high-yield home units or flats. The category of investor to grow through the first two decades of the twenty-first century was the family company. Families found that it was more attractive to hold onto the houses of their deceased parents or infirm relatives and rent them out under a family company structure than sell them. In many cases, inheritance never provided quite the flush of wealth that they had expected.[27] The strategy of renting out the house offered an ongoing income stream, the retention of an asset whose value was rising, tax minimisation, and the capacity to help children and other relatives by renting the property to them at favourable terms.

If tax reform had not been introduced by the Howard government back in 2001, family trusts would have remained the preferred investment vehicle.[28] But under the new regime they attracted a tax rate of 47 per cent compared with 30 per cent for companies. As usual, the ambiguities in the new rules were soon exploited by clever tax lawyers and accountants who found ways to split incomes within families and defer tax liabilities.[29]

On the other side of the coin, increasing numbers of Australians were destined to spend all or most of their housing career renting privately. Unless they inherited, this closed their door on wealth accumulation. Although they did benefit from the compulsory 15 per cent superannuation package introduced in 2001, relatively few tenants, and especially those renting in Sydney, had the additional income to commit to any other form of investment plan. They faced a simple fact of life in retirement: without owning their own home the outgoings for shelter would continue to the end of their days.[30]

Some new arrivals in Australia faced the prospect of a continuing battle to survive in the capital city housing markets. Australia's governments had long accepted refugees and immigrants from disadvantaged backgrounds as a way of proving their compassion to the community of nations. But too often the support these people received from government agencies was insufficient to prevent some from falling into a cycle of poverty and unemployment from which they never recovered. In this respect Australia came to mirror the United States.[31] More and more, Australia's immigrant intake split into two broad categories. There were those who brought with them the capital and qualifications that enabled them to purchase homes relatively quickly. For example, almost 30 per cent of immigrants entering on business skills and employer nomination visas either purchased outright, or had paid off their home within eighteen months of arrival.[32] The others had fewer resources and skills; they struggled to find decent jobs, and found entry into home ownership even harder. There were no up-front home owners among the humanitarian arrivals, and just 2 per cent owned their homes within eighteen months of settlement. The characteristic pattern typically found immigrants from Western Europe in the former category, and those from countries like Vietnam, Cambodia, Bosnia-Herzegovina and Croatia in the latter.

Generations and the 'wealth dividend'

By 2030 Baby Boomers were thinning out. Those born in the late 1940s were now well into their eighties, while those born in 1959 could still be considered relatively sprightly at seventy-one years of age. All things considered, the housing market had been kind to Baby Boomers. Many had bought their first homes in the 1970s and early 1980s when incomes were high and there were government schemes to assist first-time buyers into home ownership. By the time they left the paid workforce many owned a substantial asset, especially those who had made a series of upward moves in the housing market in line with career moves. This opened up a range of options for middle-class Baby Boomers in retirement—moving from expensive markets like Sydney or Melbourne to a coastal retreat or a resort complex, or into a retirement village. Others formed family companies as they, and their offspring, began to appreciate the desirability of finding ways to hold onto what they had. As well as reducing their income to the point where they would qualify for a government pension, they were just as keen to keep an appreciating asset within the family circle.

Generation X, those born in the late 1960s and first part of the 1970s, have had to deal with living in the formidable shadow cast by their parents' generation.[33] They came of age in a period of great economic and social uncertainty. They insisted on keeping their options open, and they needed to be adaptable throughout their working lives and in their domestic arrangements. Although most eventually secured their own home, purchase was generally set back by at least five years when compared with the previous generation. With the added pressure upon this generation to gain some form of post-secondary qualification or training, the overhanging liability for education fees following tertiary study certainly contributed to the delay. What set Generation X apart, in housing wealth terms, was the greater spread and disparity in the value of assets they owned.

Members of Generation X were born during the 'baby bust' years. Numbers were reduced by the decision of Baby Boomers to delay child-rearing, the contraction in immigration at that time, and the damper of economic recession.[34] As they came onto the labour market in the 1990s they had to put up with instability and low morale in the workplace, and scandalously high youth unemployment rates. Permanent jobs were hard to find and although there was greater gender equity—with males and females equally skilled and employable—only the luckiest couples secured two full-time positions from the start. As a consequence, this cohort recorded low rates of home purchase up to their thirties. This pulled down the overall rate of home purchase in Australia.

Nonetheless, many of these young adults had the benefit of being able to return to the parental home as, and when, necessary. In the long term they also stood to inherit at least some of the housing wealth that their parents had accumulated. And unlike the modest bequests that beneficiaries received in the 1990s,[35] those born in the 1970s and thereafter stood to gain much more housing wealth. For one thing, their parents had purchased more expensive housing than their grandparents, so there was a bigger cake to go round. Secondly, Baby Boomers were more likely to have some form of superannuation, so there was less of an imperative to consume the capital within the dwelling either through a sale, or through the absence of maintenance. Thirdly, the children of the 1970s came from smaller families—one or two children on average—so that the inheritance cake was cut into fewer slices.

The babies born in the 1980s came into the world in a period in which economic restructuring, competition policy, and an ethos of mutual obligation redefined the social compact between government and citizens in Australia. The expansion of the higher education sector in the early 1990s and the subsequent withdrawal of funding by federal governments resulted in one of the most competitive and ruthlessly efficient higher education systems in the world. Universities and colleges of technical and further education admitted students in larger numbers, and offered courses more closely geared to employment opportunities than at any time in the past. These graduates entered the labour market in the first decade of the twenty-first century primed for success, but mindful of the road-blocks that could lie ahead within a fast-changing global economy.

This did not necessarily ease their way into home ownership or housing wealth. Their housing careers and their opportunities to accumulate housing wealth came through avenues unlike those mapped out previously. In common with the generation born in the 1970s, they remained in the parental home for longer than was the case twenty years earlier. Likewise, those that did go on to buy a home delayed purchasing until they had cleared their debts and were sure they were in a settled relationship. Many young male and female graduates, and especially those in Sydney, had high incomes with secure superannuation. They flitted from contract to contract, spreading their savings across a broad investment portfolio as they moved between jobs. When these high-fliers eventually did decide to buy a home, it was either as outright owners or with a small mortgage.

Lastly, if the scenario painted by futurists like Lepani and her colleagues unfolds as predicted, the luckiest of those born in the 1990s entered labour and housing markets with Australia reaping the benefits of a world economy enjoying long-term growth.[36] Graduates with the ability and professional skills, and access to industry structures (including government support programmes), were able to fully exploit the opportunities arising from Australia's global orientation. But those that filled the ranks of the working poor often had to accept menial and unreliable employment. Either way, the harsh housing reality facing this generation was one of heightened competition in each of the sub-markets in which they were hunting for accommodation. Even during the 1990s, when house prices were supposed to stay flat, the value of established homes jumped by about 30 per cent across the board in Sydney and Melbourne. By the 2020s, late-comers to the housing market in Sydney or Brisbane were much less likely to be home owners or purchasers than any cohort since the 1930s. On the other hand, home ownership was still available to those living outside the major metropolises and they continued to reap the implicit subsidies of their tenure.

Diverging housing careers in 2000 and 2030

Perhaps the best way to understand the complex unfolding of these processes is to focus on two typical households from the beginning and end of the period in question. The Davis-White family lived in Melbourne in 2000. John was a sales manager with a large manufacturing firm, while Sandra had worked part-time since the birth of their first two children—Alex, five years, and Monica, two. Sandra would have liked to work longer hours, but the pressures of child-rearing and the high costs of professional child-care made that impractical. In 2000 John and Sandra were both aged thirty-five years, which made them members of Generation X. John earned \$60 000 a year, while Sandra's income fell to \$20 000 when she took up part-time work. They owned a house in the outer eastern suburbs of Melbourne worth \$230 000 which they had purchased seven years earlier, just prior to starting their family. Through hard work and accelerated repayments they now held equity of \$100 000 in their house. They had also purchased small parcels of Telstra, AMP and Commonwealth Bank shares which yielded another \$20 000 in capital. John and Sandra had decided to hold onto this more liquid equity 'just in case', rather than put it into the house. The long-term prospects for John and Sandra were bright. If they remained in employment they would eventually possess a substantial housing nest-egg, which in combination with their superannuation and other investments would tide them through their retirement years.

In the year 2030 Jarrad and Grace Carmichael were also thirty-five years of age, and they too were a middle-class household. Grace had just given birth to their first and only child, an event long planned but delayed by career and financial pressures. In real terms, Jarrad earned more than John had thirty years earlier, even though they held the same commerce degree from the same university. Jarrad worked in his own business—performing the same sales role as John—but his income was higher ($87 000 in the values of 2000). Grace worked on and off when she could find work as a doctor, but supply had long outstripped demand in that profession, at least in the big cities. Jarrad and Grace's high income had allowed them to buy a two-bedroom flat a year previously in Brisbane for $340 000. It was reasonably close to the city centre and not too far from decent amenities. John and Grace had saved hard to get into home ownership, amassing a $110 000 deposit, but interest repayments still claimed over one-third of the household's income. In some respects, Jarrad and Grace were unusual for their generation. They chose to enter home ownership and in the long run it paid off. However, they were stretched to the limit to secure a home of their own. Many people of the same age opted for an easier housing solution and chose to rent throughout their lives and, where possible, build other assets.

Citizens get the governments they vote into office. Although it can be argued that Australia was simply adjusting to the globalised economy, there is no denying that from the 1980s onwards our governments and politicians were elected with mandates to liberalise markets, reform the creaky taxation system, and curb government expenditure. The policies pursued by these governments, in conjunction with the demands of the international marketplace, increased inequality both in incomes and in housing wealth. By 2030 it was no longer possible for a social theorist in the mould, say, of Hugh Stretton, to argue that housing and housing property were more evenly distributed than other forms of income and wealth.[37] By then the differences between the haves and have-nots were simply too great. The housing markets of Sydney's North Shore and towns like Wagga Wagga were now a world apart rather than 800 kilometres as the crow flies. This in turn created a fundamental division within Australian society which fuelled more marked change within Australian society later in the twenty-first century. Australians had come to accept—and some even believed it necessary—that income and wealth inequalities were the inevitable consequence of a competitive and globalised economy.

This resignation on the part of the vast majority of Australians was perhaps the most disappointing aspect of the era. Some came to feel that Australians were no longer—as their old national anthem proclaimed—able to rejoice that they were 'young and free'. Instead these same citizens shared an uneasy sense that, consistent with Howard's vision, Australian society had indeed become more 'relaxed and comfortable' by the 2030s. But for the majority, redefining Australia in these terms also meant closing a collective mind to the fate of the losers in the highly competitive markets for schooling, health care, employment, and housing that were by then permanently in place.

CHAPTER 8

Towards Fairer Shares of Housing for All Australians

THIS BOOK IS ABOUT home ownership and housing wealth, and who gets what, where, and how in Australia. But it is a story that cannot be told without also looking at the wider housing system and the policies that have helped to shape it. In the previous chapter we forecast a troubled future for home ownership and housing wealth in Australia. The picture shows increasingly *unequal shares* of housing wealth for Australians. Moreover, it is not at all fanciful should the processes presently reshaping the housing system be allowed to run their course. It is a future where the disparities generated by the labour market are not only mirrored, but could be magnified many times over, in the housing market. Housing wealth is likely to become even more concentrated in the upper segments of the housing market—resulting from a steady polarisation of incomes along the way. The gap between regions smiled upon, and frowned upon, by economic fortune is also bound to widen.

In drawing this analysis of home ownership and housing wealth to a close, we now broaden our inquiry and ask: what's wrong with Australia's housing system, and how do we fix it? At the end of the 1990s, housing lobby groups like Shelter, the Australian Council of Social Service, and the National Council of Churches are once more raising the spectre of a housing crisis in Australia. 'At mid-century the nation made a pact that affordable housing was a right for all Australians. If at the century's end we cannot overcome the crisis before us, we will have betrayed a legacy that formed the core of the Australian nation.'[1] At the time, there were an estimated

575 000 low-income families in Australia with incomes that dropped below the poverty line after paying for their housing.[2] Similarly, there are said to be about 150 000 homeless persons in Australia—bearing in mind all the difficulties of counting the homeless.[3] Others say that 'the supply–demand gap is not of crisis proportions, but more like a slow bleed'.[4] This is the prospect in store for Australia's housing system unless remedial action is taken by federal and state governments. We follow up our diagnosis of the problem with a number of suggestions that would help move Australia in the direction of a more sustainable and fairer housing system.

What's making our housing system more unequal?

The first part of Chapter 6 relates how Australian governments responded to the housing backlog left by the war years and the swelling of the population by successive waves of migrants throughout the 1950s and 1960s. Those governments can take credit for ensuring that reasonably cheap but sound housing was made available to Australian-born and 'New Australians' alike. In his 1974 Boyer Lectures on housing and government, Hugh Stretton boldly asserted that the mode of housing provision that evolved in the postwar era was, in many ways, one of the great success stories of Australian society. In his opinion, good-quality housing and home ownership were shared more equally among all classes of Australians than income, wealth, public services, or virtually any of society's other 'goods'.[5] Further, he maintained that housing families *well* was one of the most productive investments a nation could make.

The tenure that Hugh Stretton celebrates undoubtedly generates housing wealth. Home ownership will continue to be one of the supporting pillars of Australian society. No one should take exception to *modest* domestic capital as a form of compulsory savings for retirement. It is only when the distribution of housing wealth gets out of kilter that we ought to be concerned. Housing wealth was decidedly more equal in the 1950s, 1960s, and 1970s than it is today. Virtually all households could reasonably expect to enter home ownership at some stage, and the differences between cheaper and more expensive suburbs were far less acute. But this is not to suggest that Australia could, or ought to, return to the 'economics of nostalgia'.[6] Chapters 6 and 7 show that the conditions which underlay the postwar expansion and then stability of owner-occupation are no longer with us. Nor can it really be said that federal and state governments deliberately set out to ensure that housing wealth was widely and fairly spread across income classes in the 1960s and 1970s.

Still, housing in the postwar era did reflect a general ethos within government and society. Pointedly, when Michael Pusey came to writing his widely acclaimed critique of economic rationalism in the 1990s, he subtitled the book 'A Nation-Building State Changes its Mind'.[7] For almost four decades Australia was governed by 'nation-builders' from both sides of politics. These governments got wholeheartedly involved in economic and social development, for better (the Snowy Mountains Scheme) or for worse (the Ord River Scheme)—especially where formidable amounts of capital were required. In much the same way, this postwar commitment to nation-building found expression in the implicit compact struck between the state and Australians to work for the benefit of the nation and the 'public good'. In turn, the enviable living standards and housing conditions that along with natural resources helped to make Australia the 'Lucky Country' during those years depended upon full employment and a centralised system for guaranteeing uniform wages.[8]

Global economic circumstances and new philosophies of economic management swept away this compact in favour of a hands-off approach that trusts the market to decide how resources will be allocated to competing uses. This faith in markets predates the era of conservative coalition governments led by Howard. As early as 1981, Keating, the future Labor Treasurer, and eventually Prime Minister, confided to Jenni Hewett of the *Sydney Morning Herald* that, 'For him it's the efficient market place that is the real guarantee of long-term social reform, of making everyone a middle-class success story'.[9] During the 1980s and 1990s, federal governments introduced a series of reforms with the aim of improving Australia's competitive advantage in global trade.[10] Even if it now wished to, the Australian government could not return to the protective trade policies of the past. Similar reforms to sectors of the domestic economy—to the workings of the labour market, financial deregulation, the retreat from welfare support by governments, taxation reform, changes to immigration programmes—will take Australians further down this path of no return.

In the housing sector, more of the responsibility for determining priorities and outcomes—in terms of who gets what housing—has been handed over to the market by governments. In less than a decade this change in underlying philosophy and programmes has produced outcomes that are unsustainable in the medium term. As early as 1992, Peter Williams, a British housing expert visiting Australia, declared:

> Home ownership has become more fragmented and diverse and more vulnerable to economic change and at the same time it now occupies most of the centre stage of housing policy. The insecurity of this base must be recognised. Important demographic and economic shifts are also taking place which suggests even more people will have difficulty sustaining high housing costs.[11]

We have already fleshed out the detail of these shifts in Chapters 6 and 7.

In the early 1990s, to give Labor its due, the federal government established the National Housing Strategy to study the implications of these trends for housing. Against this backdrop it reported that there is now enough housing to go round in Australia and if there is a problem, it is one of distribution.[12] Critics say there was an added problem. The National Housing Strategy team was too swayed by prevailing intellectual fashions. In retrospect, this included a willingness to uncritically adopt solutions from overseas—like community housing—and an over-reliance on markets to sort out access and equity issues. The larger subsidies received by public tenants compared with their counterparts in the private rental sector, and the tax treatment of home owners came in for the most criticism. According to the Economic Planning Advisory Council, as long as real estate remains the most tax-effective form of savings, or tax haven,[13] the temptation for middle-class Australians to over-invest in, and under-occupy, the family home is irresistible.

The National Housing Strategy also took a rather dim view of the performance of the State Housing Authorities. Partly this reflects the left's lingering mistrust of the housing bureaucracies that built the high-rise flats ringing inner Melbourne. It was also backed up by a suspicion that public housing managers were not sufficiently responsive to the needs of tenants. By proposing to fund a community housing sector along European lines, the National Housing Strategy sought to provide both another tenure of choice for low-income households, and an alternative management model to state-run housing. Comprising housing associations and co-operative housing, it set a target of 25 000 dwellings by the year 2000.[14]

By far and away the most telling argument levelled against public housing by the National Housing Strategy was an equity one: tenants renting privately were not getting as good a deal as public tenants. Rents in the public sector are set at a figure that leaves tenants with enough money in their pockets to lift household incomes slightly above the poverty line. Due to this 'growing Commonwealth concern over the disparity in subsidy levels provided to social security recipients in the public and private rental sectors, and the ensuing affordability plight experienced by the private renters', a massive funding switch has been engineered over the last decade.[15] Through its control of the purse strings, the federal government has quietly moved the thrust of housing assistance for low-income households in Australia away from the supply of public rental stock to a rental subsidy for private tenants. Since 1992, rent assistance under the federal Private Rent Assistance Scheme climbed from $0.96 billion to $1.6 billion in 1998. At the same time, capital payments to the state housing authorities fell from about $700 million to $500 million, with a further 10 per cent reduction planned for 1998/99 on the assumption that the authorities would achieve 'efficiency gains'.[16]

What also lies behind this redirection of federal funds for housing is a conviction among Department of Social Security advisers that Australia has a sufficient supply of private rental stock to house all low-income households except for those with special housing needs.[17] This includes the people with intellectual and physical disabilities, or a history of psychiatric illness, who have been turned out of state-run institutions over the last decade or so. In its 1997 submission to a Senate inquiry into housing, departmental staff argued that these people should live in public housing because the tenure was uniquely suited to cater for their particular access and security requirements.

In the housing sector, any semblance of a nationally co-ordinated approach appears to have evaporated. In the latest round of negotiations for the Commonwealth–State Housing Agreement to finalise funding arrangements for the next triennium, the state housing ministers had to wring an agreement out of the federal government. At the moment, the federal government shows little awareness of the potential social damage that lies ahead in the medium to long term if the housing system is left to the vagaries of the market, let alone enthusiasm for acting upon the warning signs. The whole history of housing provision since the middle of the nineteenth century shows that markets are no good at serving those at the bottom of the social pyramid.[18] It was to eradicate the conditions of the Dickensian poorhouse that the state in capitalist societies eventually stepped in to support not-for-profit, or cost rental, housing.

Markets do not unfailingly produce optimum outcomes in every sector of the economy—even when judged according to efficiency, let alone equity criteria.[19] Slavish adherence to the rule of markets in education, health care, housing provision, recruitment and job placement, and public transport is leading to economic and social distortions that could take more than a generation to put right. The larger problem with letting markets allocate housing to poor households is that this is always dictated by its *exchange* value at the expense of its *use* value. And when the property market is overheated, speculation distorts the process and penalises the poor even more.

Essentials for a fair and sustainable housing policy

The obvious shortcomings of the present approach to housing provision in Australia present a challenge for those who want to see a better housing future for the next generation. At the national level what would the best possible housing policy begin to look like? We can define such a policy as one that does the best by individual households—particularly those that are losing out as the Australian economy restructures—meets the expectations of a *fair-minded* community, and is sustainable. The late Peter Self, who was Professor of Public Administration at the London School of Economics before choosing Australia as his adopted country, suggested that a good housing policy would satisfy four principles:

- a generous spread of tenures so that there is plenty of choice for households as needs change during their lifetime;
- a concern for adequate housing conditions, making sure that standards in the public and private rental sectors keep up with the amenities that home buyers demand;
- housing costs that do not impose financial hardship on the poor;
- taxation and financial policies that encourage investment in not-for-profit housing and reclaim some of the socially generated wealth within the housing market.[20]

We believe there are two other principles that also need to be kept to the fore:

- households should not be unduly penalised when they move from one region or locality to another, or when their housing is no longer suitable (this often stifles movement from job-deficit to job-surplus areas or, in the case of the aged, from under-occupied dwellings into cosier housing);
- responsible tenants deserve the peace of mind that goes with security of tenure.

When these broad principles are translated into particulars like costs, standards, and control, we approach the criteria by which a sustainable and fair housing policy can be judged. There is widespread professional support in societies like ours for the belief that housing costs ought to fall beneath an acceptable threshold through a household's lifetime. The National Housing Strategy fixed on 30 per cent of net income as its benchmark for affordability for the bottom 40 per cent of households (though for several decades the state housing authorities settled for 18 to 23 per cent). Secondly, housing standards should enhance rather that detract from a sense of well-being and life chances. And thirdly, households should exercise some control over their living environment.[21] Of course, a majority of Australians access their housing via the real estate market and in the process most manage to obtain acceptable housing costs and standards, and exercise effective control over their domestic space. To extend the right to be well-housed to those remaining Australians who miss out requires a complex system of subsidies. It is this, more than anything else, that generates the heat in the debate between governments, the housing industry, consumers, and the housing lobby. With the recent breakdown of national housing policy in Australia, households most in need of housing assistance now face an increasingly raw deal.

A nation's housing system is a complex set of interacting tenures (owner-occupation, private rental, public rental, community housing) and sub-markets (house type, condition, and location). In the previous chapter, we foreshadowed a fall in Australia's home ownership rate from about 70 to 60 per cent over the next quarter-century or so. This slack will have to be taken up by the other forms of tenure. Given the ageing of the population, the stubbornness of unemployment, and the level of homelessness particularly among young people, we believe that, within this time frame, Australia should expand its public rental and community housing sector from roughly 6 to 10 per cent of the nation's dwelling stock. That leaves the private rental sector to house the remaining 30 per cent of households (up from 24 per cent).

What ought to be done?

Policies that change the tenure mix have a series of knock-on effects. The problem as we see it is that home ownership is in decline due to economic and demographic change, and the public housing sector is being downsized. These two developments will put increasing pressure on the private rental market. Yet there is no indication that governments in Australia are taking the looming supply problem at all seriously. They have a blind faith in the capacity of markets to eventually adjust to the increase in demand for private rental accommodation. But this does not allow for low-income households that get squeezed by rising rents in the bottom of the private rental market while all this re-sorting takes place. Addressing these stresses in the housing system will require: mechanisms that offer more protection to those marginal home buyers at risk in the labour market; the restoration of funding to the state housing authorities; and a much more sophisticated approach to targeted subsidies that work on the supply side of the private rental sector. That leaves the politically fraught question about the tax treatment of housing wealth and its inheritance.

This encapsulation of Australia's housing problems makes several assumptions about the future direction of economic change and the effects of current funding arrangements on the different tenures. Home ownership is never likely to be challenged as the tenure of first choice. It offers Australians undeniable benefits,[22] even though there is a worrying rise in the numbers falling out of home ownership.[23] However, as the proportion of outright home owners shrinks over the next couple of decades, the level of home ownership will steadily fall to as low as 60 per cent. Unlike the United States, there is less scope for arresting the decline by reaching underserved minorities where the ownership rate is much lower than it is for whites.[24] In Australia, the possibilities are limited to selling public rental dwellings to sitting tenants, or helping poorer households to rent privately with a home assistance package.

Except for the GST rebate, the federal government shows no inclination to prop up home ownership. For their part, the states have developed programmes to assist home buyers who are on the margins of viability.[25] Victoria's programme was known as Capil (Capital Indexed Loan). New South Wales operated HomeFund from the mid-1980s until it was suspended in 1993.[26] In 1989/90 and 1990/91, HomeFund lent almost one-fifth of the value of all loans granted in New South Wales. In South Australia, HomeStart still lends to means-tested home buyers. But these schemes are not without problems; not the least, because they extend support to households that are much more likely to face real difficulties in meeting their mortgage repayments at some stage in the lifetime of the loan. HomeStart experience shows that the households bearing the greatest risk tend to be single parents—usually women—on income support of some kind, and males aged 25–29 years employed as plant and machine operators. Both groups, and others like them, have limited ability to ride out any unforeseen crisis. Unexpected medical expenses, child-related costs, or a car breakdown usually take priority over mortgage repayments.[27] As a result, the prospect for mortgage insurers like the Housing Loans Insurance Corporation 'is a much higher level of claims in normal trading conditions than hitherto have been experienced and critically high claims in time of economic stress'.[28]

Why should the states persist with these schemes then? Ultimately it is cheaper to provide modest assistance of this nature than to provide long-term support to people in public housing or the private rental market. As HomeStart has shown, with a little extra care and in-built protection for marginal home buyers, the main pitfalls can be minimised. Having said that, these narrowly targeted home assistance packages are never likely to make great inroads among those workers at the bottom of the labour market who still dream of owning one day.

If home ownership is the tenure of first choice in Australia, the public rental sector has become the tenure of last resort. Yet, 'Public housing has been one way of ensuring the broad housing policy objectives are met'.[29] On the basis of its assessment of performance, the Australian Institute of Health and Welfare concluded that:

> public housing is achieving better outcomes for tenants than the private rental sector in most of the areas examined. The public sector performs better than the private rental sector in providing affordable housing, alleviating poverty, providing adequate dwellings, minimising the under-utilisation of houses, and in providing security of tenure for tenants. It does not perform as well with respect to facilitating access to services and employment, providing housing choice, and in meeting demand.[30]

Even the Industry Commission, with its reputation for advice devoid of all compassion, had to agree that, 'it is in the Commonwealth's interest to provide financial incentives for the States to maintain an appropriate level of public housing'.[31]

The main failings of public housing at the moment are the product of the financial clamp imposed upon the state housing authorities by the federal government. There is an undeniable sense in which the states are being asked to do more with less in the management of their housing portfolios. The funding switch engineered by the federal government in the 1990s has starved public housing agencies of the funds that they need for stock modernisation. Federal authorities point to the $32 billion asset which, after all, has been paid for by sitting tenants over the years, and urge the states to sell parts of it if they are short of funds. As well as that, some of the older public rental stock is now being transferred to community housing organisations. Although this meets the goals of self-help, tenant control, and improved leverage of the public dollar, it does not create a single *new* tenancy.

At the very least, the federal government should have honoured the National Housing Strategy's recommendation to expand the combined public and community housing sector to 6.5 per cent of the nation's housing stock, or 470 000 dwellings, by 2000. This falls well short of our social housing target for Australia of 10 per cent by 2025. In fact by 2000, stock levels owned by State Housing Authorities had fallen to 385 000, even though approximately 250 000 households were still patiently waiting to be housed.[32] With a tiny social housing sector by OECD standards (Table 1), it is incomprehensible in the face of the growing queue for public housing that the authorities are being forced to make such heavy cuts to their stock numbers.[33] At this rate, Australia is in danger of replacing the United States as the society with the meanest social housing sector in the Western world!

In the 1980s there was a tendency to dismiss private renting as a residual housing sector. It was looked upon as the left-overs after owner-occupation and public rental. Traditionally it was the tenure that everyone moved through. But now we know that 40 per cent of households have spent at least ten years renting privately.[34] The official line is that 'there is sufficient suitable private rental housing in Australia, but . . . many tenants have difficulty in affording it'.[35] Calculations done by Judith Yates contradict this.[36] By holding rents constant in real terms, she estimates that over a ten-year period, 1986–96, the proportion of houses and flats available at under $100 per week in the private rental market declined from

26 to 14 per cent. At rents below $150 per week, the corresponding fall was from 65 to 52 per cent of the nation's private rental stock. As to be expected, the greatest losses of cheap rental units have occurred in Sydney, and to a lesser extent in Melbourne. Because markets are imperfect, over 58 per cent of the households occupying the low-rent units (less than $100 per week) have sufficient income to pay more for their housing. That is, the neediest households are denied access to the cheapest rental stock. Yates points out that this mismatch between capacity to pay and the cheapest rental stock on offer is tantamount to a real shortage of 150 000 low-rent units across the country. It seems that the same kind of inequity is arising *within* the private rental sector as the Private Rental Assistance Scheme is supposed to eliminate *between* public and private tenants!

This shortfall reflects the comparatively paltry yields that are currently earned by many investors in rented housing.[37] In many parts of Australia, negative gearing no longer provides a sufficient incentive for rental investment. Besides, negative gearing is a poor way of targeting low-income tenants. It is just as likely to be applied to condominiums on the Gold Coast or loft conversion in trendy Surry Hills within spitting distance of downtown Sydney.[38] What is needed is a system of tax credits or finance provided at discounted rates to encourage the provision of affordable, purpose-built units that are available for long-term rent. For many years the German government has used a system of discounted loans to commercial housing companies and rent-setting agreements to meet its social housing objectives.[39] This is the only way to tap some of the immense reserves now held by the pension funds and life offices.

Lastly, where does the extra funding come from for an expanded social housing programme or targeted subsidies for private rental investment—assuming that Treasury would insist on it being fiscally neutral? Government should attempt to retrieve part of the wealth dividend that home owners receive from the housing market. As earlier chapters have shown, much of the capital gain accruing to property is a product of public spending on urban development. But, compared with other OECD countries, governments in Australia have shied away from wealth taxes and abolished death duties.[40] Although the federal government does tax the capital gains on property, there is an exemption for owner-occupied dwellings. In practice, capital gains taxes are problematic; any attempt to reinstate death duties or tax the imputed rent on owner-occupied homes would be politically risky.[41]

As governments grapple with tax reform, including new arrangements for tax sharing, there is an opportunity for the states to embrace a recurrent tax on property.[42] Like council or municipal rates, a tax applied to all dwellings would be low enough not to impose an undue burden in any one year, but would raise enough revenue to fund badly needed social housing. Indeed, Table 2 shows that a property tax is levied on the family home in many OECD countries. In broad terms, it would be a progressive tax: the wealthy—who own more expensive dwellings—would pay more. It could be targeted to allow exemptions for the aged and for households receiving income support. Other housing objectives could also be assisted through this mechanism: for example, it could provide full or partial exemptions for low-cost rental accommodation, or for first-time home buyers in the first five years of their purchase. If considered desirable, certain types of dwellings, such as flats or high-density units, could be granted favoured status. If sufficient revenue was raised, stamp duty on houses could be abolished, removing an impediment to labour mobility and making it more attractive for older Australians to trade down.[43] Such a tax might also contribute to economic growth, discouraging over-investment in housing while not harshly penalising the majority of home owners.

Nothing less than a paradigm shift will do

Some time ago, a colleague visiting from the Netherlands told us, 'We would never be treated the way your government treats pensioners in Australia. The Dutch government values the contribution of its senior citizens and looks after them in retirement.' In Australia we need to change a prevailing mind-set that regards the dependent in the community as an economic liability, and all social protection payments as an item of expenditure. In her contribution to the national debate on the kind of society we should aspire to in the new millennium, Bettina Cass calls for nothing less than a paradigm shift in our economic and social priorities.[44] Australia needs to approach public policy as social investment rather than social expenditure if it wishes to reduce inequality and promote social cohesion. According to Cass, 'The over-riding objective is to ensure that combinations of market income and tax/benefit support provide adequate social protection and the basis for participatory citizenship'.

In our opinion, there is no better social investment than housing. British studies, for example, highlight the direct and indirect costs of unhealthy housing conditions, the implication being that investment in adequate housing is extremely cost-effective.[45] Economic change and the under-funding of social protection are damaging the working poor as well as the unemployed in Australia. These people are hit not once, not twice, but frequently three times over: in—and out—of the labour market; in the housing market; and in the social security system. A proper social accounting system would make explicit the costs and displacement effects of inadequate housing and homelessness for the budgets of the health and employment portfolios, and the justice system. Approached this way, the case for an expanded social housing sector would be compelling.

This challenges Australians to take a hard look at whether they wish governments to continue with the housing policies of the last decade. If we do not, housing markets—doing what markets do best—will make the well-paid even wealthier, and operate to deprive needy Australians of affordable housing. So long as governments of the day are allowed to defer to the allegedly superior judgement of markets, politicians can get away with ignoring the underlying causes of income polarisation and the concentration of wealth in Australian society. Towards the end of the twentieth century we lost sight of the fact that 'The rationality of markets does not moot politics. It only alters the dynamics of influence and the mix of winners and losers . . . A decision to allow markets, flaws and all, free rein is just one political choice among many. *There is no escape from politics*' (emphasis in original).[46]

Notes

Introduction

[1] This can be seen, for example, by comparing Australian studies like Terry Kass, 'Cheaper than Rent: Aspects of the Growth of Owner-occupation in Sydney, 1911–66' and Philippa Mein Smith and Lionel Frost, 'Home Ownership in Adelaide, 1881–1911', pp. 40–55, with Richard Harris and Chris Hamnett, 'The Myth of the Promised Land: The Social Diffusion of Home Ownership in Britain and North America'.

[2] Lang Walker, founder of the Walker Corporation Property Group, reported in the *Weekend Australian*, 5–6 July 1997, pp. 53–5.

[3] Various house price series are constructed by the Valuer-General in each of the states, by the Real Estate Institute of Australia, and by consultants like JLW, Access Economics, and Residex.

[4] Ross King, 'Capital Switching and the Role of Ground Rent: 2. Switching between Circuits and Switching between Submarkets', pp. 729–35.

[5] Hugh Stretton, *Housing and Government*, pp. 35–9.

[6] Barbara Davison et al., *It's My Place.*

[7] Anne Dupuis and David Thorns, 'Meanings of Home for Older Home Owners', pp. 489–92.

[8] Two that come to mind are Sally Morgan's *My Place*, and Barbara Hanrahan's *The Scent of Eucalyptus.*

[9] Michael Harloe, *The People's Home? Social Rented Housing in Europe and America.*

[10] D. C. Thorns, 'The Creation and Transfer of Housing Wealth: The Experience of Elderly New Zealanders'.

[11] I. Welfeld, *Where We Live: A Social History of American Housing*, p. 9.

[12] Patrick N. Troy, *The Benefits of Owner Occupation*, p. 5.

[13] Alastair Greig, *The Stuff Dreams Are Made of*, pp. 71–4.

[14] M. Neutze and H. Kendig, 'Achievement of Home Ownership among Post-War Australian Cohorts', pp. 3–14.

[15] Greig, *The Stuff* . . ., pp. 71–4.

[16] Peter Saunders, *A Nation of Home Owners.*

[17] Pp. 1–2.

[18] Blair Badcock, 'Snakes or Ladders?: The Housing Market and Wealth Distribution in Australia'.

[19] M. Daunton, *A Property Owning Democracy?*

[20] *Housing Policy and Economic Power*, p. 17.
[21] M. Ball, M. Harloe, and M. Martens, *Housing and Social Change in Europe and the USA*, p. 5.
[22] Jim Kemeny, *The Great Australian Nightmare*.
[23] S. C. Bourassa, A. W. Greig, and P. N. Troy, 'The Limits of Housing Policy: Home Ownership in Australia'.
[24] According to R. Burgess and N. Skeltys in *The Findings of the Housing and Locational Choice Survey: An Overview*, p. 29, the proportion of first home owners moving 'to secure their own home' (73 per cent) is symptomatic of the undiminished desire for home ownership. In the case of satisfaction levels, 96 per cent of home owners or buyers surveyed in Sydney and Melbourne in 1991 said that the advantages definitely outweighed any drawbacks (p. 62).
[25] *Generations: Baby Boomers, their Parents and their Children*, p. 3.
[26] Mackay, *Generations*, pp. 135–76.
[27] *Trends in Home Ownership*, p. ii.
[28] M. Grattan, 'What Business Leaders Think of Costello's New Economics', p. 14.
[29] Hans Baekgaard, 'The Impact of Increasing House and Share Prices on the Distribution of Household Wealth in Australia', pp. 7–8.
[30] Baekgaard, 'The Impact of Increasing House and Share Prices . . .'
[31] Neil Chenoweth, 'Share Power—the Mass Appeal of the Market'.
[32] Australian Housing and Urban Research Institute, *Quarterly Housing Monitor*, vol. 3, no. 1, p. 3.
[33] Australian Bureau of Statistics, *Housing Australia*, p. 13.
[34] For a brief account of these programmes see Will Sanders, 'Aboriginal Housing'.
[35] Australian Bureau of Statistics, *Census of Population and Dwellings 1996, Aboriginal and Torres Strait People in Australia*, Cat. No. 2034.0.
[36] W. Sanders, 'Housing Data from the NATSIS: Can it Assist with Program Evaluation?'.
[37] M. Wulff and C. Maher, 'Long-term Private Tenants in the Australian Housing Market'.

Chapter 1

[1] Michael Ball, *Housing Policy and Economic Power*, pp. 278–9.
[2] A. E. Holmans, *House Prices: Changes through time at the National and Sub-National Level*, p. 8.
[3] Attributed to a former Governor of the Reserve Bank, Bernie Fraser, by Robert Harley, 'Hot Property', pp. 33–4.
[4] S. C. Bourassa and P. Hendershott, 'Australian Capital City Real House Prices, 1979–1993'.
[5] J. K. Galbraith, *The Culture of Contentment*.
[6] Andrew Beer, Owner Occupation and Profit: The Creation and Capture of Value through Canberra's Residential Property Market.
[7] Richard Kirwan, 'Financing Urban Infrastructure', pp. 2–3.
[8] Richard Kirwan, 'Planning for Affordable Housing', p. 17.
[9] *Social Justice and the City*.
[10] Alan Evans, *The Economics of Residential Location*.

[11] Elisabeth Tarica, 'Border Disorder'.
[12] *The Economics of Residential Location*, pp. 130–9.
[13] Blair Badcock, 'Building Upon the Foundations of Gentrification'.
[14] Reported by Stephen Ellis, 'A High Five: The Rich Let the Good Times Roll'.
[15] Planning Research Centre, 'Sydney's Housing Markets: Past and Present'.
[16] Blair Badcock, *Unfairly Structured Cities*, pp. 224–30.
[17] M. M. Li and J. H. Brown, 'Micro-neighborhood Externalities and Hedonic Housing Prices', pp. 136–8.
[18] *Social Justice and the City*, pp. 153–94.
[19] Peter Abelson, 'House and Land Prices in Sydney from 1931 to 1989', p. 1389.
[20] Abelson, 'House and Land Prices . . .', p. 1397.
[21] Abelson, 'House and Land Prices . . .', p. 1399.
[22] David Thorns, 'Industrial Restructuring and Change in the Labour and Property Markets in Britain'.
[23] 'Industrial Restructuring . . .', pp. 758–9.
[24] Chris Hamnett, 'The Postwar Restructuring of the British Housing and Labour Markets: A Critical Comment on Thorns', p. 152.
[25] *The Economist*, 'Unsafe as Houses'.
[26] From a summary of a report prepared for the Rowntree Trust by Duncan Maclennan, in Will Hutton, 'Stability Remains a Tory Pipedream', p. 21.
[27] *The Politics of Rich and Poor*, p. 184.
[28] K. E. Case and R. J. Shiller, 'A Decade of Boom and Bust in the Prices of Single-Family Homes: Boston and Los Angeles, 1983 to 1993'.
[29] 'The Impact of Increasing House and Share Prices . . .'.
[30] *Residential Property Prospects, Australian Capital Cities 1997–2000.*
[31] Hamnett, 'The Postwar Restructuring . . .', p. 154.
[32] Planning Research Centre, 'Sydney's Housing Markets', pp. 24–5.
[33] Methodological and technical issues are discussed in Badcock, 'Snakes or Ladders?'

Chapter 2

[1] R. G. Gregory, 'Aspects of Australian Living Standards: The Disappointing Decades, 1970–1990'.
[2] Bettina Cass, *The Housing Needs of Women and Children.*
[3] Maryanne Wulff, 'The Two-income Household: Relative Contribution of Earners to Housing Costs', is credited with one of the earliest studies to draw attention to the growing significance of the spread of household earnings due to the changing role of women.
[4] Nevertheless, Mariastella Pulvirenti points out that not all postwar Italian (or Greek) Australian migrants benefited from home ownership to the same degree or in the same way: 'Home Ownership, Identity and Social Polarisation'.
[5] ABS, *First Home Buyers: Australia 1988 to 1990.*
[6] M. Neutze and H. Kendig, 'Achievement of Home Ownership among Post-War Australian Cohorts'.
[7] M. T. Daly, *Sydney Boom Sydney Bust.*
[8] M. Edel et al., *Shaky Palaces: Home Ownership and Social Mobility in Boston's Surburbanization.*

9 *The Great Australian Nightmare.*
10 *A Nation of Home Owners*, p. 3.
11 *Political Essays.*
12 Hugh Stretton, 'Housing—An Investment for All'.
13 There is an early paper by David Thorns, 'The Implications of Differential Rates of Capital Gains from Owner Occupation . . .', and a later one, 'The Impact of Homeownership and Capital Gains upon Class and Consumption Sectors'.
14 Ray Forrest et al., *Home Ownership: Differentiation and Fragmentation.*
15 Badcock, 'Home Ownership and the Accumulation of Real Wealth'; Beer, 'Owner-Occupation and Profit'.
16 'Do House Prices Rise that Much?' p. 195.
17 Blair Badcock, 'Snakes or Ladders?: The Housing Market and Wealth Distribution in Australia'.
18 Beer, 'Owner-occupation and Profit', p. 193.
19 Beer, 'Owner-occupation and Profit', p. 174.
20 Readers interested in the statistical analysis that this section relies upon will find the detail in Badcock, 'Snakes or Ladders?', pp. 619–24.
21 Badcock, 'Snakes or Ladders?', p. 620.
22 John Edwards, *Keating: The Inside Story*, pp. 373–4.
23 Two aspects of the experience of these women are noteworthy. What they share is the extent to which they themselves were equally instrumental in working towards the purchase of the family home, and then paying it off. But a profound difference arises in their housing wealth, almost entirely due to the divergent fortunes of the suburbs they bought into. In terms of capital accumulation, the Elizabeth woman has nothing to show for over twenty years of repayments under the Housing Trust's rental-purchase scheme, while the other has received a dividend from the betterment produced by the staged development of up-market West Lakes.
24 S. J. Smith, 'Income, Housing Wealth and Gender Inequality'.
25 Edwards, *Keating*, pp. 373–4.
26 Rick Donald, 'Baby Boomers Go Bust', p. 17.
27 Chris Hamnett, *Winners and Losers.*
28 Michelle Gunn, 'Mortgage Belt Deals a Hiding', p. 3.
29 Mark Peel, *Good Times, Hard Times.*
30 There is no indication that his firm helped with relocation expenses, but that may well have been the case.
31 Ray Forrest and Alan Murie, 'Housing Markets, Labour Markets, and Housing Histories', p. 64.
32 Andrew Burbidge, 'Capital Gains, Homeownership and Economic Inequality'.
33 Bettina Cass, *The Housing Needs of Women and Children*, p. 20.
34 Rose Gilroy, 'Women and Owner Occupation in Britain: First the Prince, Then the Palace?

Chapter 3

1 C. Hamnett, M. Harmer and P. Williams, *Safe as Houses: Housing Inheritance in Britain.*
2 T. Thomas, 'The Inheritance Windfall'.

3 B. Mitchell, 'Nation to Inherit New Wealthy Class', p. 14.

4 See, for example, Blair Badcock, 'Urban and Regional Restructuring and Spatial Transfers of Housing Wealth'; Chris Paris, *Housing Australia*; Patrick N. Troy, *The Benefits of Owner Occupation.*

5 The main proponent here is Peter Saunders, *A Nation of Home Owners.*

6 Lisel A. O'Dwyer, Housing Wealth and the Inheritance Factor: The Nature, Impact and Implications of Housing Inheritance in South Australia.

7 Elderly households are defined as those where the household reference person was aged 65 years or more. This person may be any member of the household. The concept of 'household head' was not used in the 1991 Census. Caution is advised when comparing 1991 Census data relating to aged households with data from previous censuses.

8 Unless otherwise stated, all values are given in 1990 dollars.

9 The median is of course the better indicator of central tendency when a distribution is skewed. Interestingly, the degree of skew among deceased home owners was much less than for wealth in general. There are two reasons for this. One is the mere presence of housing wealth among these home owners. Wealth estimates relate to all households or persons, not just home owners. The more equal distribution of wealth among home owners certainly supports the popular notion that home ownership is an equalising influence. The other reason why the distribution is more equal among deceased home owners is because of their age structure—75 per cent were aged over seventy years when they died in 1990. Wealth tends to be more equally distributed within age groups than between them because each group has similar employment and housing histories.

10 B. Davison et al., *It's My Place.*

11 Transfers to surviving spouses are not defined as inheritances and are thus not included in the calculation of the average number of beneficiaries.

12 Hamnett, Harmer and Williams, *Safe as Houses*, pp. 79–80.

13 P. Travers and S. Richardson, *Living Decently: Material Well-Being in Australia.*

14 In the event, the statistical relationship between value of inheritance and value of the beneficiary's housing is very weak ($r = 0.19$, $p < 0.01$).

15 The number of cases for tenants was small, at only twenty-five cases.

16 H. Kendig, 'Housing Careers, Life Cycle and Residential Mobility'.

17 S. P. Jenkins and A. K. Maynard, 'Intergenerational Continuities in Housing', show that there is a high level of intergenerational continuity in home ownership.

18 See, for example, C. Delphy and D. Leonard, 'Class Analysis, Gender Analysis and the Family'; N. Folbre, *Who Pays for the Kids? Gender and the Structures of Constraint*; P. Somerville, 'Tenure, Gender and Household Structure'.

19 Rose Gilroy and Roberta Woods, *Housing Women.*

20 Hamnett, Harmer and Williams, *Safe as Houses*, p. 89.

21 R. Gilroy, 'Women and Owner Occupation in Britain: First the Prince, Then the Palace?'; M. Munro and S. Smith, 'Gender and Housing: Broadening the Debate'; J. Finch and L. Hayes, 'Gender, Inheritance and Women as Testators'.

22 Thomas, 'The Inheritance Windfall'.

23 Peter Saunders, *A Nation of Home Owners.*

24 H. Kendig and C. Paris, *Towards Fair Shares in Australian Housing.*

25 Peter Saunders and Peter Williams, 'The Constitution of the Home'; Ann Dupuis and David Thorns, 'Meanings of Home for Older Home Owners'.

Chapter 4

1 J. Yates, *Trends in Home Ownership*, p. ii.
2 For instance, National Housing Strategy, *Australian Housing: The Demographic, Economic and Social Environment.*
3 M. Callaghan, 'Housing Investment and the Economic Cycle'.
4 Ray Forrest and Alan Murie, 'Housing and Family Wealth in Comparative Perspective'; Michael Stegman, Joanna Brownstein and Kenneth Temkin, 'Home Ownership and Family Wealth in the United States'.
5 Callaghan, 'Housing Investment and the Economic Cycle'.
6 Department of the Treasury, *The Treasury Economic Roundup.*
7 Callaghan, 'Housing Investment and the Economic Cycle'.
8 Forrest and Murie, 'Housing and Family Wealth . . .', p. 2.
9 Stegman, Brownstein and Temkin, 'Home Ownership . . .'.
10 D. Miles, 'Housing and the Wider Economy in the Short and Long Run'.
11 'The Dynamics of Housing Wealth'.
12 'The Impact of Increasing House and Share Prices on the Distribution of Household Wealth in Australia', p. 12.
13 J. Helliwell and P. Boxall, 'Private Sector Wealth: Quarterly Estimates for Use in an Aggregate Model'; A. W. Dilnot, 'The Distribution and Composition of Personal Sector Wealth in Australia'; H. Pender, 'Public Policy and the Cost of Capital for Business Investment'.
14 C. Forster, *Australian Cities: Continuity and Change*; A. Beer and A. Maude, 'Regional Cities within the Australian Urban System'.
15 A. Beer, A. Bolam and A. Maude, *Beyond the Capitals: Urban Growth in Regional Australia.*
16 Quoted in Angela O'Connor, 'Local Price Rise Tops the Nation'.
17 K. O'Connor and R. Stimson, *The Economic Role of Cities.*
18 C. Clark, T. Geer and B. Underhill, *The Changing of Australian Manufacturing.*
19 R. Stimson, 'Processes of Globalisation, Economic Restructuring and the Emergence of a New Space Economy of Cities and Regions in Australia'.
20 Helliwell and Boxall, 'Private Sector Wealth . . .', p. 54.
21 Stimson, 'Processes of Globalisation . . .', p. 68.
22 D. Miles, 'Housing and the Wider Economy in the Short and Long Run'; D. Miles, 'Housing Markets, Consumption and Financial Liberalisation in the Major Economies'; S. C. Bourassa and P. Hendershott, *Over-investment in Australian Housing.*
23 King and Baekgaard, 'The Dynamics of Housing Wealth'.
24 *Investors in Rental Dwellings.*
25 *Investors in Rental Dwellings*, p. 7.
26 *Investors in Rental Dwellings.*
27 A. Helliwell and P. Boxall, *Australian Real Housing Costs.*
28 Chris Paris, *Housing Australia*, pp. 178–80.
29 An investment is said to be negatively geared where the income derived from the investment is exceeded by the interest cost of borrowing and the other ongoing costs of the investment. The most common example of negative gearing is the purchase, wholly or partly by debt, of a rental property by an investor.

The scheme is designed so that loan repayments (usually an interest-only loan) exceed the rental income. The resulting loss is claimed by the taxpayer as a deduction against other assessable income.

[30] D. Hayward and T. Burke, 'Gearing Up for Inflation'.

[31] G. Megalogenis, 'Capital's Gain'.

[32] J. Somers, 'Residential Property, It's the Best Investment'.

[33] *Australian Business Monthly*, 'Safe as Houses'.

[34] *Investors in Rental Dwellings*, p. 25.

[35] B. Fraser, 'Some Comments on the Economy, Deregulation and Housing'; P. Apps, *The Role of Home Ownership*; Bourassa and Hendershott, *Over-investment*; G. A. Wood, *Taxation and Housing*; National Housing Strategy, *Financing Australian Housing: The Issues.*

[36] W. Bailey, *Current Housing Policy: An Assessment.*

[37] Pender, 'Public Policy . . .'.

[38] Estimates prepared by the South Australian Treasury in the mid-1980s indicated that for every $100 million spent on public housing, 9360 jobs could be created.

[39] 'Some Comments on the Economy . . .'.

[40] Economic Planning Advisory Council, *Australia's Capital Needs in the 1990s*, p. 21.

[41] S. C. Bourassa and P. Hendershott, *On the Distributional Effects of Taxing Imputed Rent.*

[42] National Housing Strategy, *Financing Australian Housing*, p. 49.

[43] Bourassa and Hendershott, *On the Distributional Effects . . .*; Bourassa and Hendershott, *Over-investment.*

[44] J. Yates, 'Imputed Rent and Income Distribution'; R. Keever and R. Cullen, 'The Tax Commissioner's Blind Eye'.

[45] B. Badcock, *Unfairly Structured Cities*; Bourassa and Hendershott, *On the Distributional Effects . . .*

[46] Apps, *The Role of Home Ownership.*

[47] Bourassa and Hendershott, *Over-investment.*

[48] P. Hendershott and S. Bourassa, *Changes in the Relative Incentives to Invest in Housing: Australia, Sweden and the United States.*

[49] Baekgaard, 'The Impact of Increasing House and Share Prices . . .', p. 7.

Chapter 5

[1] J. Kavanaugh, 'It Pays to Figure out the Special Rate'.

[2] D. Clapham, 'Housing and the Economy: Broadening Comparative Research'; Ray Forrest and Alan Murie, 'Home Ownership in Recession'; D. Maclennan, *A Competitive UK Economy: The Challenges for Housing Policy.*

[3] K. E. Case, 'The Real Estate Cycle and the Economy: Consequences of the Massachusetts Boom of 1984–87'.

[4] J. Flood, 'Housing Subsidies, 1990–91'.

[5] National Housing Strategy, *Financing Australian Housing: The Issues.*

[6] J. Yates, *Australia's Owner Occupied Housing Wealth and Its Impact on Income Distribution*; G. A. Wood, *Taxation and Housing.*

[7] Flood, 'Housing Subsidies'.

[8] Economic Planning Advisory Council, *Australia's Capital Needs in the 1990s*, p. 21.
[9] B. Fraser, 'Some Comments on the Economy, Deregulation and Housing'; G. White 'Housing Investment: The Economic Cycle'; Chris Paris, *Housing Australia.*
[10] Fraser, 'Some Comments . . .', p. 6.
[11] Bureau of Industry Economics, *Instability in the Australian Residential Construction Industry.*
[12] *Housing Australia: A Statistical Overview*, p. 59.
[13] Yates, *Australia's Owner Occupied Housing Wealth . . .*
[14] W. Hutton, *The State We're In.*
[15] D. Clapham, 'Housing and the Economy: Broadening Comparative Research' p. 634.
[16] A. E. Holmans, *Estimates of Housing Equity Withdrawal by Owner Occupiers in the United Kingdom.*
[17] D. Miles, 'Housing Markets, Consumption and Financial Liberalisation in the Major Economies'.
[18] Hutton, *The State We're In*, p. 72.
[19] Hutton, *The State We're In.*
[20] Miles, 'Housing Markets . . .'.
[21] D. Miles, 'Housing and the Wider Economy in the Short and Long Run'.
[22] Case, 'The Real Estate Cycle and the Economy . . .', p. 174.
[23] Miles, 'Housing and the Wider Economy . . .', p. 176.
[24] Miles, 'Housing and the Wider Economy . . .', p. 182.
[25] M. Suich, 'Bank Rupted'.
[26] M. Hill, *Housing Finance in Australia.*
[27] Australian Financial System Inquiry, *The Campbell Report*; Australian Financial System Inquiry, *(The Martin Report) Report of the Review Group.*
[28] F. Argy, 'Opening Remarks'.
[29] Argy, 'Opening Remarks'.
[30] *Australian Financial Review*, 'Bank Mortgage Squeeze', pp. 1, 20.
[31] National Housing Strategy, *Financing Australian Housing*, p. 22.
[32] *Age*, 22 May 1995; *Australian Financial Review*, 28 March 1996.
[33] *Australian Financial Review*, 'Bank Mortgage Squeeze'.
[34] Kavanaugh, 'It Pays to Figure Out . . .', p. 57.
[35] White, 'Housing Investment . . .', p. 2.
[36] P. Travers and S. Richardson, *Living Decently: Material Well-Being in Australia.*
[37] F. Castles, 'The Really Big Trade-off: Home Ownership and the Welfare State'.
[38] Commonwealth of Australia, *Budget Statements, 1995–96.*
[39] P. Baldwin, Untitled address.
[40] B. Howe, *Social Justice Statement, 1995–96*; A. Harding and D. Mitchell, 'The Efficiency and Effectiveness of the Tax-transfer System'.
[41] Australian Urban and Regional Development Review, *Urban Australia: Trends and Prospects.*
[42] Castles, 'The Really Big Trade-off . . .'.
[43] Castles, 'The Really Big Trade-off . . .', p. 13.
[44] A. Harding, *The Impact of Health, Education and Housing Outlays on Income Distribution in Australia in the 1990s*; D. Johnson, I. Manning and O. Hellwig, *Trends in the Distribution of Non-Cash Benefits: An Overview.*
[45] Yates, *Australia's Owner Occupied Housing Wealth.*

[46] M. Neutze and H. Kendig, 'Achievement of Home Ownership Among Post-War Australian Cohorts'.
[47] New Zealand, with its longer tradition of home ownership, also has this in common with Australia.
[48] Castles, 'The Really Big Trade-off . . .', p. 17.
[49] Castles, 'The Really Big Trade-off . . .'.
[50] Castles, 'The Really Big Trade-off . . .'.

Chapter 6

[1] *Generations: Baby Boomers, their Parents and their Children.*
[2] R. Burgess and N. Skeltys, *The Findings of the Housing and Locational Choice Survey: An Overview*, p. 29.
[3] Patrick N. Troy, *The Benefits of Owner Occupation.*
[4] Commonwealth Housing Commission, *Final Report: 25th August 1944*, pp. 8–11.
[5] One of the subjects interviewed by Mackay, *Generations*, p. 16.
[6] Carolyn Allport, 'Castles of Security: The New South Wales Housing Commission and Home Ownership, 1941–61', p. 99.
[7] M. A. Jones, *Housing and Poverty in Australia.*
[8] Mark Peel, *Good Times, Hard Times: The Past and the Future in Elizabeth*, p. 96.
[9] Mackay, *Generations*, p. 18.
[10] J. Yates, 'Home Ownership and Australia's Housing Finance System', p. 29.
[11] S. J. Smith, 'Income, Housing Wealth and Gender Inequality', p. 76.
[12] *Social Security Journal*, 1995, Table 13, pp. 238–40.
[13] Mackay, *Generations*, pp. 62–3.
[14] Mackay, *Generations*, p. 64.
[15] Based on data compiled by the Commonwealth Treasury.
[16] Rob Keavney, Managing Director of Investor Security Group, quoted in Mackay, *Generations*, p. 63.
[17] Peter McDonald, 'Young People in Australia Today: A Socio-demographic Perspective'.
[18] M. Neutze and H. Kendig, 'Achievement of Home Ownership among Post-War Australian Cohorts', p. 11.
[19] Susan Oliver, formerly a director of the Commission for the Future, reported in Mackay, *Generations*, p. 63.
[20] John Kavanaugh, 'Managed Funds Boom as Savings Shift Direction'.
[21] Quoted in N. Chenoweth, 'Share Power—the Mass Appeal of the Market', p. 31.
[22] S. Bagwell, 'The Windfall Awaiting. The New Inheritors', p. 12.
[23] Mackay, *Generations*, pp. 137–40.
[24] *The Work of Nations*, pp. 177–8.
[25] Department of Social Security, *Meeting the Challenge—Labour Market Trends and Income Support.*
[26] Mackay, *Generations*, pp. 155–6.
[27] Anne Harding, 'The Suffering Middle: Emerging Trends in Income Inequality in Australia'.
[28] ABS estimates quoted in Don Edgar, 'Let's Make Style Get a Life'.

[29] ABS, *Australian Social Trends.*
[30] J. Yates, 'Is Australia's Home Ownership Rate Really Stable? An Examination of Change between 1975 and 1994'.
[31] Australian Housing and Urban Research Institute, 'Housing Cost Burden for Low Income Households', pp. 3–4.
[32] ABS, *First Home Buyers.*
[33] Ian Winter and Wendy Stone, *Social Polarisation and Housing Careers: Exploring the Interrelationship of Labour and Housing Markets in Australia*, p. 15.
[34] ABS, *Australian Social Trends.*
[35] Phil Malone, 'Emerging Housing Trends to the Next Millennium', pp. 14–15.
[36] These projections were prepared by the National Institute of Economic and Industry Research for the National Housing Strategy.
[37] G. A. Wood and S. Bushe-Jones, *Housing Affordability: An International Context.*
[38] Roy Eccleston, 'Profits and Losses'.
[39] Richard Salmons, 'Shares: Safer than Houses'.
[40] Eccleston, 'Profits and Losses'.

Chapter 7

[1] B. Lepani et al., *The Economic Role of Cities: Australia in the Global Economy.*
[2] Quoted in Ian Henderson, 'A Pinch of Luck, a Cup of IT, and Stir for Economic Growth'.
[3] Richard McGregor, 'Modern Conservatism Thatches the Policy'.
[4] What it's like to experience all three tenures—home ownership, private renting, public housing—is recounted by a tenant of the South Australian Housing Trust, Mrs K. Cheek, 'A Tenant's Story'. She migrated from England with her husband, built two homes in South Australia, rented privately in Whyalla when he lost his job, and shifted into a Trust unit when the owner wanted to sell; they then started again after thirty-seven years with another mortgage at seventy-four and fifty-seven years of age.
[5] A. King and H. Baekgaard, 'The Dynamics of Housing Wealth'.
[6] This vision of the future might seem to be a doomsday scenario. But in 1996 a forum met at the Australian National University to discuss the end of public housing: see R. Coles (ed.), *The End of Public Housing?* Federal government policy at present does not favour the continuation of the public rental system as we know it. The triennial review of the public housing programme in South Australia (1998) concluded that the only sensible response of the state government to the 'funding switch' that took place in the 1990s was to scale back stock numbers further from 59 000 to 43 000 rental units over the next fifteen years. See Coopers & Lybrand, *South Australian Housing Trust: Triennial Review, Volume I*, p. 8. Although some of this public rental stock has been handed over to the community housing sector to manage, this does not produce a net increase in dwelling numbers. Conservative governments in the United Kingdom also transferred large numbers of relatively poor-quality council houses to Housing Associations.
[7] ABS, *Housing Occupancy and Costs.*
[8] Queensland will overtake Victoria as Australia's second most populated state in 2030.

[9] Blair Badcock, 'Building upon the Foundations of Gentrification'.
[10] Blair Badcock, 'The Imprint of the Post-Fordist Transition upon Australian Cities'.
[11] Readers interested in the assumptions underpinning this discussion are referred to A. Beer, 'A Future of Housing Wealth?'
[12] Notable exceptions included education and banking. The Howard government also provided $300 million in funding to Tasmania and Queensland as part of the negotiations to secure the passage of the enabling legislation through the Senate.
[13] Treasury forecasts of the time suggested housing construction costs would rise by 4.7 per cent, while the Housing Industry Association and the Master Builders Association correctly predicted an 8 per cent rise.
[14] J. Sexton and M. Price, '$7000 Rebate to Buy First Home', p. 5.
[15] See R. Harley, 'Residential Investors GST Losers', p. 37.
[16] Robert Harley, 'Too Many Homes—but Rents Keep Rising', and 'Housing Industry Fears Rents Will Surge'.
[17] J. Yates, 'Changing Directions in Australian Housing Policies: The End of Muddling Through?'
[18] J. Kavanaugh, '1998 Tax Reform and Investor's Guide'.
[19] M. Lawson, '1998 Tax Shift Worth $13 bn'.
[20] Kavanaugh, '1998 Tax Reform . . .'.
[21] H. Pender, 'Public Policy and the Cost of Capital for Business and Investment'.
[22] J. Ford and S. Wilcox, 'Owner-occupation, Employment and Welfare: The Impact of Changing Relationships on Sustainable Home Ownership'.
[23] Ford and Wilcox, 'Owner-occupation, Employment and Welfare . . .'.
[24] J. Yates, 'Is Australia's Home Ownership Rate Really Stable?'.
[25] Yates, 'Is Australia's Home Ownership Rate Really Stable?'.
[26] M. Wulff and C. Maher, 'Long-term Renters in the Australian Housing Market'.
[27] Lisel A. O'Dwyer, Housing Wealth and the Inheritance Factor: The Nature, Impact and Implications of Housing Inheritance in South Australia.
[28] N. Field, 'Costello Targets Rich through Cars, Trusts, Salaries'.
[29] I. Davis, '30pc Company Rate—at a Cost'.
[30] Davis, '30pc Company Rate . . .'.
[31] B. Birrell and S. Evans, 'Recently Arrived Immigrants and Social Welfare', pp. 1–11.
[32] A. Beer and C. Cutler, *Housing Needs and Preferences of Immigrants.*
[33] M. Davis, *Gangland.*
[34] Graeme Hugo, *Australia's Changing Population, Trends and Implications.*
[35] O'Dwyer, Housing Wealth and the Inheritance Factor.
[36] Lepani et al., *The Economic Role of Cities.*
[37] See Hugh Stretton, *Housing and Government.*

Chapter 8

[1] Hal Bisset, the Director of Ecumenical Housing, as reported by Belinda Parsons, 'Churches Urge Aid to Poor Tenants'.

[2] These are National Centre for Social and Economic Modelling estimates. See the Ecumenical Housing report, *National Housing Policy: Reform and Social Justice*.

[3] Australian Institute of Health and Welfare, *SAAP National Data Collection: Annual Report*.

[4] Greg Black, general manager of the South Australian Housing Trust—a comment made at a ShelterSA workshop in May 1999 in response to the suggestion that Australia faces a housing crisis.

[5] Hugh Stretton, *Housing and Government*.

[6] Ian Macfarlane, 'The Economics of Nostalgia'.

[7] *Economic Rationalism in Canberra*.

[8] Donald Horne, *The Lucky Country*.

[9] Reported by John Edwards, *Keating: The Inside Story*, p. 154.

[10] R. J. L. Hawke, P. Keating, and J. Button, *Building a Competitive Australia*.

[11] 'Sustainable Housing Policies and the Role of Public Sector Housing Organisations', p. 26.

[12] National Housing Strategy, *Australian Housing: The Demographic, Economic and Social Environment*.

[13] An EPAC study undertaken in 1994 also shows that the family home is still the best tax haven for investors. See Michael Dwyer, 'Tax Favours the Rich: EPAC'.

[14] National Housing Strategy, *National Housing Strategy: Agenda for Action*, p. 49.

[15] Maryann Wulff and Samantha Evans, 'The Spatial Impacts of Commonwealth Rent Assistance on Australia's Low-income Households', p. 1.

[16] These financial data, which were extracted by David Hayward from Budget Papers, appear in Wulff and Evans, 'The Spatial Impacts . . .', p. 3.

[17] Department of Social Security, *Submission to the Senate Community Affairs Reference Committee Inquiry into Housing Assistance*.

[18] Tim Colebatch, 'Decades on, Housing is Still a Headache'.

[19] R. Kuttner, *Everything for Sale: The Virtues and Limits of Markets*.

[20] These principles were spelt out in a seminar given by Peter Self at the Australian National University in 1992. See Williams, 'Sustainable Housing Policies . . .', pp. 22–3.

[21] Williams, 'Sustainable Housing Policies . . .', p. 23.

[22] Patrick N. Troy, *The Benefits of Owner Occupation*.

[23] Australian Housing and Urban Research Institute, 'Housing Cost Burden for Low-income Households', pp. 3–4.

[24] Frederick J. Eggers and Paul Burke, 'Can the National Home Ownership Rate be Significantly Improved by Reaching Underserved Markets?'.

[25] For Capil, see Maryann Wulff, 'Low-income Home Ownership: The Privatisation of Squalor or the Great Australian Dream?'. For HomeStart see HomeStart Finance, *Annual Report, 1997–1998*. For HomeFund see Trevor Sykes, 'Australia's Worst Housing Disaster'. For Home see Sonia Syret, 'Qld Home Schemes under Review'.

[26] A Trade Practices Commission review of HomeFund in 1992 concluded that 'Having targeted a market to whom traditional institutions would not lend, a great many of those borrowers now find themselves locked into loans, the terms of which, in the current economic climate, will cause considerable financial hardship, if not financial ruin': *Sun-Herald*, 8 April 1993, p. 39.

[27] For more, see Gary Storkey, 'Findings and Recommendations of the Rosewood Experience'.

[28] Housing Loans Insurance Corporation, *32nd Annual Report and Financial Statements*, 1996.

[29] Williams, 'Sustainable Housing Policies . . .', p. 23.

[30] *Public Housing in Australia*, p. 7.

[31] Max Parker, 'The Industry Commission's Approach to Housing Assistance', in R. Coles (ed.), *The End of Public Housing?*, p. 19.

[32] Ecumenical Housing, *National Housing Policy.*

[33] Net additions to the public rental stock fell from 14 000 a year in 1989/90 to 4000 in 1996/97.

[34] Maryann Wulff and Chris Maher, 'Long-term Renters in the Australian Housing Market'.

[35] Senator Jocelyn Newman, Housing Reform Kit, 24 September 1996.

[36] Personal communication.

[37] G. Wood and R. Watson, 'Private Investors' Required Gross Rental Yield: Simulations'; Andrew Beer, 'Housing Investment and the Private Rental Sector in Australia'.

[38] Blair Badcock and Marian Browett, 'The Responsiveness of The Private Rental Sector in Australia to Changes in Commonwealth Taxation Policy'.

[39] G. McCrone and M. Stephens, *Housing Policy in Britain and Europe.*

[40] Gay Davidson, 'Why We Should All Be Interested in a Wealth Tax'.

[41] A death duty would raise all manner of problems in application, including the need to introduce a tax on gifts, and potentially a tax on family trusts.

[42] Victoria, the Australian Capital Territory, New South Wales and now South Australia, impose land taxes; though in the case of the first two states, on rental properties only. New South Wales introduced a 'millionaires' land tax in June 1998 which hits the top 0.2 per cent of owner-occupiers and will be indexed to move in line with property values.

[43] G. A. Wood, *Taxation and Housing.*

[44] Quoted in Michelle Gunn, 'Two Arms for Strong Social Support'.

[45] Peter Ambrose, 'Better Housing as Preventative Medicine'.

[46] Kuttner, *Everything for Sale*, p. 329.

Bibliography

Abelson, Peter. 'House and Land Prices in Sydney from 1931 to 1989', *Urban Studies*, vol. 34, 1997, pp. 1381–400.

Age, 'Australian Dollars Flow to Asia', 13 May 1994.

——, 'Home Loan War Moves into Gear', 19 September 1994, p. 18.

——, 'NAB Declares Home-loan War', 22 May 1995, p. 14.

Allport, Carolyn. 'Castles of Security: The New South Wales Housing Commission and Home Ownership, 1941–61', in Max Kelly (ed.), *Sydney: City of Suburbs*, New South Wales University Press, Sydney, 1987, pp. 95–124.

Ambrose, Peter. 'Better Housing as Preventative Medicine', *Housing Review*, vol. 46, 1997, pp. 57–9.

Apps, P. *The Role of Home Ownership*. National Housing Strategy, Background Paper No. 10, Canberra, 1992.

Argy, F. 'Opening Remarks', in *The Surge in Australia's Debt: Causes, Consequence, and Outlook*. Office of the Economic Planning Advisory Council, Canberra, 1991.

Australian, 'Non-Bank Loans Hold Their Own', 10 June 1995, p. 1.14d.

Australian Bureau of Statistics. *Australian Social Trends, 1996*. Cat. No. 4102.0, Australian Government Publishing Service, Canberra, 1996.

——. *First Home Buyers: Australia 1988 to 1990*. Cat. No. 4137.0, Australian Government Publishing Service, Canberra, 1994.

——. *Housing Australia: A Statistical Overview*. Cat. No. 1320.0, Australian Government Publishing Service, Canberra, 1996.

——. *Housing Occupancy and Costs: Australia*. Cat. No. 4130.0, Australian Government Publishing Service, Canberra, 1988.

——. *Investors in Rental Dwellings*. Cat. No. 8711.0, Australian Government Publishing Service, Canberra, 1994.

Australian Business Monthly, 'Safe as Houses', April 1993, pp. 56–9.

Australian Financial Review, 'UK Mortgage Holders Feel Pinch as Negative Equity Hits Homes Hard', 3 August 1995, p. 36.

——, 'Bank Mortgage Squeeze', 23 December 1996, pp. 1, 20.

——, 'Banks Launch Mortgage War', 28 March 1996, pp. 1, 8.

——, 'Nursing Home Plan is a Sound One', Editorial, 12 February 1997.

Australian Financial System Inquiry. *The Campbell Report*, Australian Government Publishing Service, Canberra, 1981.

——. *Report of the Review Group (The Martin Report)*, Australian Government Publishing Service, Canberra, 1984.

Australian Housing and Urban Research Institute. 'Housing Cost Burden for Low Income Households', *Quarterly Housing Monitor*, vol. 2, 1995, pp. 1–4.

——. 'Who's Moving From Home Ownership into Rental', *Quarterly Housing Monitor*, vol. 3, 1998, p. 3.

Australian Institute of Health and Welfare. *Public Housing in Australia.* AIHW, Canberra, 1994.

——. *SAAP National Data Collection: Annual Report.* AIHW Cat. No. HOU 10, 1996/97.

Australian Stock Exchange. 'The Role of the Stock Exchange', *Stock-market and the Economy*, Winter 1988, pp. 21–5.

Australian Urban and Regional Development Review. *Urban Australia: Trends and Prospects*, Research Report No. 2, AURDR, Canberra, 1995.

Badcock, Blair. *Unfairly Structured Cities.* Blackwell, Oxford, 1984.

——. 'Home Ownership and the Accumulation of Real Wealth', *Environment and Planning D: Society and Space*, vol. 7, 1989, pp. 69–91.

——. Eight-Suburb Survey of Home Ownership, unpublished data, Adelaide, 1991.

——. 'Adelaide's Heart Transplant, 1970–88: 1. Creation, Transfer, and Capture of "Value" within the Built Environment', *Environment and Planning A*, vol. 24, 1992, pp. 215–41.

——. 'Adelaide's Heart Transplant, 1970–88: 2. The Transfer of Value within the Built Environment', *Environment and Planning A*, vol. 24, 1992, pp. 323–39.

——. 'Snakes or Ladders?: The Housing Market and Wealth Distribution in Australia', *International Journal of Urban and Regional Research*, vol. 18, 1994, pp. 609–27.

——. 'Urban and Regional Restructuring and Spatial Transfers of Housing Wealth', *Progress in Human Geography*, vol. 18, 1994, pp. 279–97.

——. 'Building Upon the Foundations of Gentrification: Inner-city Housing Development in Australia in the 1990s', *Urban Geography*, vol. 16, 1995, pp. 70–90.

——. 'The Imprint of the Post-Fordist Transition upon Australian Cities', in P. Marcuse and R. van Kempen (eds), *Globalizing Cities: A New Spatial Order?* Blackwell, Oxford, forthcoming.

Badcock, Blair and Browett, Marian. 'The Responsiveness of the Private Rental Sector in Australia to Changes in Commonwealth Taxation Policy', *Housing Studies*, vol. 6, 1991, pp. 182–93.

——. 'Adelaide's Heart Transplant, 1970–88: 3. The Deployment of Capital in the Renovation and Redevelopment Sub-Markets', *Environment and Planning A*, vol. 24, 1992, pp. 1167–90.

Baekgaard, Hans. 'The Impact of Increasing House and Share Prices on the Distribution of Household Wealth in Australia', Paper presented to the Twenty-seventh Annual Conference of Economists, 28 September 1998, University of Sydney.

Bagwell, S. 'The Windfall Awaiting: The New Inheritors', *Australian Financial Review*, vol. 15, 1993, p. 12.

Bailey, W. *Current Housing Policy: An Assessment.* Discussion Paper 88/09, Economic Planning Advisory Council, Canberra, 1988.

Balchin, P. *Housing Policy: An Introduction*, 4th edn, Routledge, London, 1995.

Baldwin, P. Untitled and unpublished address to Australian Council of Social Service Conference, 12 October 1995.

Ball, M. *Housing Policy and Economic Power*, Methuen, London, 1983.

Ball, M., Harloe, M. and Martens, M. *Housing and Social Change in Europe and the USA*, Routledge, London, 1988.

Barrymore, Karina. 'Upmarket Melbourne: Heavy Demand keeps Prices Soaring', *Australian Financial Review*, 23 May 1997, p. 55.

Beer, A. Owner Occupation and Profit: The Creation and Capture of Value through Canberra's Residential Property Market. PhD thesis, Australian National University, Canberra, 1989.

——. 'A Dream Won: A Crisis Born', in C. Paris, *Housing Australia*, Macmillan, Melbourne 1993, pp. 147–72.

——. 'Housing Investment and the Private Rental Sector in Australia', *Urban Studies*, vol. 36, 1999, pp. 255–69.

——. 'A Future of Housing Wealth?', Paper presented to the South Australian Department of Family and Community Services Seminar, 19 February 1999.

Beer, A., Bolam, A. and Maude, A. *Beyond The Capitals: Urban Growth in Regional Australia*, Australian Government Publishing Service, Canberra, 1994.

Beer, A. and Cutler, C. *Housing Needs and Preferences of Immigrants*, Department of Multicultural Affairs, Canberra, forthcoming.

Beer, A. and Forster, C. 'National Overview—Australia, Urban Areas of Acknowledged Social and Economic Disadvantage', Paper prepared for the Commonwealth Department of Housing and Regional Development for presentation to the OECD, 1996.

Beer, A. and Maude, A. 'Regional Cities within the Australian Urban System, 1961 to 1991', *Urban Policy and Research*, vol. 13, 1995, pp. 135–48.

Bernheim, B. D., Shleifer, A. and Summers, L. H. 'The Strategic Bequest Motive', *Journal of Political Economy*, vol. 93, 1985, pp. 1045–76.

Bird, R. M. 'The Taxation of Personal Wealth in International Perspective', *Canadian Public Policy*, vol. 17, 1991, pp. 322–34.

Birrell, B. and Evans, S. 'Recently Arrived Immigrants and Social Welfare', *People and Place*, vol. 4, 1996, pp. 1–11.

BIS-Shrapnel. *Residential Property Prospects: Australian Capital Cities, 1997–2000*, Sydney, 1997.

Bourassa, S. C. 'Gender, Marital Status and Home Ownership in International Perspective', *Centre for Economic Policy Research, Discussion Paper No. 301*, Australian National University, Canberra, 1993.

——. *Australian Real Housing Costs*, Urban Research Program Working Paper No. 36, Australian National University, Canberra, 1993.

Bourassa, S. C., Greig, A. W. and Troy, P. N. 'The Limits of Housing Policy: Home Ownership in Australia', *Housing Studies*, vol. 10, 1995, pp. 83–104.

Bourassa, S. C. and Hendershott, P. *Over-Investment in Australian Housing*, Background Paper No. 9, National Housing Strategy, Canberra, 1992.

——. *On the Distributional Effects of Taxing Imputed Rent*, Urban Research Program Working Paper No. 35, Australian National University, Canberra, 1993.

——. 'Australian Capital City Real House Prices, 1979–1993', *Australian Economic Review*, Third Quarter 1995, pp. 16–26.

Bryant, B. L. and Nocera, D. 'The Psychological Significance of Home to Older Widows', *Psychology of Women Quarterly*, vol. 9, 1985, pp. 403–12.

Burbidge, Andrew. 'Capital Gains, Homeownership and Economic Inequality', *Housing Studies*, vol. 15, forthcoming.

Bureau of Industry Economics. *Instability in the Australian Residential Construction Industry*, Discussion Paper No. 10, Australian Government Publishing Service, Canberra, 1990.

Burgess, R. and Skeltys, N. *The Findings of the Housing and Locational Choice Survey: An Overview*, National Housing Strategy Background Paper No. 11, Commonwealth of Australia, Canberra, 1992.

Callaghan, M. 'Housing Investment and the Economic Cycle', Paper presented to Real Estate Institute of Australia Conference, 10 July 1996, Canberra.

Carroll, S. L. 'American Family Fortunes as Economic Deadweight', *Challenge*, May–June 1991, pp. 11–18.

Case, K. E. 'The Real Estate Cycle and the Economy: Consequences of the Massachusetts Boom of 1984–87', *Urban Studies*, vol. 29, 1992, pp. 171–83.

Case, K. E. and Shiller, R. J. 'A Decade of Boom and Bust in the Prices of Single-Family Homes: Boston and Los Angeles, 1983 to 1993', *New England Economic Review*, March–April, 1994, pp. 40–51.

Cass, Bettina. *The Housing Needs of Women and Children*, National Housing Strategy Discussion Paper, Australian Government Publishing Service, Canberra, 1991.

Castles, F. 'The Really Big Trade-off: Home Ownership and the Welfare State', Paper presented to the Urban Research Program, Australian National University, Canberra, 1996.

Challen, M. *National Needs and Tax Reform*, Submission by the Brotherhood of St Laurence to the National Tax Reform Summit, 3–5 October 1996, <http://www/vicnet.net.a.../taxpaper.htm>, 1996.

Cheal, D. J. 'Theories of Serial Flow in Intergenerational Transfers', *International Journal of Aging and Human Development*, vol. 26, 1988, pp. 261–73.

Cheek, K. 'A Tenant's Story', *Shelter Newsletter*, February 1999, pp. 16–17.

Chenoweth, N. 'Share Power—the Mass Appeal of the Market', *Australian Financial Review*, 13–14 September 1997, pp. 30–1.

Clapham, D. 'Housing and the Economy: Broadening Comparative Research', *Urban Studies*, vol. 33, 1996, pp. 631–47.

Clark, C., Geer, T. and Underhill, B. *The Changing of Australian Manufacturing*, Productivity Commission Staff Information Paper, Australian Government Publishing Service, Canberra, 1996.

Colebatch, Tim. 'Decades on, Housing is Still a Headache', *Age*, 23 April 1991, p. 15.

Coles, R. (ed.). *The End of Public Housing?* Urban Research Program, Australian National University, Canberra, 1997.

Commonwealth of Australia. *Budget Statements, 1995–96: Budget Paper No. 1*, Australian Government Publishing Service, Canberra, 1995.

Commonwealth Housing Commission. *Final Report: 25 August 1944*, Ministry of Post-war Reconstruction, Canberra, 1944.

Coopers & Lybrand. *South Australian Housing Trust: Triennial Review, Volume I*, Adelaide, 1998.

Cornell, Andre. 'Australia's $44 Billion Binge Buying is on the Home', *Australian Financial Review*, 24 July 1995, pp. 1, 24.

Correll, D. *Summary of Main Issues*, Submission by the Council on the Ageing (Australia) to the National Tax Reform Summit, <http://www.impactservice.../submission/dcorrell.htm>, 1996.

Crook, A. and Kemp, P. 'Reviving the Private Rental Sector?', in D. Maclennan and K. Gibb (eds), *Housing Finance Subsidies in Britain*, Avebury, Aldershot, 1993, pp. 67–86.

——. 'The Revival of Private Rented Housing in Britain', *Housing Studies*, vol. 11, 1996, pp. 51–68.

Daly, M. T. *Sydney Boom Sydney Bust: The City and its Property Market, 1850–1981*, George Allen & Unwin, Sydney, 1982.

Daunton, M. *A Property-Owning Democracy?* Faber, London, 1987.

Davey, J. 'Putting Housing Wealth to Work: Implications for Social Policy', Paper presented to the National Social Policy Conference, University of New South Wales, Sydney, 1995.

Davidson, Gay. 'Why We Should All be Interested in a Wealth Tax', *Australian Society*, vol. 7, 1989, pp. 36–7.

Davis, I. '30pc Company Rate—at a Cost', *Australian Financial Review*, 14 August 1998, p. A4.
Davis, Mark. *Gangland: Cultural Elites and the New Generationalism*. 2nd edn, Allen & Unwin, Sydney, 1999.
Davison, B., Kendrig, H., Stephens, F. and Merrill, V. *It's My Place*, Australian Government Publishing Service, Canberra, 1993.
Davison, G. 'The Past and Future of the Australian Suburb', in L. Johnson (ed.), *Suburban Dreaming*, Deakin University Press, Geelong, 1994, pp. 99–113.
Daw, R. 'Gender Bias and Family Law', *Reform*, no. 67, Winter, 1995, pp. 14–20.
Delphy, C. and Leonard, D. 'Class Analysis, Gender Analysis and the Family', in S. R. Crompton and M. Mann (eds), *Gender and Stratification*, Polity Press, Oxford, 1986.
Department of Social Security. *Meeting the Challenge—Labour Market Trends and Income Support*, Australian Government Publishing Service, Canberra, 1993.
——. 'Social Security Statistics', *Social Security Journal*, December 1995, pp. 238–40.
——. *Submission to the Senate Community Affairs Reference Committee Inquiry into Housing Assistance*, Canberra, 1997.
Department of the Treasury. *The Treasury Economic Roundup, Summer*, Australian Government Publishing Service, Canberra, 1990.
Dilnot, A. W. 'The Distribution and Composition of Personal Sector Wealth in Australia', *Australian Society*, vol. 9, 1990, pp. 14–17.
——. 'The Distribution and Composition of Personal Sector Wealth in Australia', *Australian Economic Review*, First quarter, 1983, pp. 33–40.
Donald, Rick. 'Baby Boomers Go Bust', *Age*, 30 November 1992, p. 17.
Dorling, Daniel and Cornford, James. 'Who Has Negative Equity? How House Price Falls in Britain Have Hit Different Groups of Home Buyers', *Housing Studies*, vol. 10, 1995, pp. 151–78.
Duncan, S. S. 'Do House Prices Rise That Much? A Dissenting View', *Housing Studies*, vol. 5, 1990, pp. 195–208.
Dupuis, Ann. 'Financial Gains from Owner Occupation: The New Zealand Case 1970–88', *Housing Studies*, vol. 7, 1992, pp. 27–44.
Dupuis, Ann and Thorns, David. 'Meanings of Home for Older Home Owners', *Housing Studies*, vol. 11, 1996, pp. 485–501.
Dwyer, Michael. 'Tax Favours the Rich: EPAC', *Australian Financial Review*, 9 January 1994, p. 4.
Eccleston, Roy. 'Profits and Losses', *Weekend Australian*, 20–21 June 1998, p. 30.
Economist, 'Unsafe as Houses', 8 August 1992, pp. 41–2.
Economic Planning Advisory Council. *Australia's Capital Needs in the 1990s*, Council Paper No. 43, EPAC, Canberra, 1990.

Ecumenical Housing. *National Housing Policy: Reform and Social Justice*, Melbourne, 1997.

Edel, M., Sclar, E. D., and Lauria, D. *Shaky Palaces: Home Ownership and Social Mobility in Boston's Suburbanization*, Columbia University Press, New York, 1984.

Edgar, Don. 'Let's Make Style Get a Life', *Weekend Australian Review*, 17–18 October 1998, p. 29.

Edwards, John. *Keating: The Inside Story*, Penguin, Ringwood, Vic., 1996.

Eggers, Frederick J. and Burke, Paul. 'Can the National Home Ownership Rate be Significantly Improved by Reaching Underserved Markets?', *Housing Policy Debate*, vol. 7, 1996, pp. 83–101.

Ellis, Stephen. 'A High Five: The Rich Let the Good Times Roll', *Australian Financial Review*, 2 September 1997, pp. 1, 11.

Ermisch, J. ' An Ageing Population, Household Information and Housing', *Housing Studies*, vol. 6, 1992, pp. 230–9.

Eslake, S. 'Housing Investment: The Economic Cycle', Paper presented to Real Estate Institute of Australia Conference, Canberra, 1992.

Evans, A. W. *The Economics of Residential Location*, Macmillan, London, 1973.

Evans, M. 'Tax Free Inheritance: Pro and Con', *National Social Science Survey*, 2, Research School of Social Sciences, Australian National University, Canberra, 1991, pp. 6–8.

Field, N. 'Costello Targets Rich through Cars, Trusts, Salaries', *Australian Financial Review*, 14 August 1998, p. A4.

Finch, J. and Hayes, L. 'Inheritance, Death and the Concept of the Home', *Sociology*, vol. 28, 1994, pp. 417–33.

——. 'Gender, Inheritance and Women as Testators', in L. Morise and S. Lyons (eds), *Gender Relations in Public and Private*, Macmillan, London, 1996.

Finch, J. and Wallis, L. 'Death, Inheritance and the Life Course', in D. Clark (ed.), *The Sociology of Death: Theory, Culture, Practice*, Blackwell, Oxford, 1993.

Flood, J. 'Housing Subsidies, 1990–91', Paper presented to the Institute of Australian Geographers Conference, Monash University, September 1993.

Flood, J. and Yates, J. 'Housing Subsidies Study, Final Report', AHRC Project 160, Australian Government Publishing Service, Canberra, 1987.

——. 'Housing Subsidies and Income Distribution', *Housing Studies*, vol. 4, 1989, pp. 193–210.

Folbre, N. *Who Pays For the Kids? Gender and the Structures of Constraint*, Routledge, New York, 1994.

Forbes, S. 'Death Duty "Time Bomb"', *Advertiser*, 13 November 1995, p. 40.

Ford, J. and Wilcox, S. 'Owner-occupation, Employment and Welfare: The Impact of Changing Relationships on Sustainable Home Ownership', *Housing Studies*, vol. 13, 1998, pp. 623–39.

Forrest, Ray, Kennett, Patricia, and Leather, Philip. *Home Ownership in Crisis? The British Experience of Negative Equity*, Ashgate, London, 1999.

Forrest, Ray and Murie, Alan. 'A Differential Accumulation: Wealth, Inheritance and Housing Policy Reconsidered', *Policy and Politics*, vol. 17, 1989, pp. 25–39.

——. 'Housing Markets, Labour Markets and Housing Histories', in J. Allen and C. Hamnett (eds), *Housing and Labour Markets: Building the Connections*, Unwin Hyman, London, 1991.

——. 'Home Ownership in Recession', *Housing Studies*, vol. 9, 1994, pp. 55–74.

——. 'Housing and Family Wealth in Comparative Perspective', in R. Forrest and A. Murie (eds), *Housing and Family Wealth*, Routledge, London, 1995, pp. 1–7.

Forrest, Ray and Williams, Peter. *Home Ownership: Differentiation and Fragmentation*, Unwin Hyman, London, 1990.

Forster, C. *Australian Cities: Continuity and Change*, Oxford University Press, Melbourne, 1999, 2nd edn.

Fraser, B. 'Some Comments on the Economy, Deregulation and Housing', *Reserve Bank of Australia Bulletin*, March 1991, pp. 1–8.

Frazer, N. 'From Redistribution to Recognition? Dilemmas of Justice in a "Post-Socialist" Age', *New Left Review*, vol. 212, 1995, pp. 68–93.

Galbraith, J. K. *The Culture of Contentment*, Penguin, London, 1992.

Gilroy, R. 'Women and Owner Occupation in Britain: First the Prince, Then the Palace?', in R. Gilroy and R. Woods (eds), *Housing Women*, Routledge, London, 1994, pp. 31–56.

Gilroy, Rose and Woods, Roberta (eds). *Housing Women*, Routledge, London, 1994.

Goody, J. 'Inheritance, Property and Women: Some Comparative Considerations', in J. Goody, J. Thirsk and E. P. Thompson (eds), *Family and Inheritance: Rural Society in Western Europe, 1200–1800*, Cambridge, 1976.

Grattan, Michelle. 'What Business Leaders Think of Costello's New Economics', *Australian Financial Review*, 10 July 1997, p. 14.

Greene, K. V. 'Inheritance Unjustified?', *Journal of Law and Economics*, vol. 16, 1973, pp. 417–9.

Gregory, R. G. 'Aspects of Australian Living Standards: The Disappointing Decades, 1970–1990', *Economic Record*, vol. 69, 1993, pp. 61–76.

Greig, Alastair. *The Stuff Dreams Are Made of: Housing Provision in Australia, 1945–1960*, Melbourne University Press, Carlton, Vic., 1995.

Gunn, Michelle. 'Mortgage Belt Deals a Hiding', *Australian*, 5 October 1998, p. 3.

——. 'Two Arms for Strong Social Support', *Australian*, 5 May 1999, p. 14.
Halifax Building Society, 'The UK Housing Market: from Recession to Recovery', *The Halifax Viewpoint*, Autumn 1992, pp. 1–7.
Hamilton, I. 'Capital Gains Death Tax by Stealth', *Advertiser*, 21 November 1994, p. 36.
Hamnett, Chris. 'The Postwar Restructuring of the British Housing and Labour Markets: A Critical Comment on Thorns', *Environment and Planning A*, vol. 16, 1983, pp. 87–109.
——. 'A Nation of Inheritors? Housing Inheritance, Wealth and Inequality in Britain', *Journal of Social Policy*, vol. 20, 1991, pp. 509–36.
——. 'The Geography of Housing Wealth and Inheritance in Britain', *Geographical Journal*, vol. 158, 1992, pp. 307–21.
——. 'Housing Inheritance and Inequality: A Response to Watt', *Journal of Social Policy*, vol. 24, 1995, pp. 413–22.
——. 'Social Polarisation, Economic Restructuring and Welfare State Regimes', *Urban Studies*, vol. 33, 1996, pp. 1407–30.
——. *Winners and Losers: Home Ownership in Modern Britain*, University College London, London, 1998.
Hamnett, C., Harmer, M. and Williams, P. *Safe As Houses: Housing Inheritance in Britain*, Paul Chapman, London, 1991.
Hanrahan, Barbara. *The Scent of Eucalyptus*, Hogarth Press, London, 1989.
Harbury, C. D. and Hitchens, D. M. W. *Inheritance and Wealth Inequality in Britain*, Allen & Unwin, London, 1979.
Harding, A. *The Impact of Health, Education and Housing Outlays on Income Distribution in Australia in the 1990s*, NATSEM Discussion Paper No. 7, University of Canberra, Canberra, 1995.
——. 'The Suffering Middle: Emerging Trends in Income Inequality in Australia. 1982 to 1993/94', Paper presented to the Australian Population Association Eighth National Conference, 6 December 1996, Adelaide.
Harding, A. and Mitchell, D. 'The Efficiency and Effectiveness of the Tax-Transfer System in the 1980s', *Australian Tax Forum*, vol. 9, 1992, pp. 277–304.
Harley, Robert. 'Still More Legs in Soaring Sydney Market', *Australian Financial Review*, 23 May 1997, p. 61.
——. 'Sydney Housing Boom Warning', *Australian Financial Review*, 11 July 1997, p. 65.
——. 'Hot Property', *Australian Financial Review Weekend*, 6–7 September 1997, pp. 33–4.
——. 'Too Many Homes—but Rents Keep Rising', *Australian Financial Review*, 3 August 1998, p. 35.
——. 'Housing Industry Fears Rents Will Surge', *Australian Financial Review*, 14 August 1998, p. A4.
——. 'Residential Investors GST Losers', *Australian Financial Review*, 15–16 August 1998, p. 37.

Harloe, M. *The People's Home? Social Rented Housing in Europe and America*, Blackwell, Oxford, 1995.

Harris, Richard and Hamnett, Chris. 'The Myth of the Promised Land: The Social Diffusion of Home Ownership in Britain and North America', *Annals of the Association of American Geographers*, vol. 77, 1987, pp. 173–90.

Harvey, D. W. *Social Justice and the City*, Edward Arnold, London, 1973.

Hawke, R. J. L., Keating, P. and Button, J. *Building a Competitive Australia: Statements by the Prime Minister, Treasurer and Industry Minister, 12 March*, Australian Government Publishing Service, Canberra, 1991.

Hayward, D. and Burke, T. 'Gearing Up for Inflation', *Australian Society*, March 1989, p. 33.

Helliwell, J. and Boxall, P. 'Private Sector Wealth: Quarterly Estimates for Use in an Aggregate Model', *Economic Record*, vol. 54, 1978, pp. 45–64.

Hendershott, P. and Bourassa, S. *Changes in the Relative Incentives to Invest in Housing: Australia, Sweden and the United States*, Urban Research Program Working Paper No. 34, Australian National University, Canberra, 1992.

Henderson, Ian. 'A Pinch of Luck, a Cup of IT, and Stir for Economic Growth', *Australian*, 12 May 1999, p. 55.

Henretta, J. C. 'Parental Status and Child's Home Ownership', *American Sociology Review*, vol. 49, 1984, pp. 131–40.

Hill, D. G. 'The President's Page', *Taxation in Australia*, May 1985, pp. 878–9.

Hill, M. *Housing Finance in Australia*, Melbourne University Press, Carlton, Vic., 1974.

Holmans, A. E. *House Prices: Changes Through Time at the National and Sub-National Level*, Government Economic Service Working Paper No. 10, London, 1990.

——. *Estimates of Housing Equity Withdrawal by Owner Occupiers in the United Kingdom, 1970–90*, Government Economic Service Working Paper No. 116, Department of the Environment, London, 1991.

Holmans, A. E. and Frosztega, M. *House Property and Inheritance in the UK*, Department of the Environment, London, 1994.

HomeStart Finance. *Annual Report, 1997–1998*, Adelaide, 1998.

Horne, Donald. *The Lucky Country: Australia in the Sixties*, 2nd edn, Angus and Robertson, Sydney, 1968.

Housing Industry Association. *Housing Towards 2000*, HIA, Canberra, 1990.

Housing Loans Insurance Corporation. *Thirty-second Annual Report and Financial Statements, 1995/96*, HLIC, Sydney, 1996.

Howe, B. *Social Justice Statement, 1995–96*, Australian Government Publishing Service, Canberra, 1995.
Hugo, Graeme. *Australia's Changing Population*, Oxford University Press, Melbourne, 1986.
Hurd, M. D. 'Research on the Elderly: Economic Status, Retirement and Consumption and Saving', *Journal of Economic Literature*, vol. 28, June 1990, pp. 565–637.
Hutton, W. 'Stability Remains a Tory Pipedream', *Guardian Weekly*, 10 July 1994, p. 21.
——. *The State We're In*, Jonathan Cape, London, 1995.
Ioannides, Y. M. 'Heritability, Intergenerational Transfers and the Distribution of Wealth', *International Economic Review*, vol. 27, 1986, pp. 611–23.
Jacobs, B. 'The National Potential of Home Equity Conversion', *The Gerontologist*, vol. 26, 1986, pp. 496–504.
Jenkins, S. P. and Maynard, A. K. 'Intergenerational Continuities in Housing', *Urban Studies*, vol. 20, 1983, pp. 431–8.
Johnson, D., Manning, I. and Hellwig, O. *Trends in the Distribution of Non-Cash Benefits: An Overview*, Australian Government Publishing Service, Canberra, 1995.
Jones, M. A. *Housing and Poverty in Australia*, Melbourne University Press, Carlton, Vic., 1972.
Kass, Terry. 'Cheaper Than Rent: Aspects of the Growth of Owner-Occupation in Sydney 1911–66', in Max Kelly (ed.), *Sydney: City of Suburbs*, New South Wales University Press, Sydney, 1987, pp. 77–94.
Kavanaugh, J. 'It Pays to Figure out the Special Rate', *Weekend Australian*, 14–15 October 1995, pp. 56–9.
——. 'Surging Shares Tempt Property Players: Retiring Strategy Requires Patience', *Weekend Australian*, 9–10 August, 1997, p. 10.
——. '1998 Tax Reform and Investor's Guide', *Weekend Australian Personal Finance*, 29–30 August 1998, p. 1.
——. 'Managed Funds Boom as Savings Shift Direction', *Weekend Australian*, 21–22 November, 1998, p. 6.
Keever, R. and Cullen, R. 'The Tax Commissioner's Blind Eye', *Australian Society*, March 1990, p. 10.
Kemeny, Jim. *The Great Australian Nightmare*, Georgian House, Melbourne, 1983.
——. *The Myth of Home Ownership*, Routledge and Kegan Paul, London, 1981.
Kendig, H. 'Housing Careers, Life Cycle and Residential Mobility: Implications for the Housing Market', *Urban Studies*, vol. 21, 1984, pp. 271–83.
——. 'Housing Tenure and Generational Equity', *Ageing and Society*, vol. 4, 1984, pp. 249–72.

——. 'The Cumulation of Inequality: Housing Costs and Income Support in Old Age', *Australian Journal on Ageing*, vol. 3, 1984, pp. 8–15.

Kendig, A. and Paris, C. with N. Anderton. *Towards Fair Shares in Australian Housing*, A Report prepared for the National Committee of Non-Governmental Organisations, International Year of Shelter for the Homeless, Highland Press, Canberra, 1987.

King, A. and Baekgaard, H. 'The Dynamics of Housing Wealth', Paper presented to the Eighth National Conference of the Australian Population Association, Adelaide, 3 December 1996.

King, R. J. 'Capital Switching and the Role of Ground Rent: 1. Theoretical Problems', *Environment and Planning A*, vol. 21, 1989, pp. 445–62.

——. 'Capital Switching and the Role of Ground Rent: 2. Switching Between Circuits and Switching Between Submarkets', *Environment and Planning A*, vol. 21, 1989, pp. 711–38.

Kirwan, R. 'Financing Urban Infrastructure: Equity and Efficiency Considerations', *Urban Futures*, vol. 1, 1991, pp. 1–5.

——. 'Planning for Affordable Housing: A Challenge for the 1990s', *Urban Futures*, vol. 2, 1991, pp. 17–22.

Kuttner, R. *Everything for Sale: The Virtues and Limits of Markets*, Alfred Knopf, New York, 1997.

Langbein, J. H. 'The Inheritance Revolution', *The Public Interest*, vol. 102, 1992, pp. 15–31.

Landt, J., Percival, R., Schofield, D. and Wilson, D. *Income Inequality in Australia: The Impact of Non-Cash Subsidies for Health and Housing*, NATSEM Discussion Paper No. 5, University of Canberra, Canberra, 1995.

Laurence, M. 'Debt Crisis Hangs over Suburbia', *Business Review Weekly*, 10 April 1995, pp. 38–41.

Lawson, M. '1998 Tax Shift Worth $13 bn', *Australian Financial Review*, 14 August 1998, p. A3.

Lepani, B., Freed, G., Murphy, P., and McGilvray, A. *The Economic Role of Cities: Australia in the Global Economy*, Australian Government Publishing Service, Canberra, 1995.

Li, M. M. and Brown, J. H. 'Micro-neighbourhood Externalities and Hedonic Housing Prices', *Land Economics*, vol. 56, 1980, pp. 125–41.

Lomax, J. 'Housing Finance: An International Perspective', *Bank of England Quarterly Bulletin*, February 1991, pp. 56–66.

McCaffery, E. J. 'The Political Liberal Case Against the Estate Tax', *Philosophy and Public Affairs*, vol. 23, 1994, pp. 281–312.

McCallum, J. and Beggs, J. 'Determinants of Household Wealth: Assets of Divorcing Couples in Australia', *Australian Economic Review*, vol. 96, 1991, pp. 47–67, 57–66.

McCrone, G. and Stephens, M. *Housing Policy in Britain and Europe*, UCL Press, London, 1995.

McDonald, Peter. 'Young People in Australia Today: A Socio-demographic Perspective', in R. Thanki and C. Thomson (eds), *Mortgaging our Future? Families and Young People in Australia*, Reports and Proceedings No. 129, Social Policy Research Centre, University of New South Wales, Sydney 1996.

Macfarlane, Duncan. 'Dearer Homes Gain More Value', *Australian Financial Review*, 13 November 1997, p. 50.

Macfarlane, Ian. 'The Economics of Nostalgia', *The Sydney Papers*, vol. 9, 1997, pp. 79–89.

Mackay, Hugh. *Generations: Baby Boomers, their Parents and their Children*, Macmillan, Sydney, 1997.

Maclennan, D. *A Competitive UK Economy: The Challenges for Housing Policy*, Joseph Rowntree Foundation, York, 1994.

McNames, S. J. and Miller, R. K. 'Estate Inheritance: A Sociological Lacuna', *Sociological Inquiry*, vol. 59, 1989, pp. 7–29.

Madigan, R., Munro, M. and Smith, S. J. 'Gender and the Meaning of the Home', *International Journal of Urban and Regional Research*, vol. 14, 1990, pp. 624–47.

Maher, Chris. 'Housing Prices and Geographical Scale: Australian Cities in the 1980s', *Urban Studies*, vol. 31, 1994, pp. 5–27.

Malone, Phil. 'Emerging Housing Trends to the Next Millennium', Paper presented to the Eighth National Conference of the Australian Population Association, 3–6 December 1996, Adelaide.

Manning, I. *Deficiencies of the Current Tax System*, Paper presented to the National Tax Reform Summit, <http://www.impactservice...cci/summary/imanning.htm>, 1996.

Mant, John. 'The City Syndrome', *Advertiser*, 8 April 1980, p. 5.

Marcuse, P. *Is Australia Different? Globalisation and the New Urban Poverty*, Occasional Paper No. 3, Australian Housing and Urban Research Institute, Melbourne, 1996.

Meade, J. E. *Efficiency, Equality and the Ownership of Property*, Allen & Unwin, London, 1964.

Megalogenis, G. 'Capital's Gain', *Weekend Australian*, 25–26 September 1999, pp. 33–4.

Mein Smith, P. and Frost, L. 'Home Ownership in Adelaide, 1881–1911', *Australian Economic History Review*, vol. 35, 1995, pp. 40–55.

Miles, D. 'Housing and the Wider Economy in the Short and Long Run', *National Economic Review*, February 1992, pp. 64–77.

——. 'Housing Markets, Consumption and Financial Liberalisation in the Major Economies', *European Economic Review*, vol. 35, 1992, pp. 1093–136.

Mitchell, B. 'Nation to Inherit New Wealthy Class', *Sunday Age*, 25 April 1993, p. 14.

Mitchell, Deborah. 'The Sustainability of the Welfare State: Debates, Myths, Agendas', *Just Policy*, vol. 9, 1997, pp. 3–13.

Morgan, Sally. *My Place*, Fremantle Arts Centre Press, Fremantle, 1987.

Mullins, P. *Exploring the Line of Descent in the Intergenerational Transmission of Domestic Property*, Urban Research Program Working Paper No. 55, Australian National University, 1996.

Munro, M. 'Housing Wealth and Inheritance', *Journal of Social Policy*, vol. 17, 1988, pp. 417–36.

Munro, M. and Smith, S. 'Gender and Housing: Broadening the Debate', *Housing Studies*, vol. 4, 1989, pp. 3–17.

Murie, A. and Forrest, R. 'Wealth, Inheritance and Housing Policy', *Policy and Politics*, vol. 8, 1980, pp. 1–19.

National Housing Strategy. *Australian Housing: The Demographic, Economic and Social Environment*, Issues Paper No. 1, Australian Government Publishing Service, Canberra, 1991.

——. *Financing Australian Housing: The Issues*, Australian Government Publishing Service, Canberra, 1991.

——. *National Housing Strategy: Agenda for Action*, Australian Government Publishing Service, Canberra, 1992.

Neutze, M. and Kendig, H. 'Achievement of Home Ownership among Post-War Australian Cohorts', *Housing Studies*, vol. 6, 1991, pp. 3–14.

Norbury, K. 'High Interest Rates Erode Home Equity', *Sunday Age*, 12 April 1992, p. 10.

O'Connor, Angela. 'Local Price Rise Tops the Nation', *Sunday Age Property*, 7 March 1999, p. 3.

O'Connor, K. and Stimson, R. *The Economic Role of Cities*, Australian Government Publishing Service, Canberra, 1995.

O'Dwyer, Lisel A. Housing Wealth and the Inheritance Factor: The Nature, Impact and Implications of Housing Inheritance in South Australia, PhD thesis, Flinders University of South Australia, 1997.

Paris, Chris. *Housing Australia*, Macmillan, South Melbourne, 1993.

Parsons, Belinda. 'Churches Urge Aid to Poor Tenants', *Age*, 15 November 1997, p. 3.

Peel, Mark. *Good Times, Hard Times: The Past and the Future in Elizabeth*, Melbourne University Press, Carlton, Vic., 1995.

Pender, H. 'Public Policy and the Cost of Capital for Business and Investment', *Capital Income Taxation in Australia*, EPAC Background Paper No. 20, Australian Government Publishing Service, Canberra, 1992.

Phillips, Kevin. *The Politics of Rich and Poor: Wealth and the American Electorate in the Reagan Aftermath*, Random House, New York, 1990.

Planning Research Centre 'Sydney's Housing Markets: Past and Present', Housing Markets and Housing Assistance Options Paper No. 1, Planning Research Centre, University of Sydney, June 1997.

Pulvirenti, Mariastella. 'Home Ownership, Identity and Social Polarisation', in K. Gibson et al., *Restructuring Difference: Social Polaris-*

ation and the City, Australian Housing and Urban Research Institute Working Paper No. 6, Melbourne, 1996, pp. 59–66.

Pusey, M. *Economic Rationalism in Canberra: A Nation-Building State Changes its Mind*, Cambridge University Press, Cambridge, 1991.

Reich, Robert B. *The Work of Nations*, Alfred Knopf, New York 1991.

——. *Locked In Cabinet*, Random House, New York, 1998.

Reserve Bank of Australia. *Bulletin*, Reserve Bank, Sydney, various years.

Riley, B. 'Mortgages that Threaten Ruin', *Financial Times*, 17 October 1992, p. xxiv.

Rossi, Peter H. and Weber, Elanor. 'The Social Benefits of Homeownership: Empirical Evidence from National Surveys', *Housing Policy Debate*, vol. 7, 1996, pp. 1–35.

Salmons, Richard. 'Shares: Safer than Houses', *Sunday Age Business*, 18 April 1999, p. 21.

Sanders, W. 'Aboriginal Housing', in C. Paris (ed.), *Housing Australia*, Macmillan, South Melbourne, 1993, pp. 212–27.

——. 'Housing Data from the NATSIS: Can it Assist with Program Evaluation?', in J. C. Altman and J. Taylor, *The 1994 National Aboriginal and Torres Strait Islander Survey: Findings and Future Prospects*, Research Monograph No. 11, Centre for Aboriginal Economic Policy Research, ANU, Canberra, 1996, pp. 106–17.

Sassen, S. *The Global City: New York, London, Tokyo*, Princeton University Press, Princeton, NJ, 1991.

Saunders, Peter. *A Nation of Home Owners*, Unwin Hyman, London, 1990.

Saunders, Peter and Williams, Peter. 'The Constitution of the Home: Towards a Research Agenda', *Housing Studies*, vol. 3, 1988, pp. 81–93.

Schrader, D. E. and Winfrey, J. C. 'Is There Property After Death?', *Human Rights Quarterly*, vol. 6, 1984, pp. 107–24.

Sexton, J. and Price M. '$7000 Rebate to Buy First Home', *Australian*, 14 August 1998, p. 5.

Simms, M. 'The Politics of the Assets Test: The Political Peril in Daring to Attack "Home Sweet Home"', in H. Kendig and J. McCallum (eds), *Grey Policy: Australian Policies for an Ageing Society*, Allen & Unwin, Sydney, 1990.

Smith, S. J. 'Income, Housing Wealth and Gender Inequality', *Urban Studies*, vol. 27, 1990, pp. 67–88.

Social Security Journal, Table 13—Age Pensioners: Home Ownership by Age Group by Sex, June 1995, December 1995, pp. 238–40.

Somers, J. 'Residential Property, It's the Best Investment', *Australian Financial Review*, 30 October 1992, pp. 43–4.

Somerville, P. 'Tenure, Gender and Household Structure', *Housing Studies*, vol. 9, 1994, pp. 329–49.

South Australian Department of Lands. Sales Reports, unpublished, various years.

South Australian Valuation Office. Sales Reports, unpublished, various years.

Stegman, Michael A., Brownstein, Joanna and Temkin, Kenneth. 'Home Ownership and Family Wealth in the United States', in R. Forrest and A. Murie (eds), *Housing and Family Wealth: Comparative International Perspectives*, Routledge, London, 1995, pp. 86–107.

Stilwell, F. *Economic Inequality: Who Gets What in Australia*, Pluto Press, Leichhardt, New South Wales, 1994.

Stimson, R. 'Processes of Globalisation, Economic Restructuring and the Emergence of a New Space Economy of Cities and Regions in Australia', in J. Brotchie et al. (eds), *Cities in Competition*, Longman, Melbourne, 1995, pp. 58–87.

Storey, L., Wilson, P. and Kendig, H. *Home Equity Conversion in Australia*, Australian Government Publishing Service, Canberra, 1994.

Storkey, Gary. 'Findings and Recommendations of the Rosewood Experience', in B. Badcock and K. Harris (eds), *Revitalising Housing Areas: Proceedings of the 1998 National Urban Renewal Seminar*, Australian Housing and Urban Research Institute, Melbourne, 1998, pp. 253–60.

Stretton, Hugh. *Housing and Government: 1974 Boyer Lectures*, Australian Broadcasting Commission, Adelaide, 1974.

——. 'Housing—An Investment for All', in J. Brian McLoughlin and Margo Huxley (eds), *Urban Planning in Australia: Critical Readings*, Longman Cheshire, Melbourne, 1986, pp. 259–73.

——. *Political Essays*, Georgian House, Melbourne, 1987.

——. *Ideas for Australian Cities*, 4th edn, Georgian House, Melbourne, 1989.

Suich, Max. 'Bank Rupted', *Independent Monthly*, May 1991, pp. 14–16.

Sykes, Trevor. 'Australia's Worst Housing Disaster', *Bulletin*, 2 November 1993, pp. 65–70.

Syret, Sonia. 'Qld Home Schemes under Review', *Australian Financial Review*, 14 May 1996, p. 41.

Tarica, Elizabeth. 'Border Disorder', *Sunday Age Property*, 5 October 1997, pp. 1–2.

Thomas, T. 'The Inheritance Windfall', *Business Review Weekly*, 14 December 1990, pp. 44–9.

Thorns, David. 'The Implications of Differential Rates of Capital Gains from Owner Occupation for the Formation and Development of Housing Classes', *International Journal of Urban and Regional Research*, vol. 5, 1981, pp. 205–30.

——. 'Industrial Restructuring and Change in the Labour and Property Markets in Britain', *Environment and Planning A*, vol. 20, 1982, pp. 745–63.

——. 'The Impact of Home Ownership and Capital Gains Upon Class and Consumption Sectors', *Environment and Planning D: Society and Space*, vol. 7, 1989, pp. 292–312.

——. 'Housing Wealth and Inheritance; The New Zealand Experience', in R. Forrest and A. Murie (eds), *Housing and Family Wealth*, Routledge, London, 1995.

——. 'The Role of Housing Inheritance in Selected Owner Occupied Societies (Britain, New Zealand, Canada)', *Housing Studies*, vol. 9, 1994, pp. 473–92.

——. 'The Creation and Transfer of Housing Wealth: The Experience of Elderly New Zealanders', *Urban Policy and Research*, vol. 12, 1994, pp. 242–52.

Torrey, B. B. 'Assets of the Aged: Clues and Issues', *Population and Development Review*, vol. 14, 1988, pp. 489–97.

Travers, P. and Richardson, S. *Living Decently: Material Well-Being in Australia*, Oxford University Press, Melbourne, 1993.

Travers Morgan and Applied Economics. *Housing Costs Study, Study 3: Determinants of the Prices of Established Housing*, Australian Government Publishing Service, Canberra, 1992.

Troy, Patrick N. *The Benefits of Owner Occupation*, Urban Research Program Working Paper No. 29, Australian National University, Canberra, 1991.

United States Department of Housing and Urban Development. 'New National Homeownership Strategy Can Create 8 Million New Homeowners by Year 2000', HUD No. 95–117, 5 June 1995.

Wagner, R. E. *Inheritance and the State*, American Enterprise Institute for Public Policy Research, Washington, DC, 1977.

Walsh, M. 'Capital Outflow Could Backfire', *Age*, 3 August 1994.

Welfeld, I. *Where We Live: A Social History of American Housing*, Simon and Schuster, New York, 1988.

White, G. 'Housing Investment: The Economic Cycle', Paper presented to Real Estate Institute of Australia Conference, Canberra, 1996.

Williams, Peter. 'Sustainable Housing Policies and the Role of Public Sector Housing Organisations', Unpublished paper prepared for the Urban Research Program, Australian National University, Canberra, 1992.

Winter, Ian and Stone, Wendy. *Social Polarisation and Housing Careers: Exploring the Interrelationships of Labour and Housing Markets in Australia*, Australian Institute of Family Studies Working Paper No. 13, Melbourne, 1998.

Wood, G. A. *Taxation and Housing*, Background Paper No. 5, National Housing Strategy, Canberra, 1991.

Wood, G. A. and Bushe-Jones, S. 'Financial Deregulation and Access to Home Ownership in Australia', *Urban Studies*, vol. 27, pp. 583–90.

——. *Housing Affordability: An International Context*, Background Paper No. 3, National Housing Strategy, Canberra, 1991.

Wood, G. A. and Watson, R. 'Private Rental Investors' Costs: Why Who You Are Matters', Paper presented to the Australian Housing and Urban Research Institute and Department of Family and Community

Services Seminar on Australia's Housing Choices, 19 February 1999, Canberra.

Wulff, Maryann. 'The Two-income Household: Relative Contribution of Earners to Housing Costs', *Urban Studies*, vol. 19, 1982, pp. 343–50.

——. 'Low-income Home Ownership: The Privatisation of Squalor or the Great Australian Dream?', *Housing Studies*, vol. 5, 1990, pp. 229–41.

Wulff, Maryann and Evans, Samantha, 'The Spatial Impacts of Commonwealth Rent Assistance on Australia's Low-income Households', Paper presented at the Australian Population Association Ninth National Conference, Queensland, 29 September–2 October 1998.

Wulff, Maryann and Maher, C. 'Long-term Renters in the Australian Housing Market', *Housing Studies*, vol. 13, 1998, pp. 3–18.

Yates, J. *Australia's Owner Occupied Housing Wealth and Its Impact on Income Distribution*, Reports and Proceedings No. 92, Social Policy Research Centre, Sydney, 1991.

——. 'Imputed Rent and Income Distribution', *Review of Income and Wealth*, vol. 40, 1994, pp. 43–66.

——. 'Home Ownership and Australia's Housing Finance System', *Urban Policy and Research*, vol. 12, 1994, pp. 27–39.

——. 'Changing Directions in Australian Housing Policies: The End of Muddling Through?', *Housing Studies*, vol. 12, 1997, pp. 265–78.

——. *Trends in Home Ownership*, Department of Urban Affairs and Planning, Sydney, 1997.

——. 'Is Australia's Home Ownership Rate Really Stable? An Examination of Change Between 1975 and 1994', *Urban Studies*, vol. 37, 2000, pp. 319–42.

Index

References to figures and tables are indicated by an f or t, respectively.